Historic
Inverness

An illustration from Pennant's Tour of Scotland (1769) showing the ruins of former Fort George on Castle Hill.

Historic
Inverness

A. Gerald Pollitt

With thirty-six photographs and two maps

1981
The Melven Press

PERTH

© A. Gerald Pollitt 1981
Published by the Melven Press, 176 High Street,
Perth, Scotland.

ISBN 0 906664 14 4

Set in 11/13 Times and printed by John G. Eccles Printers Ltd., Inverness,
Scotland.

Gerald Pollitt is an adopted son of Inverness and his love of the town has led him to research various facets of its past. These researches have resulted in this most illuminating account of its early history and the more recent historical details of many facets which are known to the older Invernessian.

I have known Gerald Pollitt for many years and as a fellow Councillor on Inverness Town Council I was aware of his deeply held interest in current municipal affairs.

I feel sure that this book will commend itself to all those who love Inverness, those who are exiles from it, those who have spent some part of their life here and also those living here now who would like to know more about the town, its history and traditions.

Inverness has produced many "characters" in its time and Gerald Pollitt, an incomer who has unveiled so much of our past, must surely be regarded as a most interesting member of that distinctive band.

Aly Bella.

PROVOST.

Contents

Preface   6

Beginnings   8

Chapter 1 — Buildings   14
   Cromwell's Fort; Greyfriars' Yard —
   Blackfriars Friary; the Old High Church;
   Dunbar's Hospital; Town House; the
   Castle; Ness Bridge; St. Andrew's
   Cathedral; Royal Northern Infirmary.

Chapter 2 — Streets   68
   Background; Castle Street; High Street,
   with Eastgate and Bridge Street; Church
   Street; Academy Street; Chapel Street and
   Shore Street; 'Bewest the waters of the
   Ness'.

Chapter 3 — Names and Institutions   132
   Earl of Inverness; Baillie of Dochfour;
   Cuthbert; Forbes of Culloden; Gordon;
   Grant; Inglis; Eden Court; Inverness
   Courier; Inverness Scientific Society and
   Field Club; Northern Meeting; Post Office;
   Sett; Stent.

Chapter 4 — The locality and its customs   180
    The Boar Stone; The Broadstone;
    Drumden; The Islands; The Longman;
    Sunday Observance; Thursday Market.

Chapter 5 — Trade and Industry   190
    The Sea; Other Trades; Brewing and
    Distilling; Commerce.

Appendix A: Town Charters   208

Notes   216

Bibliography   226

Index   230

List of Illustrations

Front endpaper
John Hume's Plan of Inverness, 1774

Frontispiece
Fort George, Castle Hill, 1769

Back endpaper
Wood's Map of Inverness, 1822

Between pages 52 & 53

1   Clock Tower of Cromwell's Fort
2   Friar's Street
3   Dunbar's Hospital
4   The Old Townhouse

Between pages 84 & 85

5   The Townhouse today
6   The Exchange and High Street with Forbes Fountain
7   Aerial view of the Town Centre and Ness Bridge
8   The Suspension Bridge, c. 1890
9   Another view of the Suspension Bridge, c. 1890

Between pages 116 & 117

10   The second Castle Tolmie
11   Saint Andrew's Cathedral
12   The Castle endangered by a landslip, 1932
13   The Castle Street landslide, 1932
14   The Steeple today
15   The south side of Bridge Street
16   Interior of St John's Church

Between pages 148 & 149

17 Station Square, c. 1883
18 The Market Arcade
19 The Academy built in 1792
20 The original Black Bridge
21 Aerial view of Highland Region headquarters
    and Eden Court
22 Chisholm's Close, c. 1900
23 Greig Street

Between pages 180 & 181

24 Cottage industry
25 Laundry bleaching, c. 1860
26 Tomnahurich and Millerton Bridge
27 Torvean and Caledonian Canal
28 Academy Street, with Empire Theatre
29 The Post Office of 1820
30 The Post Office of 1888
31 Commercial salmon fishing

Between pages 212 & 213

32 Inverness Harbour, c. 1896
33 Kessock Ferry in the days of sail
34 Kessock Ferry in its last days
35 Kessock Bridge under construction
36 Washing fleeces for Gilbert Street Tannery

Preface

It is with no pretensions to literary merit or even historical interpretation that I present this volume; rather this is the accumulation of knowledge acquired through extensive and pleasurable reading over many years and now marshalled into some sort of order so that part of the considerable history of Inverness may be absorbed by others without laborious and time-consuming research. The format is based on notes written by Thomas D. Wallace, F.E.I.S., F.S.A (Scotland) who died in 1926. He had been rector of the High School, was founder member, past-president and for many years secretary of the Inverness Scientific Society and Field Club. Obviously he had intended to publish, and his notes are a book in manuscript form. Those notes are now in private hands and were loaned to me by Miss May Fraser, lately of the Town Clerk's Department. The copy that I now have, I intend to place in the Inverness Branch of the Public Library for the benefit of future researchers. I have adopted his theme without unduly plagiarising his material.

Kenneth MacDonald, then Town Clerk, speaking in 1898 of Queen Mary's Inverness, said that it was 'a little settlement of Saxon and Fleming traders in the middle of a Celtic population,' and although he would not have claimed that this was more than a generalisation I have more and more come to accept its principle as a basic factor in the growth and development of Inverness. Hostility between town and landward areas has always existed, and persists today, explaining many incidents otherwise inexplicable.

For those whose appetite is hereby whetted I strongly commend a browse amongst the excellent collection of books on local history in the Inverness Public Library, the source from which much of my material has been collected. To the staff of that Library I extend my very sincere thanks; led by Miss Carol Goodfellow they have all been most generous in their efforts to assist me and have made what could so easily have become a chore into an enjoyable experience.

To my wife who has patiently edited my rambling writings, and seldom if ever complained when I immured myself for extended periods, and to the many friends who have contributed advice and information, far too many to enumerate, I also offer my grateful thanks. I hope that they may find my effort worthy of the assistance they so readily gave.

With the exception of two, all the photographs are reproduced by permission of the Inverness Museum and Art Gallery. I would especially like to thank the curator, Richard Higginbottom for all his help. Photographs 34 and 35 are reproduced by permission of James Anderson, Inverness.

Beginnings

Inverness is undoubtedly a very ancient settlement although the actual date of its foundation was long before recorded history. Two early Scottish historians, Boethius and Buchanan writing in the sixteenth century, assert that it was founded by Evenus II, fourteenth King of Scots in Scotland, who died sixty years before the birth of Christ but there is little evidence to support such a claim. Since we now know that it was not until at least five centuries later that the Scots first crossed to settle in what is now called their land it can hardly be accepted that one of their kings could have founded a town in the Highlands at that early date and certainly he could not have been their king "in Scotland". Nor can firm conclusions be reached on another claim for its existence some two hundred years later. There is a traditional belief that, in those days the Beauly Firth did not exist but that the Ness and Farrar united to form one river flowing through what is now that Firth joining the sea somewhere east of Chanonry Point. The same Boethius records that, in 1093, the land of Moray was "desolated by the sea, castles sub-verted from their foundations and some towns destroyed" which gives support to the tradition of the Beauly Firth being formed in this upheaval. In the year AD 140 Lollius Urbicus, Imperial Lieutenant, placed a Roman station at Ptoroton, the chief town of the Vacomagi Tribe, which is described as being

8

in North Britain near the mouth of the Vararis. But where was Ptoroton and which was the river Vararis? Nobody can be certain, Forres and Burghead are both strong contenders but so too is Inverness with the Farrar as the Vararis. Support to this claim is given by the small Roman fort known to have been at Bona, some six miles south-west of the town, the place where Columba was later to encounter a monster living in Loch Ness. What is quite certain is that there were people inhabiting the area as is shown by the many stone circles of which traces still exist and the vitrified fort on Craig Phadric, itself one of the great Scottish enigmas. Hill forts of similar basic construction usually dating from the Bronze Age are common throughout Europe but none, even in other parts of Britain, are vitrified. The one on Craig Phadric was built about BC 350 and consists of an area of some 2250 square yards enclosed by a rampart nearly 20 feet thick and over 25 high. At a later date the whole was enclosed in a further rampart built, like the first, of rock and conglomerate boulders with wooden beams between the courses of stone. It was the intense heat generated when these wooden beams burned which caused the rock to melt and anneal but why where they burned? Surely not accidentally, it simply is not credible that seventy such accidents can have happened all and only in Scotland. Attempted destruction or the expulsion of defenders by invading forces? Again difficult to accept since the enormous quantity of brushwood needed to ensure the eventual ignition of the embedded timber could hardly have been transported to the hilltop and stacked against the ramparts whilst defenders were within the fort or in the vicinity. Could it have been just the reverse, a means of strengthening the ramparts or was it, as Dr. Muir suggests, a ritual purging by fire of a captured fortress, a practice widely used by Celtic tribes in Scotland?[1]

Four centuries further later, we are on much firmer ground. In AD 565 Brude MacMaelchon, King of the Northern Picts, had his capital near the River Ness and it was to this place that Columba came from Iona to convert him to Christianity. Columba was, in fact, seeking permission to build a small cell or place of worship on St. Michael's Mount, the site of the present Old High Church. Since Brude's fortress would presumably have been of wattle and daub, and the homes of his followers merely tents of skins and tree branches in keeping with the building standards of the day, no trace remains and the site cannot be identified with any certainty. The hill on which Victoria Terrace now stands has natural advantages which make it a strong contender but Torvean and Craig Phadric, [which had the Gaelic name of 'Larach an Tigh Mhor'. The site of the great house] cannot be ruled out. Undoubtedly such a house, and almost certainly the early town, would have been built on the higher land rather than what is now the town centre, since at this early period there was little dry ground on the lower flat. Blue clay, containing sea shells, was uncovered whilst digging foundations for buildings in Bridge Street, and red deer antlers were unearthed in Church Street; these suggest swampy ground subject to flooding from tide and river. There is other evidence that the town was once centred in the Crown area in that a point at Maryfield, on Midmills Road, has long been known as the former location of the town cross and since we know that the Castle, until it was razed by Malcolm Canmore and then re-built on Castlehill, was in this area it would be natural for the town to have developed in its shadow. The removal to the present site, following the transfer of the castle to its present site by Malcolm Canmore, would account for the regularity of the streets at right-angles to High Street and the lanes down to the river at proper distances along Church Street would suggest planned development rather than casual growth.

Until the time of Malcolm Canmore Scottish Kings were Celtic. His sons, doubtless due to his English wife, were trained in Saxon and Norman usages and when in power tried to make Scotland as like England as possible. The Celts around Inverness were naturally rebellious about this change in their way of life and the presence of the Castle, complete with a royal garrison, which was built to strengthen the King's power over them. Similarly lowland burgesses were settled in the town to spread southern influence by trade and commerce.

Carruthers says that 'The early records of the Highland Capital show that Inverness was, in great measure, a town of Lowland people, customs and manners. The Celtic people mingled little in trade but seem to have occasionally plundered and annoyed the industrious burghers. Little intercourse was maintained betwixt Inverness and the neighbouring districts — owing most probably to the hostility of the clans and the want of roads and other means of communication. A remarkable instance of this occurs in the Town Council books. 'Little more than a century ago (written in 1843) a depute from the Council was sent to Dingwall — just twelve miles distant by ferry or twenty-one by mail road — to ascertain and report what sort of a place it was. On 20th August 1733 he reported that they had no prison, that they had a lake close by the town which kept people from kirk or market from want of a bridge, that they had no trade and that those who were inclined to carry on a trade could not do so for want of a harbour and that the state of the building of the town was very ruinous'.[2]

Apart from a few skirmishes history has little to tell us of Inverness from Brude's time until the eleventh century; a silence suggesting it had already ceased to be a Pictish Capital even before AD 843 when such a distinction was made superfluous with the union of the Pictish and Scottish crowns in the person of Kenneth MacAlpin. In 1180 King William the Lion granted charters which affected the development of the town for many centuries to come.

These charters have five main provisions. (1) Burgesses of Inverness were to be free from toll and customs throughout the whole land, (2) No one could buy or sell in the Burgh, or exercise any merchandising therein, unless he were a Burgess or had their permission, (3) The Burgesses agreed that the King should make a *fosse* (ditch) around the Burgh whilst they would enclose the whole Burgh within that fosse by a good paling which they would maintain in good order*, (4) For the support of the Burgh the Burgesses received "that land beyond the Burgh called the Burgh Halve (Haugh) viz. between the hill and the water".** and (5) the right was given to hold a weekly market every Sunday. Amongst the

11

far-reaching results of these privileges was that the Burgh's position close to a Royal Castle and its gratitude for these precious rights made it faithful to the Crown no matter what might happen in the vicinity; it made the Burgh an Island of peaceful trading in a very unsettled part of the country and, from its start as a Burgh, meant that amongst its foremost Burgesses were men bearing lowland or even foreign names.*** These characteristics remained true of Inverness right until 1746. As far back as written records go Inverness has always been a peaceful marketing centre supporting the ruling monarch, an English-speaking town set in the midst of a Celtic and Gaelic speaking population.

*This fence remained as a defence as late at 1689
**This land at Island Bank and Lower Drummond, not the present Haugh which remained in the hands of the Keeper of the Castle.
***A signature on one of the Charters is that of the first Burgess of whom we have a record — Geoffrey Blund.

Chapter 1 — Buildings

Cromwell's Fort; Greyfriar's Yard-Blackfriar's Friary; Old High Church; Dunbar's Hospital; Town House; Castle; Ness Bridge; St. Andrew's Cathedral; Royal Northern Infirmary.

Cromwell's Fort

True to their traditions the citizens of Inverness were firmly supporting the King in 1650 when the Council ordered that 'A company of able bodied men be raised and sent to the army at this time of exigence, when it is the duty of every well-disposed Christian to bestir himself, when religion, the King's interest and all the liberties of this ancient kingdom are all lying at the stake and threatened most proudly to be ruined, by the perfidious army of secretaries, now lying in the bowels of this kingdom under the command of that wicked tyrant Oliver Cromwell'.[1] Their efforts were in vain. By September that year Cromwell was in Edinburgh prior to the defeat of the King's Scottish Army at Dunbar, and his advance the following year to Perth — the limit of his personal incursion into Scotland. By September 1651, the Royal Armies had been finally defeated and 'the wicked tyrant' was in control of the whole of Britain.

Inverlochy (Fort William) and Inverness were to be the locations of the two forts by which the Highlands were to be controlled. Work in Inverness was started in May 1652, and Mr Hanes, 'a German ingenire', was ordered to 'lay out the line'. Since he is known to have been in England for most of the summer and in France during the autumn it is unlikely that he spent much time in Inverness. Work appears to have proceeded somewhat slowly, and when General Monck made an inspection in August 1655 he found that, 'Inverness will

14

cost a great deal of money before it be done though I gave them orders twelve months since to begin no more new buildings but to finish what they had begun'.[2] His estimate was that £500 would be needed each month for the next two years which, added to the original £30,000 allocation, would suggest that the final cost must have been about £50,000 or even the £80,000 stated in the Wardlaw Manuscript.[3] It was demolished in 1662. Throughout its short existence it was manned by a force of about a thousand men.

Two eye-witness accounts remain to us, one by the Reverend James Fraser and another most grandiloquent one by Richard Franck.

'North and by east, near the forcible streams of the Ness, stands the fortress or pentagon, drawn out by regular lines, built all with stone, and girt about with a graff that commodes it with a convenient harbour. The houses in this fair fortress are built very low, but uniform; and the streets broad and spacious, with avenues and intervals for drilling of foot or drawing up horse. I must confess such and so many are the advantages and conveniences that belong to this citadel, it would be thought fabulous if but to numerate them; for that end I refer myself to those that have inspected her magazines, providores, harbours, vaults, graffs, bridges, sallyports, cellars, bastions, horn-works, redoubts, counterscarps &c. Ocular evidence is the best judge, and gives the plainest demonstration, which, without dispute, will interpret this formidable fortress a strength impregnable; and the situation, as much as any, promises security by reason it's surrounded with boggy morasses, standing in swamps on an isthmus of land that divides the Ness from the Orchean Seas.[4]

The Reverend James Fraser gives a much more realistic description:

'The Citadel of Inverness is now on a great length, almost finished. They had first built a long row of buildings, made of bricks and planks, upon the river side, to accommodate the regiment; and ramparts

and bulwarks of earth in every street of the town; and
also fortified the Castle and the bridge, and the main
court of guard at the Cross. They bought a large plot of
ground from the burghers, called Carseland, where they
built the Citadel, founded May 1652, and now finished
— a most stately scene! It was five-cornered, with
bastions, with a wide trench, that an ordinary bark might
sail in at full tide; the breastwork, three storeys, built all
of hewn stone, limed within, and a brick wall; centinal
houses of stone in each corner; a sallyport to the south,
leading to the town; and on the north the great entry or
gate, called the port, with a strong draw-bridge of oak,
called the blue bridge, and a stately structure over the
gate, well cut with the Commonwealth's arms and the
motto, 'Togam Tuentur Arma'. This bridge is drawn
every night, and a strong guard is within. Ships or
shallops sailing in or out the bridge was heaved to give
way. The entry from the bridge into the Citadel was a
stately vault about seventy feet long, with seats on each
side, and a row of iron hooks for pikes and drums to
hang on. In the centre of the Citadel stood a great
four-square building, all hewn stone, called the
magazine and granary; in the third storey was the
church, well furnished with a stately pulpit and seats, a
wide bartisan at top, and a brave great clock, with four
large dials and a curious ball. South-east stood the great
English building, four storeys high, so called, being built
by English masons; and south-west the Scotch building
of the same dimensions, built by Scotch masons;
north-west and north-east lower storeys for
ammunition, timber, lodgings for manufactories,
stables for horses, provision, brewing houses, a great
long tavern quhar all manner of wines, viands, beer, ale,
cider, was sold by one Master Benson; so that the whole
regiment was accomodat within these walls. A
cinquoport or conduit run under ground from the one to
the other side, with grates of iron at ends, which at
flowing and ebbing carried away the filth and odor of all
the Citadel. All their oak planks and beams were carried

16

out of England in ships to Kessock rode; all their firr
logg, spar rofe beames were sold them out of Hugh
Fraser of Struy's woods. I saw that gentleman receive 30
thousand merks at once for timber. Most of their best
hewn stone was taken from Chanory, the great
Cathedrall and Steeple, the Bishop's Castle, to the
foundation, rased, the Church and Abbey of Kinloss
and Beauly, the Gray Friars and St Mary's Chappell at
Inverness and many more so that it was a sacriligious
structure and therefore could not stand.

   'At the digging of the trenches, every man got a
shilling sterling wages a day, so that all the country
people flockt in to that work, and hardly could you get
one to serve you; and the soldiers made more money
attending it than their daily pay amounted to. This great
work was finished in five years and commissary Coup,
who advanced the money to masons, carpenters, and
others, told me that the whole expense of it amounted to
about 80 thousands pounds sterling.[5]

An ardent Royalist, the Reverend Fraser also gives a
delighted report of the destruction of the Citadel and the
departure of the troops.

   'In the close of July, by an act of the Parliament, an
order is issued out to slight and demolish the citadels
of the kingdom which were built by the English. This
of Inverness had not stood ten years. The first part
they seized upon was the sentinel houses, neat turrets
of hewn stone, curiously wrought and set up on every
corner of the rampart wall, these now all broken
down by the soldiers themselves. The next thing was
the Commonwealth's arms, pulled down and broken
and the King's arms set up in their place; the blue
bridge slighted, the sally-port broken, the magazine
house steeple broken, and the great bell taken down
— all this done with demonstrations of joy and
gladness, the soldiers shouting 'God save the King',
as men weary of the yoke and slavery of usurpation
which lay so long about their necks . . . In the
beginning of April the garrisons of Scotland were

given up. The regiment at Inverness was ordered to muster and be ready to march. On the eleventh 400 of the English removed in arms, rank and file, with their wives and children, for Leith. Next morrow other 400 marched with their arms, commanders and colours, to the great grief of all the English soldiers. Never people left a place with such reluctancy. It was sad to see and hear their sighs and tears, pale faces, and embraces, at their parting farewell from that town. And no wonder. They had peace and plenty for ten years in it; they made that place happy and it made them so.[6]

Little now remains of the Citadel. Amongst a mass of oil storage tanks stands a somewhat dilapidated lower portion of the tower, re-roofed and with a new time-piece to replace the 'brave great clock', and two or three earthen ramparts from the perimeter of the fort. It is interesting to know that one of these ramparts, made nearly three centuries earlier, was used as an air raid shelter in the Second World War.

Greyfriar's Yard, Blackfriars' Friary

The name commonly given to the burial ground off Friars Street and now hemmed in by the Telephone Exchange is a complete misnomer. It is almost the only remnant of the Dominican (Black, or Teaching, Friars) Friary and has never had any connection whatsoever with the Franciscan Order, the Greyfriars whose name it has come to bear. The Dominicans, whose normal dress was a white robe and hood covered by a black cloak when away from the cloister, were a teaching and preaching Order founded by Saint Dominic in Toulouse and turned into a universal mission by Pope Honorious III in 1216. They spread quite quickly and were established in England within five years, crossing the Border very soon afterwards. There is some uncertainty about the date of their arrival in Inverness since all their early Charters were lost either in a fire of 1372 or at the Reformation. Dr Alexander Ross, the eminent Inverness architect, gives the date as 1217; but he must surely be mistaken since they could hardly have reached here only one year after first receiving Papal blessing. The more usually accepted date is 1233 when Alexander II made them a grant of a piece of land stretching from Kirkgate (now Chapel Street) to the river where they built their Friary.

The Dominicans seem never to have been a numerous body in Inverness although we only twice have any record of their numbers. In 1523 there was a prior, a sub-prior and just three brethren and the inventory of goods handed to the Magistrates thirty-six years later bears the signatures of the prior and three brethren only. Of course it is possible that neither indicate the total number of friars attached to Inverness; as a missionary order there could well have been others away on preaching journeys. The number of friars in no way related to the extent of the buildings, for Dominican practice was to have quite extensive premises since they aimed to attract large congregations. In addition, it was common for the buildings to be used as Royal residences during visits of the Court, and as places for national or ecclesiastical assemblies. Despite its sparsity of residential friars, Inerness appears to have been no exception.

Their constitution ordained that every Dominican Friary must have a school, with a Doctor of Divinity as Rector, and it is from this edict that Inverness Royal Academy claims its origin. From a Council minute of 1574 it appears that the original school was just outwith the Friary walls at the corner of what is now Friars Lane and Church Street. In the cellar of a house on the north-east side of Friars Street is the remains of a Friar's cell and in the burial ground stands a seven-foot high hexagonal pillar which was once part of an arch in the Friary. Built into a wall enclosing the ground is the effigy of an armed knight said to be from the tomb of Alexander Stewart, Earl of Mar and natural son of the Wolf of Badenoch, who died in Inverness on 26 July 1435. These are all the tangible remains apart from a very tenuous connection that may exist with Ness Islands and Dunbar's Hospital. When the Friary came to be demolished its stones were sold to Col. Lilburn for the building of the Citadel and its material was, in turn, used for Dunbar's Hospital and the new bridge of 1681.

That latter structure was afterwards replaced and its stones used to strength the islands, so it is just possible that stones once part of the Friary now prevent the river from eroding this amenity. Amongst the intangible legacies are the street and place names, the Royal Academy and the main achievement in the armorial bearings of the District Council. It has been decided that a bridge still to be built near the Friary site will be called the Friars Bridge.

North-West of where the Friary stood, between the river and what is now Waterloo Place lies the Maggot, a very old name said to be a corruption of Margaret, a saint who may once have had an altar there, and this too was granted to the Order by Alexander. In the Charter it is described as an island, the river in those days having quite a delta. Friars' Croft, across Chapel Street and between Manse Place and the Chapel Yard, was granted by the Monastery of Arbroath in a mood of generosity not to be continued in later dealings. It was apparently kept under tillage, its crops grown for the friars' own use. They also held about an acre in the Shipland, north of Chapel Yard, and a piece of land in the centre of the town at the corner of Bridge Street and Castle Wynd. On the west side of the river they had two plots of land in the vicinity of Young Street and Alexander Place. Outwith the town they had ground at Western Kessock in the Black Isle and, strangely, the Island of Cava in Scapa Flow, Orkney. This small island, only about a mile long and a quarter of a mile wide, had a ruined chapel and four houses with about forty inhabitants in 1851, but it is now uninhabited and used only for sheep-grazing. Altogether it can have been of little value to the friars unless it was bought or gifted to provide a mission station for their work of preaching and teaching in those northern parts. In the general scramble for the lands of the Friary after its dissolution Cava was feued by William Cumming, Town Clerk of Inverness. It must, however, have reverted to the Burgh later since, in 1675, it was sold by the council to James Moncrieff of Edinburgh for £133.6s 8d with a feu duty of £2, both Scots. Since twelve Scots pounds equalled one pound sterling the island sold for the English equivalent of £11.2s 3d with a feu duty of 3s 4d, or 16½ pence.

This duty continued to be paid until 1874 when, with other small dues diverted from the Church at the Reformation, it was waived as being too trivial to justify the costs of collection.

Apart from these territorial possessions the friars had a pension, an annual payment of £10 Scots granted by Robert Bruce, and payable to them by the Burgh from the rents paid by the Burgesses through it to the Crown. After the Reformation Queen Mary diverted this pension, with a later additional 8s 6d payable in the same way, to be paid to the hospital for the benefit of the poor and they were still deducted from the payments made to the Crown by the Burgh until it ceased to exist in 1975. There is no trace of a single penny ever having been handed over to the hospital or to the poor.

Soon after their arrival in Inverness the friars became involved in national affairs. In 1262 the Earl of Ross supported by other mainland nobles had been raiding Skye and the Western Isles, doubtless with a view to incorporating them into the Kingdom of Scotland. The island chieftains appealed to their sovereign, Haco of Norway, who prepared to invade Scotland but was defeated at the Battle of Largs on 2 October 1263 and died in Orkney eleven weeks later. Alexander, King of Scots, promptly brought the Isles under his sway and entered into negotiations for their cession by Norway, an embassy being sent there in 1264. In the Inverness accounts for that year is an entry 'To the expenses of the Preaching Friars going on an embassy of the Lord King of Norway 47s 7d.'[7] By the 'Annual of Norway' the Western Isles were finally ceded to Scotland in 1266, the treaty being ratified in Inverness in 1312 when Bruce, who had succeeded Alexander, was accompanied by at least four bishops and three Earls whilst Magnus, the Norwegian King, had one Archbishop, two Bishops, one Earl and two Barons. It is almost certain that they all stayed in the Friary which was probably the only place large enough to accommodate two such large retinues, the pension granted the next year presumably being in recognition of the hospitality given.

In 1372 the Friary and part of the town were burned by an armed band sent by the Abbot of Arbroath. William the

Lion, in an ill-judged zeal to the memory of Thomas à Becket had given control of the town's church and its revenues to the Monastery of Arbroath which thereafter persistently starved it of funds. Perhaps the Abbot could see no reason for not owning all church property in Inverness or, there was some dispute about possible payments due for the feu of the lands granted to the Friars by his predecessor. In the proceedings of a Justiciary Court of the Regality of Moray held in 1376 a Charter of the Earl of Moray, left for safe keeping in the house of the Preaching Friars of Inverness, was stated to 'have been burned there and completely destroyed at the time of the burning of the said house.'[8] It was common practice for the laity to leave valuables in ecclesiastical care where undoubtedly they were far safer until the friars reversed the procedure and left their treasures in the care of the laity as they did at the time of the Reformation. Whilst violence accompanied the changes in many Scottish towns, Inverness seems to have accomplished the transformation peacefully but the friars, fearing trouble, provided for the safety of their sacred vessels and charters by delivering them to the Magistrates for protection.[8a] Provost George Cuthbert took them into his own care and they disappeared without trace. After his death an application for their return was made in the Courts but failed to unearth any trace of them, his widow denying any knowledge of their ever having been in his keeping.[8b]

After the dispersal of the friars Queen Mary issued a charter transferring the possessions of the Church to the Burgh to be used 'for the poor and the hospital of Inverness' and the scramble began. The Town Clerk obtained the feu of Cava, and he also got the Mill of Kessock for a combined feu duty of only 14 merks. Bailie John Ross acquired both the fishings and the croft but undoubtedly the Provost fared best of all. He got the Friary itself and all the yards and crofts within the walls thereof for a perpetual feu duty of £4 Scots and later he feuded the 'Auld Scule' for a further 5s yearly. Three weeks later he explained to the Burgh Council that the wall at the riverside which protected these feus had been damaged in a spate and requested them to make the repairs or alternatively to cancel his current debt to them of £50. A sympathetic Council wiped off two-thirds of the account. The Friary lands remained in the Cuthbert family until 1640 when the Presbytery started proceedings for their recovery to provide glebes for the first and second charges, a transaction not completed until 10 January 1648. Thus, 415 years after its foundation, the Friary and its possessions passed into history.

Old High Church

It is reasonably certain that the small chapel Columba built on land given to him by Brude MacMaelchon was on the small riverside mound of Saint Michael's Mount, the site of the present Old High Church, but the simple materials with which it was constructed would not be capable of enduring, so that no trace of it exists today. When the Roman Church replaced such structures with more permanent buildings it almost invariably erected them on the venerated sites of their predecessors and dedicated them to some saint. The church in Inverness was dedicated to the Virgin Mary and certainly was on Saint Michael's Mount, doubtless the ancient site. At some date between 1164 and 1171 William the Lion made a grant to this church in these terms: 'William, by the Grace of God King of Scots, to all good men in his whole land; Greetings. Know that I have given and granted to God, and the Church of Saint Mary in Inuirnys, and Thomas, Priest, parson of the said Church, one plough of land in perpetual mortification. Whereof I will that the foresaid Thomas hold the foresaid land as freely and peaceably held. Witness — Nicholas, chancellor; Matthew, Archbishop of St. Andrews; David Olifard, Richard Comyn. At Elgin'.[9] But it was not long before the same William granted the church and its revenues to the Monastery of Aberbrothoc (Arbroath) whose Abbots thereafter consistently starved it of funds. In 1371 the Bishop of the Diocese described the church as 'a noble, strong and distinguished place', but its roof was in disrepair.[10] A part of that church — a portion of its tower — is still traceable in the tower of the present church. By 1769 it was in a ruinous condition and was demolished to be replaced by the building we still have, the town church of Inverness. Here during the lifetime of the Burgh, the 'Kirking of the Council' took place on the Sunday following the Annual Meeting. The Provost and Magistrates occupied the front centre of the gallery which is furnished with arm-chairs for their comfort instead of the usual pews. Each chair is fronted by a large Bible, embossed with the Town Arms and bears the date 1775. The Town Council used to assemble at the Provost's house every Sunday and process to church. Then back to the Provost's for Hollands and bread and cheese before returning to church for afternoon service before dispersing to their own homes. This continued until 1775 when there was a dispute about precedence. A tailor turned merchant claimed the higher position given to merchant councillors over tradesmen. The dispute continued even after the minister had entered the pulpit. Next day a specially convened meeting of the Council decided that the two pews should be converted into one so that all members could be accommodated equally and at the same time agreed to proceed from the Town House instead of the Provost's residence. This continued until 1894 when the single pew was restored to its original two and the weekly attendance dropped to an annual visit and attendance on national days of prayer or thanksgiving only. The Minister of the Old High Church continues to be Chaplain to the Town and now District Council.[11]

The reformation seems to have passed reasonably peacefully in Inverness with an easy transition to Protestant Ministers, MacLaughlan claiming that a son-in-law of John Knox, Robert Pont, 'was sent as superintendent of the Church and laboured here for five years', whilst many others record that Thomas Howieson (or Houston), formerly a priest, was the first Protestant Minister being appointed in 1565. These statements may not be in conflict if Pont is regarded as not having been appointed to the church but rather as someone to oversee it. Yet another competitor for the distinction of being first is David Rag, described in court proceedings as 'our Minister' in December 1561. This case was for slander against one Arthur Byrnaye who had accused the Minister of adultery with his wife.

Howieson had been a schoolmaster and continued to teach after his appointment. In a deed of 1550 he had been described as 'Master of Arts, Clerk of the Diocese of Aberdeen and Notary under Apostolic licence' and in June 1561 he had been sworn in as Burgh clerk along with two others by the Inverness Magistrates; obviously he was a 'lad o' pairts'. Between 1661 and 1689, when Episcopacy was dominant the Kirk Session continued to function as before and the church building was used by both the 'English' and 'Eirshe' churches and 'when a chaplin was here they had Church of England service at another hour.'[12] The Kirk Session at this time was hardly distinguishable from the magistracy, the personnel being identical and meetings of both bodies often being on church premises.

After the Battle of Culloden the Church was used by Government forces to house prisoners, and in the churchyard can still be seen two stones in a direct line nine paces apart; one stone has two curved hollows and the other a V-shaped groove. It is thought that Jacobite prisoners were led out to the first stone and either sat or were made to kneel in it whilst their executioners rested their muskets in the groove of the other.

Whilst stationed in Inverness at this time, prior to his transfer to Canada and death at Quebec, Lieut-Colonel James Wolfe made a regular practice of attending worship in the Old High Church.

Except for the period of the Second World War the church bell has run curfew on every week-day since 1720. In a show-case in front of the pulpit is a copy of the King James Bible, first edition, of 1611 commonly known as 'the great "He" Bible' because Verse 15 of Ruth 3 reads 'and he went into the city', whereas others translate the words as 'and she went into the city'.

Dunbar's Hospital

The first civilian hospital in Inverness of which we have definite information is Dunbar's, built in 1668 and like several others of about that date built partly with stones from Cromwell's Fort. Still standing in Church Street, it is one of the oldest buildings in the town. There are, however, earlier references to hospitals but scant information given. Royal Charters of 1567 and 1591 granted to the Burgh both mention a hospital, and the records of the Kirk Session of Inverness show that there was such an institution in 1661 and imply an existence twenty years before that. Where these were situated is unknown except that a resolution to build a Grammar School in 1664 states that it is to be built 'beside the house used as a hospital', and since other evidence shows that about that time there was a school at the corner of Bank Street and Bank Lane it is presumed that 'the house used for a hospital' was also in that vicinity. It would have been maintained by voluntary subscription and have operated more as a poor house than a hospital as we understand the title today. Control over it was exercised by the Kirk Session, a joint body of the Inverness charges — two until 1706, thereafter until the present day three Old High, St. Mary's (Gaelic) and West, the Gaelic one then being in Church Street but later transferred to Dalneigh as English speaking. Until 1950 none of these churches had individual control of their affairs which were wholly in the hands of the Session along with the administration of most of the charitable funds of the town. Even today those funds, including the ownership of Dunbar's, are administered by a joint Session made up of representatives of those same three churches.

An old volume of accounts of this hospital still exists with the first part left blank as though to allow for the insertion of earlier transactions, the earliest recorded ones covering the years 1657 to 1663 when Bailie John Hepburn was Treasurer. Like most of his successors he was a prominent citizen and a member of the Town Council; like all of them he was appointed by the Kirk Session to whom he rendered his statement of accounts after they had been audited by a committee also appointed by that body. These first recorded ones are dated 5 December 1663 when he was leaving office, apparently the only time any treasurer had his transactions audited and approved by Session. His were audited by the two Ministers, two Bailies, a past Bailie and a ruling Church Elder. They show that he had paid out £1091 19s 0d for the hospital house and that he was able to hand on to the new treasurer £5994 6s 8d 'be bonds, precepts or decreits, infeftment or money in hand'.[13]

John Hepburn was succeeded as Treasurer of the Hospital by Alexander Dunbar, later to serve three terms as Provost. It appears obvious that he was a dynamic activist able to galvanise others into action in the wake of his own efforts. The building which rightly bears his name is the fruit of his endeavours, but it is clear that there had already been some other building since John Hepburn had spent over a thousand pounds on the 'hospital house', chiefly on lime and sand for repairs or additional building and on pynerfies (cartage). Within five years of taking office Alexander Dunbar had built the building which still stands, on land he owned and at his own expense. He had cajoled an impressive number of other prominent citizens into subscribing to maintain it, and influenced many others to mortify (bequeath) further funds for the same purpose. Entered amongst these mortifications in his account book is an item, '1668 — Mortified be the said Alex. Dunbar, Provost of Inverness, Hospitall Treasurer, the ground right of the Hospitall and yard yroff, with the whole Hospitall, skoole, weyhouse, and all the casualties within the same, all wch he bought and buylded on his own expensis, wch extends to . . . and wch Hospitall and yard has been mantient and repared on ye said Provost his expenssis since the buylding therof till the tearme of Martmas sixteen hundred and four skore thrie yiers'.[14] It is to be noted that he failed to enter the value of this mortification.

The old Hospital is substantially and well-built of stone and lime and slated. The walls on the ground floor are about three feet thick. Its length about 72 feet, its width about 27 feet. It stands abutting the street, the level of which has been altered by lowering it at a later date; and the north end stood so close to the carriage way that part of the wall has there been reduced in thickness for several feet up to give more room to foot passengers.

The building is three-storied, the lower consisting formerly of the Grammar School on one side, and the Weyhouse on the other side of the entrance door, which has a Norman arch above it. An entrance hall leads to a stone staircase giving access to the upper floors. The roof, which is of a high pitch, had formerly a small steeple or belfry in the centre. The ground-floor had formerly six windows, a floor above six also, and two small ones besides, and the attic floor six dormer windows. Each of these has an inscription on the pediment above it; these are as follows, reckoning from the north end:— The pediment of the first has the figure of a bedesman and the date 1668 and the words 'This poor man cryed', that of the second the words 'And the Lord heard him, and saved him out of his tryel', the pediment of the third has 'A little that a righteous man hath is better nor the' and that of the fourth '1668' and 'Riches of many wicked men'. The pediment of fifth has 'He that giveth to the poor leneth to the' and that of the sixth '1668' and 'Lord and Hie wil paye them sevean tymes mor'. The first, second and fourth have fleur de lis at the top of the pediments. The tops of the third and fifth are much worn and have carvings which may be meant for thistles. The sixth has apparently an angel— some of them, in addition, griffins or scrolls on the upper part. Above the entrance door is a tablet bearing the date 1676 with the arms of Provost Dunbar and the motto 'Suum cuique tribue' and the words cut thereon 'Alexander Dunbar, Provest of Invernes. This weyhouse belongs to the Hospital of Invernes, the rent thereof payable be the master of the weyhouse to the Treasurer of the said Hospital'. At the back there are four dormer windows; on two of the pediments is inscribed 'Invernes', on two the date '1668'. Apparently there were once two more, one having been altered into

28

a chimney stalk, into which the pediment, with date, has been built.[15]

Provost Dunbar retired from the Treasurership in 1683 when he handed over to his successor assets of £11,164 6s 4d, but his liberality to the hospital did not cease, for he made two further gifts of 2000 merks Scots each. One was for the benefit of 'such indigent deserving persons as should be called by Mr Gilbert Marshall, then Minister at Inverness, or his successors as ministers there, and by James Barbour of Mullderg and James Dunbar, Bailie of Inverness and their aires or representatives, the purpose being that the rents should be employed (1st) For building a stone dyke about the yaird of the Hospitall in conjunction with the other rents of the Hospitall and weighouse kept yrin; and (2ndly) for maintaining the poor persons that should be called by the said Trustees, with a preference for any of the name Dunbar.' The other was for use 'and behoof of eight poor, weak, old and indigent persons within the Burgh of Inverness only, that the yearly interest thereof might be divided among them towards their relief and helping of maintenance and clothing'.[16] His mortification of 1668, previously apparently only recorded in the Treasurer's Account Book, was formally shown in the Session Minutes of 18 September 1711 when some minor additions were made. The lower room was to be used as 'a Grammar Skoole ffor the use off the towne off Inverness for ever' was now specified as being 'in the South end' whilst the Weyhouse is stated to be 'in the North end', its rent 'at present ffourtie-twa punds Scotts money' to be used 'ffor upholding the whole ffabrick, and all the roumes above for the use of the poor'.[17] Alexander Dunbar served as Provost from 1666/69, 1674/79 and 1680/83 and as was customary he was given the courtesy title for the remainder of his life. He donated 1000 merks to the fund for building the Ness Bridge (a name not officially used until 1961) which was started in 1681 and completed in 1685 and was honoured by having his arms placed on the eastern archway facing Bridge Street.[18] The date of his death is not recorded, but twice in 1701 he is referred to as 'the deceast Alexr. Dunbar of Barmuchatie, late Provost of Inverness'.

Wimberley points out that the hospital got very little, if any, good from the two later gifts from the Provost. 'Both sums were deposited in the hands of Bailie James Dunbar, or James Roy Dunbar of Dalcross as he is frequently designed, merchant in Inverness, who seems to have been resolved not only to be custodier of the funds, but to employ them in his own business without paying any interest thereon.'[19] There were, it appears, no less than three different James Dunbars concerned in the affairs of the hospital at this time; James Dunbar elder and James Dunbar junior who were both deacons of the parish and who both signed 'docquets' appended to the accounts of different treasurers; but another signature of the same name also appears in this capacity, and one of these three became Hospital Treasurer from 1712 to 1719. It is not clear which, if any, were related to the Provost nor whether Bailie James, sometimes James Roy, was one of them. It does, however, appear that the Bailie was his son since there is a reference in 1712 to 'Alexr. Dunbar of Barmuchatie, only lawful son and apparent heir to said deceast James Dunbar of Dalcross'. The fact that this heir had the same Christian name as the late Provost and that both were 'of Barmuchatie' would suggest that the one was grandson of the other, making James Dunbar of Dalcross son of the Provost. The private use of the Provost's bequests by the Bailie caused considerable perturbation in the Session and references to his failure to pay interest or to account for the capital are in the Minutes of 1 July and 17 July, 2 November 1701 and again on 11 September 1711 when the Treasurer was instructed to use 'the utmost diligence, both personal and reall, against the said Bailie for recovering the poor's money lying in his hands'. As a result of this diligence the Treasurer received a half-cobble's fishing as security, a pledge which the next year, was shown as having a value of £2000 Scots (£166 13s 4d sterling) against a debt of 2000 merks plus unpaid interest of a further 1600 merks. Between the giving of the security and the recording of this valuation the Bailie had died and his heirs were now shown as owing a further 2000 merks with arrears of interest (a total of £222 4s 5d sterling) on the other of Provost Dunbar's mortifications and

£609 16s 0d for an unspecified reason. For these accumulated debts 'the lands above the hill' (Gallowmuir and Milnfield) were given as security and not redeemed for fifty years.[20] These lands, lying to the south of the town, roughly between Kingsmills and Muirfield Roads, had been granted to the Burgesses in the 'Great Charter' of 1591.

The embarrassment and lack of real drive in seeking repayment of these unauthorised borrowings is explained, not just by the apparent relationship of the offender to the donor, but also by the composition of the Kirk Session in those days. A little earlier, in 1674, the Session Records show that the elders then were the Provost, the four Bailies, two former Provosts, three former Bailies, the Dean of Guild, the Burgh Treasurer and the landward lairds of Culloden, Dunean elder and younger, Moorton, Holme and Gillespie McBean. There were twenty deacons for the English (High, now Old High) Church and thirteen for the Irish (St Mary's Gaelic). Very soon after the Reformation a large number of new elders was appointed, including still the Provost and all, or nearly all, the Bailies with several merchants, so that sometimes the Session is said to 'consist of the Minister, Magistrates and Elders' and sometimes 'the Ministers with the Magistrates and remnant members of the Session'. With himself and his fellow-Bailies all such influential members, active pursuit of their claims by the Session would be delicate to say the very least. Litigation continued long after the Bailie's death and the Hospital retained possession of the lands and fishings until they were redeemed in 1762.

Nor were the troubles of the Hospital authorities confined only to these financial problems. It is quite clear that the worthy Provost's intention had been that the upper floors were to be used by the poor people of the town, chosen by the Trustees he had named, with preference given to those of the name Dunbar. The rent from the weigh-house, after the provision of a dyke, was to be used to maintain the property whilst that of the other mortifications was to maintain 'the deserving poor' residents. The deserving poor may have been maintained but certainly not as residents. In

September 1711 the future Hospital Treasurer, James Dunbar was protesting that both the upper floors should 'be made void and redde for receiving the poor, according to the will of the mortifier' to which one of the Magistrates replied 'Possess the rooms who will next year, the Magistrates have decerned in favour of him to whom it was set for this year and that they will own it'.[21] Obviously the Magistrates were letting these upper floors without consent of Session and without any regard to the wishes of the donor. In fact it appears that no 'deserving poor' ever lived in the Hospital except for a very few years after 1845.

The first petition for assistance which is recorded in the Session Minutes was lodged at Martinmas 1687 by Thomas Dunbar, merchant and burgess, who on 26 March the following year was granted 80 merks annually 'whyll he wear a gown suitable for his pentuine'. Many similar grants make the same condition and some even include the provision of such a gown as part of the benefit. In 1781 the Minutes record,

> The Session having considered that there has not been a Collection for the Infirmary at Aberdeen for these Twenty years past, and that several diseased persons have been sent from this place, and notwithstanding our neglect to collect for a long time, the Managers till very lately received objects into the Infirmary, and treated them with as much care and attention as if regular Contributions had been made and remitted to them; but believing that no Contributions were to be expected from this place in future, they at length resolved to receive no diseased from this place or parish, and accordingly returned Objects recommended to them without administrating any advice or medicine. The Session therefore appoint Intimation to be made first Lord's Day from the pulpit that a Collection might be made on the Monday following.[22]

Fifteen years later there is note of a similar decision, clear evidence that the wishes of the donor were still being ignored. Amongst the varied uses to which the upper floors were put the Minutes record:

20 June 1721 'The upper loaft let to the Magistrates to be a Hospital for the Regement of Fusaleers. Rent £3 stg.'

10 November 1778 'Let to the Magistrates for Writing School and English School.'

21 August 1792 Proposed 'to let the whole house to the Magistrates and Council as a Poorhouse for the town.'

22 May 1810 The whole, except the weighhouse was let to Hon. A. Fraser of Lovat for seven years. Rent £15 stg. yearly.

'About the year 1750 there was a company in Inverness for encouraging manufacturers. They rented a loft above the library in Dunbar's Hospital. It is interesting to learn, although difficult to believe, that so much lint was stored in the loft that the weight of it broke the great joists, and as might be expected the Session saw to it that the company repaired them.'

In 1845 'occupied as a Poorhouse till 1862 when the new house for the poor at Muirfield was opened.'[23]

Only the James Dunbar who became Hospital Treasurer in 1712 appears to have been at all concerned about the blatant disregard of the Provost's wishes. Eighteen months after the protest already mentioned he was stating that 'Provost Dunbar during his lifetime had placed Bedmen in the Hospital' and that 'in one of his mortifications of 2000 merks left for subsisting of the poor he appoints the yearly annl. rent thereof to be bestowed on such poor persons as shall be brought into the said house.' He also refers to his having 'consulted an expert advocate in Edinburgh, how he should obtain possession of the uppermost storie for which he had applied to the Magistrates and Council'.[24] All appears to have been in vain. Later he argued, 'It is evident that the said Provost Dunbar appointed the said house for lodging of the poor and not for to be set on rent or bestowing it for private use', but still without attaining his ends — or the Provost's.

In January 1710 we find Mr John Laying (Laing), Master of the Grammar School, 'craveing that the Session (as Patrons of the Hospital) would be pleased to allowe and grant him libertie to possess the Chamber above the school with the closet thereto belonging, both being fire rooms, in the south end of the Hospital, to the end that he might better attend his school and wait upon the Librarie; the Session, taking the same into consideration and seeing that none of the hospital poor did possess the same and being vacant, did grant the Petitioner's desire, and hereby allows the said Mr John to possess the same during the vacancie and their pleasure.'[25] Apparently there was no James Dunbar present that day to remind the Session that the reason none of the 'hospital poor' occupied these rooms was that the Session had never allowed them so to do. Two years later Mr Laying resigned from his post and claimed £25 Scots for arrears of salary and 'fiftie-eight shillings sevenpence sterling' which he had spent improving the chambers of the Hospital. His salary arrears were paid without demure but the Session decided 'to consider the other claim'. In November of that year a dispute arose about the appointment of his successor, the Magistrates and Town Council claiming the exclusive right, the Session claiming a joint right with them, one basis for this claim being their control of the school building. Eventually the Magistrates and Council called Mr James MacKenzie of Ferintosh 'without advice or consent of the Session' which thereupon 'for peace sak' agreed to call Mr James MacKenzie to be school-master at Inverness and referred his to the Presbytery to be tried according to Act of Parliament.[26] By 1715 the new Master, as well as the Session Clerk, was complaining because his salary was in arrears. In 1719 ' a strange and unauthorised schoolmaster set up school and began to teach in the Green of Muirtown' and on 28 April the Session asked Presbytery to examine this Donald Forbes 'to find out by what authority he sets up school there, the Magistrates to order the Burgesses not to support "such ane unorderly man" and that the matter be laid before the Justice of the Peace.'[27]

Six years later the Minutes record that 'A letter from Mr Alexander Dundas, Doctor of Medicine, and Preseise to the Society for the propogateing Christian Knowledge in the Highlands and Islands of Scotland was presented before the Session and Read, it being Anent An Important affair; viz, of Raining's Mortification for a School &c. The consideration of it was referred to the Committie on the Hospital Accompts.'[28] This was indeed 'an important affair' since it was the start of Raining's School which so long existed on Barnhill, and which is still commemorated in the stairway from near the foot of Castle Street to the school-site at the end of Ardconnel Street — 'The Raining Stairs'. John Raining, a Scottish merchant resident in Norwich, left £1000 to the General Assembly of the Church of Scotland 'to plant a school in any part of the North Britain where they think it is most wanted'. The General Assembly of 1724 handed this bequest over to the Society for Promoting Christian Knowledge in Scotland who, after discussions with the Session and the Town Council of Inverness, agreed to use £200 to set up a school there. Initially it was housed in Dunbar's, in the upper part with the Grammar School continuing to operate below it; two schools in the one building. By 1757 however new premises were built and Raining School moved to the site it was to occupy until its absorption into the High School (now the Crown Primary School) in 1894. The Grammar School continued in the Hospital until 1792 when it was replaced by the Academy in what is now called Academy Street. Undoubtedly the most notable scholar to have studied at the Grammar School is General Wolfe, victor of Quebec, who took lessons in mathematics whilst stationed in Inverness after the Battle of Culloden. Another famous visitor was John Wesley who, on one of his four visits to Inverness, preached at seven in the morning 'in a commodious room in Dunbar's Hospital.'[29]

With the closure of the Grammar School the Magistrates represented to the Session that 'that part of the Hospital which had long been used as a school-room, and the large cellar formerly used as weigh-house, would not be wanted for these purposes, and as a Poorhouse was very much wanted it would be very proper to employ the whole fabrick in that way, as it is evident that the worthy man who mortified the House did intend that the whole of it, except the weigh-house and grammar school, would be occupied as a Hospital or Poorhouse.'[30] This belated recognition of Provost Dunbar's intentions was approved by the Session — and allowed to drop. For some time after this the space had many and varied occupants; it was a female school, female work society rooms and flats for private residence. The town's first fire appliance was housed there. In 1817 it was used as a soup kitchen for the poor and then, in 1845 it at last became a Poorhouse — but only for sixteen years, and even then it was an isolation hospital for part of that time during a cholera epidemic. More recent uses have included Boy Scout Headquarters and now a social centre for the care of senior citizens.

Mention has been made of the school master in 1710 suggesting that he might 'better attend his school and wait upon the Librarie', a reference to one of the Sessions most notable possessions, the Session Library.

The re-establishment of Presbyterian form of Church Government in 1690 was closely followed by a movement to form libraries in remote districts of the Highlands. In the year 1704 The General Assembly of the Church of Scotland declared their approval of a scheme devised by some pious people in England and Scotland for providing libraries in the Highlands of Scotland and, in the following year, by Act of Assembly, they divided the whole of the books into territorial libraries of two kinds, presbyterial and parochial. Of the former Inverness (including the shire it is presumed) was to get one and of the latter three. From this originated the Kirk Session Library, although there is no trace of any of the three proposed parochial libraries.[31]

By the beginning of 1706 'the Kirk Session had under its control the nucleus of a good library'. In one old book in that library is written, on the first page, 'A catalogue of the books sent by piously disposed persons in London to the town of Inverness as the beginning of a Presbyterial Library in that bounds, with an account of the value put upon the said books by Mr Henderson, Stationer, Edinburgh.'[32] Thereafter about 200 volumes are listed. In addition there were also received 30 Irish (i.e. Gaelic) Bibles and New Testaments bound together, 45 Irish New Testaments, 150 Catechisms, 12 copies of 'A Plain Man's Reply to the Roman Missionaries', the whole valued at £775 0s 8d.

The Library at first put the ministers into something of a dilemma; a library cannot be kept together without a suitable place to keep the books in. The ministers do not appear to have had any proper place for the purpose and at last they were obliged to make representations to the Kirk Session who provided a room in Dunbar's Hospital which, however, seems to have been contrary to the intentions of the founder of the Hospital.[33]

From this circumstance the control of the Library passed wholly into the hands of the Kirk Session.

Frequent benefactions were made, the chief from James Fraser, son of Rev. Alex. Fraser, Minister of Petty from 1633/81 who was Secretary of Chelsea Hospital. Not only did he give books and cash but he also chose, purchased and dispatched books to the Library.

The oldest book in it is dated 1529. Many of the books are no doubt rare and valuable as well. They are mostly standard works of their time in all branches of literature, including treatises on Philosophy and Medicine, works on Theology, Polemics, Social and Political Economy, History, Biography, Geography, Travel and Adventure. There are also dictionaries in Gaelic, English, Latin, Greek, French, German, and to bring up the rear, a Low Dutch Grammar.[34]

When the Grammar School merged with the Academy the Library followed and was in the Academy Hall until 1817 when it was moved back to Dunbar's. There it remained until the Hospital became a Poorhouse in 1845, when it was moved into the Session House of the Old High Church and then, in 1891, 'to one of the rooms in the Female School, lately used as a Kindergarten School in Academy Street.'[35] This school had now become the Halls of the Old High Church and here the Library remained, largely ignored and seldom consulted, until it was recently handed over to the Highland Region Council Library for cataloguing and safe-keeping.

The Town House

For a town of such antiquity Inverness has remarkably few really old buildings so that sites rather than edifices tend to be the more interesting. Although not old, the Town House is notably an exception to this general rule.

Centuries ago the council and the Kirk Session had almost wholly the same personnel, and from the records it appears that they were not too careful in differentiating between these different functions. They usually met in the Parish Church, presumably in its vestry, but later moved to the Laigh Council House at the Bridge End where they remained until 1670 when they purchased a dilapidated tenement building built for his own town house by Lord Lovat some sixty-five years earlier. Here, on the site of the present Town House they may have met until 1708, when the building was demolished and a new meeting place erected at a cost of £600 sterling.

The new building was a three-storied building with a news-room on the ground floor, the Town Hall on the first and above that a sewing and spinning room, later the Guildry Room, and somewhere there must have been a Town Clerk's office since it is mentioned at a later date. Such was the building known to Burt as 'A plain building of rubble, and there is one room in it where the Magistrates meet upon the Town's business, which would be really handsome, but the walls are rough, not white-washed or so much as plastered, and no furniture in it but a table and some rough chairs, and altogether immoderately dirty.'[36] These spartan premises were to be used for well over a century and a half. In view of the troubled times and the fact that the town was open and defenceless it was decided in 1745 that the 'records, charters and papers' should be moved from the Town Hall and the

Town Clerk's Office to the Charter Room of the Tolbooth Steeple across the road. When the Bridge was demolished in 1849 it was decided that its stone bearing the Burgh Arms should be built into the walls of the Town House. There it is to this day although in a different building, in the west gable overlooking Castle Wynd.

Burgh Arms

The armorial bearings of the Burgh until its demise were, in non-heraldic language, a crucifix in natural colours on a red shield under a crest of a cornucopia mounted on a Crusader's helmet. Standing on their hind legs on a grassy mound an elephant and dromedary supported the shield with their forelegs. The motto ws *Concordia et Fidelitas*.

These bearings were curious in two ways. The 'livery colours', the ceremonial colours used by the owner of any armorial bearings, are properly the first colour and the first metal mentioned in the description of the arms. Since Inverness had no metal mentioned it should strictly have used only red but since the Cross was invariably pictured as yellow this was taken as the metal gold and so the livery colours used were red and yellow. Over the years heraldry has caused various animals to assume all sorts of peculiar poses but surely none so bizarre as ungainly animals such as the elephant and the dromedary prancing on their hind legs trying to support a shield which, no matter how clever the artist, inevitably appeared to be supporting them. The use of supporters was a rare privilege for Scottish local authorities and the honour of having them was lost to Inverness at the death of the Burgh.

All Scottish Burghs, royal or baronial, had from their earliest period a Common Seal usually bearing the image of their patron saint. Thus the Inverness seal bore the figure of Christ on the Cross on the obverse with, on the reverse, the Virgin and Infant (the parish church being dedicated to Saint Mary) with a lily, a star and a crescent in the background. Lord Lyon, King of Arms, the supreme authority in Scotland on all heraldic matters, is of the opinion that the crucifix represented the Dominican Friary whilst the lily and crescent are recognised emblems of the Virgin. The crescent also typifies a ship whilst the star as a symbol of sailors is often used by harbour towns.

On the staircase of the Town House are two wooden panels found many years ago in the cellar of the old Burgh Court-house. One bears on its front the Royal Arms of the seventeenth century and the initials 'C.R.' said to be for Charles Rex. On the reverse is the Scottish Royal Shield and the figures 86 in a heart-shaped border, taken to indicate 1686 — but Charles the Second died in 1685. The reverse may, of course, have been painted later than the front. The second panel, obviously contemporary with the first, has the oldest authentic representation of the Inverness Arms, 'Gules, a camel statant contourne or; Supporters two elephants rampant proper; Crest a cornucopia; Motto *Concordia et Fidelitas.*' So at that time the recognised arms were a camel (not a dromedary) on a red shield with two elephants, even then prancing, as supporters. About the same time Lord Lyon ordered all Burghs to register their Arms but, like many another, Inverness failed to comply in spite of having resolved to do so in 1680. Then, in 1683, they ordered James Smith, a Master Mason in Edinburgh, to cut the Arms in a stone to be incorporated into the bridge then being built. For his guidance they described the Arms as 'Our Saviour on the Cross supported a dromedarie on the dexter and an elephant upon the sinister.' Three years later Smith was writing the Council to complain that although he had cut the stone according to the original order he now had instructions to cut the dromedarie for the Arms supported by two elephants. Apparently the Council itself was not sure what their Arms were — or had they doubts about the permanence of the reign of James II and so wanted Arms which could not be suspected of favouring Roman Catholicism? In fact they did use the stone as originally ordered — the stone that is now built into the west wall of the Town House. It bears the date 1686, the same as that thought to be indicated on the wooden panel, and shows the supporters standing on their four legs holding up the shield with their heads, a much more natural posture. The motto is *Fidelitas et Concordia* a reversal of the usual order of words. Above the front door of the Town House is a later representation of the Arms, but has the hind legs of the elephant jointed the wrong way!

The Arms were finally matriculated in March 1900 when the helmet first appeared. This was included to commemorate the building in Inverness of a ship for Count St Pol to use in the Crusades. The elephant and the dromedary are said to be emblematic of the seaborne trade Inverness had in ancient times with eastern and Mediterranean ports. Another story is that they were granted by William the Lion in recognition of the contribution the town made towards his ransom when he was held captive in England. Whatever the truth of this story it is most unlikely that he granted them as supporters since such additions to armorial bearings appear to have been unknown until the fourteenth century.

These Arms ceased to be used in 1975 when the Burgh became part of the Inverness District and that larger authority assumed new bearings on 15 May of that year. These still have the Crucifix on a red ground as the main feature but with a crescent and a star on that ground, a return to a feature of the old town seal. In the chief, the upper part of the shield, separated from the red field by a wavy band of white to represent the Ness and Beauly Rivers are a cornucopia on a blue ground, a rampant wild cat on gold and a fraise (strawberry) flower also on blue the first being the old Burgh crest and the latter representing the two chief clans of the District, MacIntosh and Fraser. The motto remains *Concordia et Fidelitas* but, in accordance with an edict of Lord Lyon that no District Countil be allowed supporters and that they must all have a gold coronet of thistles as a crest, the elephant and the dromedary, the oldest elements in the Burgh Arms, have gone, and the cornucopia has moved to the shield itself.

And so back to the Town House. The old building was demolished in 1878 and the present one completed four years later. It was opened by the then Duke of Edinburgh and cost £13,500 of which £5000 was from a bequest by Duncan Grant of Bught. Because of this bequest the centre windows in the Hall have the Grant crest, a burning rock, and the MacRae crest, a hand brandishing a short sword — Mrs Grant was born a MacRae. Except for the full-length portrait of Lord President Forbes and the smaller ones of Prince Charles Edward Stuart and Flora MacDonald all the portraits in the Hall are of ex-provosts whilst the sculptures, with one exception, are of prominent citizens who never were Provosts. The exception is the fine head of Sir Alexander MacEwen who was Provost from 1925 to 1931. The windows on the length of the Hall each bear the shields of Scottish Clans, the interesting point being that those ancient foes Campbell and MacDonald are placed at the two extremities, as far apart as they can be. They are: Argyll (Campbell), MacLeod, MacKay; Grant, Stewart of Appin, MacGregor; MacKenzie, Ross, Matheson and then beyond the central windows MacLean, Munro, Robertson; Cluny (MacPherson), MacIntosh, Locheil (Cameron); Glengarry, Sleat and Clanranald all three MacDonalds. In one of the end windows are parts of the bearings of the three most prominent clans in the locality, the portions representing their names which are Chisholm, Fraser and Forbes whilst at the opposite end are the Royal Arms with Scottish Quarterings, Inverness Burgh and the Scottish Royal Shield with those of the six Incorporated Trades of Inverness below: Tailors, Bakers, Hammermen, Carpenters, Masons and Skinners.

Next to the Hall is the Council Chamber and it was here that a really historic event took place. Not for the first, nor the last, time Ireland was in ferment and a crisis arose. The Prime Minister was on holiday at Gairloch, his deputy at Beaufort and King George V at Moy so instead of them going to London they summoned the Cabinet to meet in Inverness, the only time it has ever convened outside the vicinity of London. From this meeting emerged the 'Inverness Formula' which formed the basis of the discussions at the conference where the Treaty creating the Irish Free State (Eire) was agreed. The meeting was in the Council Chamber at 11 a.m. on 7 September 1921, the members sitting round the horseshoe table, not using the dais. The Council Officer, William Bain, was alert enough to pass round a sheet of plain paper which each member signed, a paper still in the Council's possession. A facsimile is on display, the original having shown signs of fading. Present were: Lloyd George, Prime Minister; Austen Chamberlain, Lord Privy Seal; Viscount Birkenhead, Lord Chancellor; Sir Robert S. Horne, Chancellor of the Exchequer; Edward Shortt, Home Secretary; Edward S. Montague, Secretary for India; Viscount Derwent, Lord Lieutenant of Ireland; Sir Hamar Greenwood, Irish Secretary; Sir Eric Geddes, Minister of Transport; Stanley Baldwin, Secretary of the Board of Trade; Sir Alfred Mond, Health Minister; Sir Laming Worthington-Evans, Secretary for War; Sir Arthur Griffiths-Boscawen, Minister for Agriculture and Fisheries; Robert Munro, Scottish Secretary; Dr T.J. Macnamara, Minister of Labour and Winston S. Churchill, Colonial Secretary. After the Cabinet Meeting the Prime Minister returned to Gairloch but first called at John Macpherson and Sons, gunsmiths and fishing tackle suppliers, to augment his gear for fishing at Loch Maree. The following Sunday the proprietor, John Macpherson, had a telephone call from Miss Frances Stevenson (later Lloyd George's second wife) the Premier's private secretary asking if he could arrange for a dentist to go to Gairloch to extract one of the Prime Minister's teeth. He could, and a well-known dentist in the town, David Lees Provan, made the round trip of some one hundred and fifty miles to remove the offending molar.

On one wall of the Council Chamber, underneath the Press Gallery, are three portraits of past Provosts, W. Simpson, Phineas MacKintosh and Cuthbert. There is little to say of the first except that he was in office from 1846 to 1852 and not as shown below his picture, and that he is said to have fled to London with someone else's wife at the end of that term. The third is not given any forename or even initial and there was no serving Provost Cuthbert in 1730, the date on his frame.

For the remainder of their lives ex-Provosts, were, and still are, given the courtesy title of Provost, and this must apply here for the last of several Cuthberts to hold that office left it in 1689. No matter which Provost Cuthbert it represents he must have been an old man in 1730. From 1600 to 1689, one member or other of the Cuthbert of Drakies family held the Provostship for forty-five years. At one time there was a Provost, a Bailie, two Councillors and the Town Clerk all of that family, and twenty years later there was again a Provost Cuthbert with a Town Clerk and a Deputy Town Clerk all related to him and bearing the same name. It might with reason be asked why these three should be specially chosen for the honour of overseeing the deliberations of their successors when all other ex-Provosts are in less-frequented rooms. To explain the machinations of Phineas it is necessary to give a short history of the Common Good Fund.

Common Good Fund

In the early days, before rates and government grants to finance local needs had been though of, such civic requirements as arose were mainly paid for by endowments from the Crown, and these were the foundation of the Common Good Fund from which Burghs were able to spend money on projects not provided for in any enabling legislation. For example there is no Act giving power to spend money entertaining distinguished guests nor in mounting a campaign against some proposal detrimental to the town; the Common Good Fund can provide that cash.

Royal Burghs were built on Royal lands, and the burgesses qualified as such by having a piece of land at least a rood in extent for which, in Inverness, they paid a rent of five shillings to the King. A rood was a narrow strip with a road frontage of twenty feet — the space need for a house. Together with fines, great customs (duties on foreign imports and exports), petty customs (duties on internal trade) and other minor dues, these rents were collected by the Bailies and periodically paid to the King's High Chamberlain. Gradually it became the practice for these revenues to be leased to the Magistrates for short periods at fixed annual amounts, thereby saving the preparation of detailed accounts for the Chamberlain. Eventually these leases were converted into a permanent feu right; the Burgh itself, except for the great customs, was feued to the burgesses whose representatives collected the various revenues on their behalf. This mutual ownership of the lands and revenues became the Common Good and instead of the burgesses being direct tenants of the King, the Burgh became the King's vassal. Comparing feu duty gives some indication of the importance of various towns in the mid fourteenth century; Aberdeen paid £213 6s 8d Scots, Inverness £53 6s 8d and Edinburgh £34 13s 4d.

In those days the Burgh was quite compact, its boundaries being the fosse built by William the Lion which ran approximately along what are now Chapel Street, Academy Street, Ardconnel Terrace and thence to the river near Castlehill and, on the other side, Alexander Place, King Street and Duff Street to the river again at Huntly Place. All the land within this boundary, except for the Castle and its environs which remained in the possession of the Crown, was then in the ownership of the burgesses. Outwith these limits other lands were granted by charter, the first being the Burgh Haugh at Island Bank and Lower Drummond and then, in 1236, the Merkinch, with a feu duty of one pound of pepper every year at Michaelmas. Other grants followed including the fishings in the river and the Burgh Mills known as Kingsmills. To this day residents in the old Burgh bounds are allowed to fish the river freely every tenth day. Shore dues on goods landed at the harbour, tolls on the Ness Bridge, fees payable by burgesses on admission to the freedom of the Burgh, and those paid by apprentices on being articled all went into the Common Good Fund, which managed to meet all normal demands. Only when the demand was exceptional was a voluntary stent (levy) imposed. With the Reformation came further extensive grants from what had been Church lands, but also large scale fueing of valuable areas to favoured individuals at nominal prices, so that a potentially wealthy Fund was considerably depleted. The whole of the Bught estate was feued for £6 16s 8d Scots, only 11s 5d sterling and Raigmore, from Culcabock to Culloden Burn for £1 4s sterling.

A Royal Commission on Municipal Corporations in Scotland reporting in 1833 said of Inverness,

A large part of the Landed Property of the Burgh has been alienated at different times so that this portion of the funds is now comparatively small. The alienations were not, in every instance, made either after public intimation or by public roup but were authorised by acts of council upon reports of committees. Except in a very few cases engineers, surveyors or men of professional skill were not consulted. In some instances the alienations were highly censurable, by reason of having been made privately, for an inadequate value and to members of the council. Of this description was the sale of the lands of Drumevan or Drummond, made to the Provost on 15 September 1783. In 1785 the prescription was interrupted by the burgesses, via facti, upon which proceeding a formal instrument was taken.

Other lands, called Campfield, of inferior extent and value, were afterwards acquired by him from the Burgh. At the time of the sale of Campfield, 11 and 18 January 1796, the purchaser was one of the councillors of the Burgh and had for several years previously been its provost. The minutes of the council bear that the lands were barren and of no use whatsoever to the community and, accordingly, they were sold for £20 and a feu duty of 20/-. Their extent is about 20 acres and, as they are situated adjoining to the lands immediately surrounding the Provost's residence (as the Commissioners ascertained on inspection) they necessarily formed a desirable acquisition. The description of them given in the minutes of the council was substantially untrue, as was proved by the examination of a gentleman who was a member of the council at the time of the sale

and who is well acquainted with the different modes, and the necessary expense of improving land. By his declaration it appears that the purchaser has not expended any considerable sum on meliorations, for that the land was not difficult to improve, as merely ploughing and liming would be sufficient.
Notwithstanding, the purchaser, about two or three years after the date of sale, received a rent of about £35. This transaction was entirely private and, although the Commissioners were unable to recover evidence, they ascertained that it was commonly believed that a higher offer had been made and refused.

Another sale also appears to have been made under circumstances of a suspicious nature although the Commissioners were unable to obtain explicit evidence of malversation. On 11 January 1796 an application was made to the council by one of the bailies for a feu of part of the Burgh property which immediately adjoined his own lands. On 18 January, after a report by a committee, a sale was made to him for £50 and annual feu duty of £2 10s. which was said to be the rent under the existing lease. *1st* no specification of the extent of the ground is given; *2nd* the acquisition was obviously desirable; *3rd* the purchaser was a member of the council and *4th* the transaction was private.

Whilst these sales were thus made to members of the council by private bargain there appear to have been other sales and feus made after public intimation and by public auction to persons not of the council.[37]
The Provost referred to, Phineas MacKintosh, served for four terms between 1770 and 1791 each of three years with a similar interval between each term when one or other of his cronies filled the office, yet he is one of the three ex-Provosts chosen to look down on the activities of his successors.
Common Good accounts for the period 1730-90 make interesting reading. At the start of that period the gross revenue was about £250, by the end it had risen to £1000, this revenue going to payment of the Crown feu-duty and other burdens, salaries of officials, public works and repairs and, a

frequently recurring item, expenses for 'the honour and interest of Royalty'. This last appears to have been roistering in the Town House both on the King's and the Queen's birthdays when several dozen bottles of 'strong claret' were consumed. Another much-repeated item for 'glasses broken' surely speaks for itself. In the years 1732-34 the expenditure on 'entertainments' was almost £50 annually — out of a total revenue of only £250. Public works and repairs took only £29 and public burdens, which included £22 for the stipends and house rents of two ministers, came to £54. The town's advocate, Duncan Forbes of Culloden, later to be Lord President of the Court of Session and whose portrait has already been mentioned, received a fee of 120 guineas Scots (10 guineas sterling), and the headmaster of the Grammar School £16 13s 4d sterling. The scavenger, who was the proprietor of the Bught no less, received £24 Scots (£2 sterling) and the Provost £6 13s 4d Scots (11s 2d sterling) but the Town Clerk was not paid at all. The first salary paid to a Town Clerk was in 1736 when the Provost's salary ceased. The four Burgh Officers each had £18, the Dempster (Court officer and hangman) £16 whilst the drummer received £20, all Scots. Apparently the drummer was three times as useful as the Town Clerk. Significantly in a town consistently loyal to the throne, nothing appears in these accounts for entertainment of the Jacobites whilst they were here in 1746, but various items of expenditure are recorded after the Duke of Cumberland arrived — for the comfort of the troops, for the improvements to the appearance of the Town House used, with hotel next door, as his headquarters, for the burial of the bodies of those executed and for the cleansing of the streets, 'on the order of the Magistrates upon a message from H.R.H. the Duke of Cumberland'.

The Common Good Fund continued to meet the expenses of running the town until 1808 when an Act was passed allowing the Council to make an assessment for the purpose of extending and improving the harbour, building a bridge (Waterloo or 'Black' Bridge), constructing a quay at Thornbush, providing a water supply, police, street lighting and other highly desirable amenities. From then the Fund gradually ceased to meet the Burgh expenses in general and became, what it is to the District Council to-day, a useful Fund to meet special requirements not covered by Statute.

And so back once again to the Town House. The magnificent crystal chandeliers in the Council Chamber and above the main staircase used to hang in the Northern Meeting Rooms in Church Street and are still on loan from the Northern Meeting Society.

On the staircase are the wooden panels already mentioned and three stained windows with the Royal Arms, Scottish quarterings (although strangely with the motto of the English Order of the Garter), the old Burgh Arms and the Scottish Standard with the motto of the Order of the Thistle. On the ground floor, in the entrance hall, is a wooden beam which was part of Cromwell's Fort later recovered from the river. There is also a portrait, painted around 1715, of James Fraser of Castle Leather (now Castle Heather but originally Castle Lethoir) who, with only three words of French in his vocabulary, set off on foot to France to persuade the Chevalier to allow Lord Lovat (the 'Fox) to return to his Clan. There is a duplicate of this picture in the National Portrait Gallery in Edinburgh but which is original and which copy is not known. It will be noted that, ardent Jacobite though he was, he is here shown bearing the black cockade of the House of Hanover on his bonnet.

The Castle

We cannot be certain about who built the first castle on the present site. The old one was certainly destroyed by Malcolm Canmore and a tradition, mentioned as early as 1412,[38] claims that he built the new one, but a convincing case has been made for it being the work of his son David I.[39] Nor is it certain what material was used; stone castles were a rarity in Scotland at that time, so that it was more likely to be a stockade with wooden palisadings, although some doubt is cast by references to the use of lime in expenditure accounts for this building at a later date. These accounts do not, however, make any reference to stone so that the dubiety is not resolved.

In 1163 Shaw MacDuff, second son of the 5th Earl of Fife, came north with Malcolm IV and helped to suppress a rebellion in Moray, for which services he was made hereditary Constable of Inverness Castle. At the same time he took the name of MacIntosh (Son of the Leader). Except for short periods when it passed into English hands, the honour of governing the Castle remained with his family for over two centuries. When Edward I of England became arbiter during the contested succession to the Scottish throne many castles, Inverness amongst them, were voluntarily handed into his control and Sir William de Braytoft was given command both of Inverness and Dingwall in 1291. Edward, however, was not satisfied with simple surrender; he demanded an oath of allegiance to himself from the dignitaries of Church, nobility, landowners and burgesses, all those north of the Spey being ordered to swear fealty in the Castle at Inverness. The following year the English garrison was withdrawn and the castle given into the care of Baliol, but with the outbreak of war four years later it was captured by Edward's forces. The next year, 1297, saw the start of Wallace's fight for independence in which he was ably supported by Andrew de Moray who owned castles at both Petty and Avoch. Moray concentrated his earlier efforts in the north, particularly against Urquhart Castle, whilst so harrassing Sir Reginald le Chen, Governor in Inverness, that no assistance could be sent to Urquhart for its defence. Finally he was successful in capturing both Urquhart and Inverness.

Six years later Inverness Castle again fell to the English, and remained in their hands until 1307 when Bruce regained it and, in accordance with his usual practice, caused it to be 'levelled with the ground'.[40]

Throughout these turbulent times and quick changes of control one other name stands clear — Alexander Pilche, Burgess of Inverness. Chief Lieutenant to Andrew de Moray, Pilche was with him when Fitzwarine, Constable of Urquhart, was ambushed and utterly routed, two of his principal followers captured, and several of lesser rank killed. Pilche fought at the Battle of Stirling Bridge when Moray was killed and then, deeming the conquest of Scotland complete, reluctantly accepted Edward's peace, even to the extent of being appointed Constable of the Castle. His sympathies, however, remained unaltered and he took the lead in raising the province of Moray in favour of Bruce, who eventually rewarded him by appointing him Sheriff of Inverness. Two of his sons were later to become Provosts of the town. Writing of this period in his book *Inverness and the MacDonalds*, Dr Barron says:

> It was with the aid of the burgesses of Inverness that the first blow in the War of Independence was struck in 1297, when Andrew de Moray of Petty and Avoch, a near neighbour of the town, with Alexander Pilche, Burgess of Inverness, as his Chief Lieutenant, led a revolt which resulted in the Battle of Stirling Bridge. It was from Inverness and neighbourhood that Bruce gained some of his earliest and staunchest adherents, and it was to Inverness that he came in the crisis of his fate in the autumn of 1307. It was with Inverness as his base, and with an army drawn from Inverness and its neighbourhood, that he rallied the Highlands to his side, humbled the Earl of Ross, who had surrendered his Queen to Edward, and embarked on his career of victory.[41]

There is no record of any re-building after Bruce's demolition, nor of how complete that destruction really was; but in a Charter of 1313 granting royal lands in the Burgh and its vicinity to Randolph, Earl of Moray, the site only was reserved to the Crown, implying a vacant plot without buildings. By 1383, however, there was a castle occupied in the name of the King. It was destroyed by Donald, Lord of the Isles, in 1411, either on his way to the Battle of Harlaw or, more probably, on his way home again. The next year Alexander Stewart, Earl of Mar (incidentally a cousin of Donald), was ordered to rebuild a fortalice in Inverness as protection against rebellious Highlanders. The Exchequer volume of the time reads,

> One of the means adopted for introducing order into
> the Highlands was the reconstruction on a larger
> scale of the important Castle of Inverness, on whose
> site a stronghold had existed since the time of
> Malcolm Canmore. The new buildings were erected
> under the superintendence of the Earl of Mar, and
> the expenditure connected with the constructing and
> garrisoning of them is given in the Exchequer
> accounts in considerable detail, the items enumerated
> amounting in all to nearly £640.[42]

Just how effective Mar's efforts were in controlling the turbulent chiefs is questionable, for in 1427 James I visited Inverness and imprisoned Alexander, Lord of the Isles, his mother the Countess of Ross and several others. The Lords of the Isles, however, continued to be troublesome, and in 1463 another Donald at the instigation of Edward IV seized the Castle and proclaimed himself king. Edward had promised to divide Scotland between Donald and the Earl of Douglas, to reign as his puppets. This manoeuvre was short-lived, and Donald retired with ample booty to his island fastness. In 1491 the Castle was again captured by the MacDonalds, this time by Alexander of Lochalsh who claimed to be head of the Clan although John of the Isles and his son still lived. This, too, was more of a gesture than a serious attempt to occupy the stronghold.

1 *The truncated clock tower of Cromwell's Fort*

2   *Friar's Street and the tower of the Old High Church*

3 *Dunbar's Hospital*

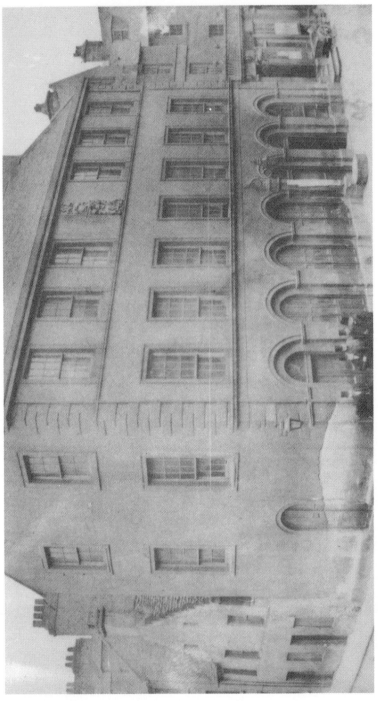

4 *The Old Town House, demolished in 1878*

In 1508 the Earl of Huntly was appointed Heritable Sheriff of Inverness and Governor of the Castle, and was ordered to add to the existing structure a hall of stone and lime upon vaults, 100 feet long, 30 feet wide and 30 feet high with a slated roof and a kitchen and chapel attached. This work was eventually done — nearly forty years later.

The Castle next seems to have made history at the time of the ill-fated Mary, Queen of Scots. When in 1562 Mary visited Inverness she was forced to find lodgings in a house on the north side of Bridge Street, for Alexander Gordon, Huntly's deputy, refused her admission to her own Castle. Her supporters eventually did manage to capture it and Gordon was hanged. For the next 70 years or so the Castle seems to have enjoyed a period of relative unimportance, but in 1639 'the clans' showed their feelings: 'they brake up the doors, gates and windows of that stately Castle, spoiled the pleasant plenishing and rich library of books, and brocht all to nocht within that house, inferior to few in the kingdom for decorment.'[43] Repairs must have been made, for it was only four years later that the Duke of Montrose besieged it until General Middleton arrived to relieve it. Another four years and it was again taken, this time by Royalists who expelled the Parliamentary soldiers and demolished the fortifications. From then on it appears to have again been neglected and allowed to deteriorate until it was refurbished in 1715 to aid the House of Hanover against Highland Jacobites. For a short time that year it was held for the Earl of Mar by William MacKintosh of Borlum, but his troops were quickly expelled by loyalists under Rose of Kilravock. The end came in 1746 when Prince Charles ordered the Castle's destruction to prevent it falling into the hands of the Hanoverians.

A story is related of the engineer officer, a Frenchman, who applied the fuse to the train laid for its destruction. Supposing it to have gone out, he approached to relight it, and as he came near the explosion took place, blowing him into the air along with the materials of the fortress. He landed a mutilated corpse on the green on the opposite side of the river, 300 yards distant from the spot he was on duty. But though he himself was killed, the little dog which accompanied him is said to have performed the journey unhurt. Other authorities say both fell into the river and were carried out to sea. Thus ended the Castle of Inverness as a fortress.[44]

Two descriptions exist of the Castle up to this time. From the *Archaelogia Scotica*:

The ground floor was vaulted, the upper floors were of wood and the roof when last inhabited was flat and leaded and surrounded by a low parapet. Within the North Entrance a handsome stone stair led to the upper floors. The walls were of great thickness and almost entirely composed of that mixture of lime and small stones of every shape frequently met with in structures of very ancient erection. In each of the Chambers exposed in the three upper floors there was an alcove or recess formed in the walls of the castle of sufficient dimensions to contain a bed.[45]

Another is by Sir Aeneas MacKintosh in his history of his time:

The original consisted of two towers with a stone wall round the whole, the stone being connected with run lime became solid as a rock. The next change it underwent was the two towers being connected by two walls built in the same manner and formed a square building four stories high and contained six large halls besides vaults etc. etc. and in 1727 the sides of the squares built of bricks and of the same height were added capable of holding 400 men and the old castle was divided into twelve rooms for the Governor and other public offices. At the south side was a very neat English chapel and a Magazine. The works round it humouring the form of the hill the Castle stands on, come nearly to an oblong square having four irregular bastions the longest side of the place being near the river. The bastions have scarcely any gorge. The two eastern bastions are still entire, but the other two with the ramparts are destroyed by the inhabitants who build houses with the stones; of the brickwork none is extant and of the Castle little except the two ends and part of the side wall which has a melancholy appearance.[46]

After Culloden the Duke of Cumberland set about building a new fort — to be called Fort George — to replace the old Castle and, of course, considered a new building on the same site. Ex-Provost Hossack, father of pretty daughters, led the opposition to any such proposal because of the effect on the young ladies of Inverness of the 'wild and licentious soldiery'. The new fort was built at Ardersier.

Apart from the ruins the site remained empty for nearly a century until the Duke of Gordon, descendant of the Huntly heritable Constables, whose family had managed to acquire ownership (without payment) during the royal dynastic changes, sold the Castlehill for the building of a Courthouse and Jail. The building of the courthouse started in 1834 and was completed two years later, whilst the Jail was finished in 1849. 'A suite of county buildings which covers the Castle Hill was erected in 1835 at a cost in the region of £7000 after a design by Mr Burn of Edinburgh and strongly arrests the eye of a stranger. The commanding site of the edifices, the neatness of their architecture, their resemblance to a spacious English Castle and their interior commodiousness and beauty, unite to render them superior to most Scottish buildings of their class.[47]

Mr W.T. Jack, last Burgh Architect, gives a description of the style of architecture:

The architectural style is typical of the period when the classical tradition of the previous century was giving way to a movement attempting to create something new. The design is an early Victorian example of a mixing of previous styles from Jacobethan (a mixture of Elizabethan with the style of the Stuarts) with a touch of Gothic and Georgian reminiscent of the earlier Culzean Castle in Ayrshire built 1777-90. The result is a severity of style in square block outline, round corner towers facing the river, castellated parapets and vertical pinnacles out of character but suggesting look-out towers thrusting upwards and not in the traditional manner.[48]

Describing the older buildings as it was in his day Cameron says:

> The primary object in the erection of it was to afford sufficient accommodation for the Circuit Court of Justiciary which sits here once a-year on cases from the whole of the northern counties and, in fixing the site, room was reserved to the north of it for building a new jail as soon as the necessary funds could be procured. The Castle contains a splendid court-room, a robing-room for the Judges, jury-rooms, witness-rooms and cells for prisoners previous to their trial, the Sheriff-clerk's office, an apartment for meetings of the Heritors and Commissioners of Supply, Stamp and Tax Offices, Assessment Office, library-rooms possessing a complete set of Acts of Parliament, vaulted rooms for the county records and other apartments not yet appropriated to any particular use besides accommodation for the keeper and his family.[49]

That building remains largely unaltered internally and externally. The jail followed quite quickly, 'the necessary funds' apparently having been acquired. It remained in use until the present jail at Porterfield was built in 1901. It then became the headquarters of the Inverness-shire Police, whilst the large room on the first floor was the Council Chamber of the Inverness-shire County Council. On the demise of this Council the Chamber was converted to become the District Court-room.

In 1809 a well was discovered between the two buildings and is now protected by a low surrounding wall and a cover. The statue of Flora MacDonald, gazing down the Great Glen for a fresh sight of her prince, was erected in 1899 in front of the seldom-used main doors.

Ness Bridge

From time immemorial the most important settlement in the Highlands has been near the mouth of the Ness, the focal point for communications in all directions and the most convenient crossing place over the waters of the Great Glen. Long before there was any bridge over the Ness the main route from Moray and Badenoch, from Aberdeen and Edinburgh, to the north and west was through the centre of the present town along what are now High and Church Streets to a ford in the vicinity of Abban Street and thence by Clachnaharry or Leachkin according to the destination. Paradoxically the first reference we have to a bridge over the river is the report of its destruction. Described as one of the finest in the kingdom, this early bridge was of wood and hence susceptible to fire, a factor in favour of Donald of the Isles in 1411.

Donald was claiming the Earldom of Ross and wreaking vengeance wherever he failed to gain support. From his native isles he marched through Dingwall to Inverness on his way to Aberdeen, which he was prevented from attacking by the Earl of Mar who met him in battle near Inverurie at 'Red Harlaw'. The battle was generally accepted as a draw but, since nothing less than outright victory could serve Donald he must be counted the loser. At Inverness he had gained little support but neither had he met any serious opposition, only one burgess is reported as having made any effort against him. 'John Cumine, a gentleman burgher of the town, putting on his armour and head piece and two-handed sword, made such stout resistance at this nearest end of the bridge against the M'kdonels that Jo. Major the historian saith, Si essent decem tales in Invernesia nec pons urbs comburerenter (and had there been but ten more like him in Inverness neither bridge nor burgh had been burnt).'[50]

Centre of communications though Inverness undoubtedly was, there are remarkably few references at this time to any bridge. In 1561 it is recorded that 'the Provost, Bailies and Council has ordainit the officers to pass and arrest the brig that nae manner of man free or non-free should carry 'muck' our it under all hurt and pain and charge that after may follow.'[51] The following year, possibly after pressure from Queen Mary who was in Inverness at the time, the same body appointed a master of works for the bridge and found new offences for which they could impose fines to be dedicated to 'the bridge wark'. There is no indication as to whether this appointment and funding were for repairs or re-building, but in 1613 steps were taken for repairing and 'upholding' the bridge, the estimated cost being 3000 merks Scots of which the Provost and Bailies undertook to provide 1000, the remainder to come from a stent (tax) on the lands. This bridge was also of oak, and we must assume that it had no handrail since a woman carrying a bundle of heather was blown off it and drowned. It was destroyed by a flood in 1620 and we read that 'Sir Simon Fraser of Inverallochy, having died at Dalcross, they were desirous of carrying his body to Beauly, but could not do so on account of the destruction of the bridge and the swollen state of the river and he was interred in St Catherine's aisle of the Rood Church of Inverness.'[52]

After an interval of four years a new bridge was built of timber supplied by the laird of Glenmoriston at a cost of 1000 pounds Scots. It was later described by one of Cromwell's officers as 'the weakest that ever straddled over so strong a stream' — with some justification for in 1664 it too fell into the river. A person living near Inverness reported:

> The great old wooden bridge of Inverness repaireing, and by unadvertancy of a carpenter cutting a beame that lay fast 'tuixt two cuples, to set up a new one, the bridge tending that way ten of the old cupples fell flat on the river, with about 200 persones, men, women, and children upon it. 4 of the townes men broke leggs and thighs; some 16 had their heads, arms, and thighs bruised; all the children safe without a scart; and, by Providence, not one perished, a signall instance and dreadful sight, at 10 houres forenoon. Immediately, a great inundation happened, that the river run over the banks; the passage all that winter by a great cobble over it.[53]

He does not explain how it came about that there were two hundred people on the bridge at ten o' clock in the forenoon! Maybe the fascination of watching men at work was as potent then as it is to-day. One writer has said that there was an aquatic display at the time but it appears unlikely at that hour on a morning in late September. Once again Inverness was without a bridge, and for the next twenty-one years had to rely on the 'great cobble' to ferry people and goods across.

To modern minds it appears strange that such long intervals between destruction and replacement could be tolerated, but it must be remembered that wheeled vehicles were uncommon in the Highlands in those times. In 1731 it was said that few carts were needed in the town, heavy goods being carried slung between four horses; but country folk did sometimes bring one in. One type had two long shafts extending far behind the body of the cart and dragging on the ground.[54] It was not until 1760 that the first post-chaise was brought into Inverness and for a considerable time it was the only four-wheeled carriage in the district. By 1822 there were still only about forty private carriages and post-chaises in the town and the parish.

Now for the first time a stone bridge was to be provided, mainly using material salvaged from Cromwell's Fort. It was built in 1685 at a cost of £1300 raised by public subscription, Macleod of MacLeod being a large contributor. For this reason his Arms, with those of the Burgh, were placed in the arch at the eastern end. At the western end were two pillars supporting a gate, which had fatal consequences for Jacobites fleeing home after the Battle of Culloden some sixty years later. Just after the battle the Campbells and the Argyllshire militia decided that they would cut off any retreat through the town and rushed to close this gate before anyone could pass through. The Highlanders came down High Street and into Bridge Street with the Redcoats in hot pursuit and then found themselves hemmed in. Dispirited they almost accepted their fate until one of the Glenmoriston men shouted 'An tuit sibh mar choin?' (will you be slaughtered like dogs?) and roused them to a further battle. Many clansmen managed to escape by fording the river south of the bridge. The purpose of the gate was to ensure payment of the toll of a boddle (one sixth of a penny), an imposition frequently evaded by wading across the river. Many of the residents on the west of the river who chose to play shinty on the bleaching green then facing the Castle claimed inability to pay this toll as the reason for not attending church on the Sabbath. At the behest of the Minister the bridge was made toll-free on Sundays only!

This bridge comprised seven arches and between the second and third from the eastern end was a prison twelve feet long, nine wide and six high. There was no fireplace and access was through a trap-door in the pavement leading to a short stair. In the floor was a hole through which a pitcher could be lowered to obtain water from the river. Light and ventilation came from an iron grating. The original prison later became a mad-house until it was sealed off in 1770.

In 1808 a second bridge was started, now called Waterloo Bridge. It also was subject to toll but was built of wood so dark in colour that it earned the colloquial name of the 'Black Bridge' and though it was replaced in 1896 by a metal structure, made at Rose Street Foundry, Inverness, the name persists. Next, in 1829, came a link from Ness Bank to the Islands followed five years later by another to complete the crossing of the river by joining the Islands to the Bught.

Another disastrous flood in 1849 washed away both the stone bridge and these new ones at the Islands. The Caledonian Canal had burst its banks and poured into the river causing it to overflow in many places. The area where shinty had been played was especially affected. A sailor, Matthew Campbell, who incidentally was a classics medal winner at Inverness Royal Academy, was the last person to cross the bridge when returning from assisting people in this area. It fell at 6.15 a.m. on 25 January, and once again Inverness had no bridge on its main route. A temporary foot-bridge was soon erected but six years were to pass before vehicles could cross the river at Bridge Street. It was not decided to build on the same site until several other locations had been carefully considered, and then there was lengthy debate about the type of construction to be used. Only on 10 June 1852 it was announced that the contract had been given to Messrs. Thomas Hutchins and Co. who were already engaged in railway construction work in Moray. Work commenced a week later on 17 June and ceased four months after that, the firm having gone bankrupt. A new contractor was found early the following year but he, too, failed a year later. At this point the Council drew up a memorial of protest to the Commissioners on Highland Roads and Bridges, who were responsible for the building of the bridge. They pointed out that five years had passed and not one pillar had yet been completed. By March, however, a new company had been appointed and work was proceeding; the new bridge was opened on 23 August 1855.

It was in one respect a rather curious erection. At one end was a high archway whilst at the other, the western, were two much lower towers giving the appearance of only half of a much longer bridge which, in fact, some claim it to have been. It was a suspension bridge with a span of 225 feet, and made a fitting foreground to the newly erected castle. Two further crossings, the Infirmary and Greig Street Bridges, were to follow thirty years later, both suspension bridges, both for pedestrians only, and both made in Inverness.

The constriction imposed by the narrow opening in the arch at the eastern end and the rapidly growing weight and volume of traffic made consideration of a replacement for the Suspension Bridge essential,, and eighty years after its opening a report by Sir Murdoch MacDonald, eminent engineer and both a native of and Member of Parliament for Inverness, said that repairs were urgently needed and that a new bridge was the only solution. He advised that in the meantime a speed limit of ten miles per hour should be imposed. For some time thereafter a man with a red flag controlled traffic using the bridge, to ensure that it was never over-loaded, and in 1939 a contract was tendered for a new bridge, to be constructed of Shap granite. To allow traffic to flow whilst work proceeded a temporary wooden bridge was built a few yards upstream, the seventh bridge over the Ness. The Brahan Seer is said to have predicted that when there were seven bridges over that river 'much bloodshed would ensue'. Now, and in 1939, that number had been reached.

Can Inverness Town Council therefore be held accountable for the Second World War? The outbreak of that war caused the removal of the man with his red flag and prevented the work of rebuilding until 1959 when a somewhat lighter design was adopted.

The old Suspension Bridge was closed on 31 August with a minor ceremony, the Council and Officials ceremonially parading from the Town House at midnight, led by a pipe band, to cross in each direction. After that no further traffic was allowed to cross. It is even reported that one Councillor carried a hip-flask so that he and at least some of his colleagues could have a parting dram in the centre of the bridge.

The new bridge was opened in heavy rain on 28 September 1961 — by coincidence the precise anniversary of the collapse of 1664. It is 62 feet wide with a carriageway of 44 feet and two footpaths each of 9 feet. The centre span is 120 feet in length, the two end spans each 62½ feet.

Saint Andrew's Cathedral

The story of St Andrew's Cathedral really begins with an election. In 1850 there were two candidates for the vacant Bishopric of Moray and Ross in the Scottish Episcopal Church; they were James MacKay of St John's, Inverness and Robert Eden of Leigh, Essex. Each received four votes. Shortly after the election, one of those who had supported Eden joined the Roman Catholic Church and yet, at a second election the following January, the votes were five to two in Eden's favour. It proved to be a notable and historic appointment which was to last for 35 years.

Until this time the seat of the Bishopric had been in Elgin but Bishop Eden soon realised the advantages of Inverness and as early as 1853 proposed that a new Cathedral should be built there. Little support was given initially but when, in 1864, Caithness was added to the Diocese a new purpose was given to the proposal. There was a small Episcopal Church in Bank Street to provide a nucleus for this great enterprise and

Eden's faith, enthusiasm and driving power were sufficient to achieve the laying of a foundation stone on 17 October 1866, by the Archbishop of Canterbury. Completed and dedicated three years later, consecrated in 1874, it was the first Cathedral built in Britain since the Reformation — a part of the revival enjoyed by the Episcopalian Church in the nineteenth century.

The cathedral was designed by the outstanding local designer Dr Alexander Ross 'The Christopher Wren of the Highlands' and Inverness is fortunate in that he was also responsible for the developments in the neighbouring Ardross Street and Ardross Terrace, so that there is sympathy of treatment for a whole environment. For over 50 years Ross was the premier architect in Inverness, and indeed of the whole Highlands. He was born in Brechin but came to Inverness at a very early age when his father, also an architect, came to live in Church Street. Here he also had a business office, as was usual in those days. Alexander was educated at Dr Bell's Institution, Farraline Park and there does not appear to be any record of further formal education. His father died in 1853 and the following year, at the age of 20, he became an architect in his late father's firm after, presumably, having been an apprentice there since he left school. About six years later he became factor to Sir Alexander Matheson MP of Ardross who had recently purchased the Muirtown Estates and so Alexander Ross became responsible for the planning and development of the whole area on the west of the river from Muirtown to the Cathedral. He was also responsible for the development of Union Street, and around 1865 he built a new house for his own occupation — Riverdale — now Ach-an-Eas and used as an Old Folk's Home. In 1881 he joined the Town Council and eight years later was elected Provost, a post he then held for the next six years. Schools, churches, houses, factories and even the earlier cinemas throughout the Highlands and Islands, and beyond, all came within the scope of his designing genius.

The original design of St Andrew's Cathedral shows spires a hundred feet high rising from the twin towers, themselves of that height, and a chancel some fifty-four feet longer than that eventually built. For years there has been a quite erroneous story that it was the lack of these spires that prevented Inverness from being created a city, the status usually accorded a cathedral town. On the arch surrounding the transept window overlooking the river are carved a wheel and a horse and there is an interesting story to explain their presence. During the building the stones were raised by means of a pully and horizontal wheel which was turned by a horse. At a late stage in the work, one of these stones slipped and killed the horse which is now commemorated in this carving. Inside the church are several sculptured heads including those of Saint Margaret (Canmore's Queen), Charles I, Dr Ross and Bishop Eden.

The Bishop's Palace, Eden Court, was built just after the Cathedral, and like the Episcopal Primary School was named after the Bishop not the Garden of Eden. When it became too large for modern style of living it was used as a nurse's training school and residential home for nurses at the nearby Infirmary. To-day it forms part of the Eden Court complex, the civic theatre and conference centre opened in 1976.

Royal Northern Infirmary

On 28 December 1797 an advertisement appeared in the *Edinburgh Evening Courant*, verbose as was the habit in those days. It spoke of the impossibility of affording effectual aid to the sick and the poor in the Highlands in their own homes and of the need for an Infirmary in Inverness for their treatment. Subscriptions for this laudable project were invited and the names of the Chairman, Treasurer and Secretary were appended. William Inglis, Chairman, was in his first year of office as Provost but had long taken a prominent part in the development of the town and was generally accepted as one of the ablest Magistrates and Provosts Inverness had ever known. The Treasurer, Thomas Gilzean, was another notable figure who became Provost from 1807-10, and again in 1813. Thus was launched what we today know as the Royal Northern Infirmary, or more commonly, the R.N.I.

A contract for the building was agreed in March 1799 with a penalty clause to be effective if work was not completed by 1 August 1800. Land had been feued from Mr Fraser of Torbreck in Ballafery and, from the start, the committee were determined to be moderate in their plans, the reply to John Fraser of Achnagairn who had submitted alternative proposals being that they were 'too gaudy for us; our object is to erect a decent building which will do credit to the liberality of the subscribers but by no means forget that it is to be inhabited by the sick poor for whom to provide anything beyond comfortable accommodation would be absurd'. In addition to physical cases provision was also to be made for mental patients.

The whole enterprise was to be on a voluntary basis and the restrictions thereby imposed were recognised at a very early stage: 'the extent of what may be done will in a great measure depend upon the extent of the free funds now in the Treasurer's hands or which may afterwards be collected from new subscriptions'. It is of interest that a metal collection box with a locked door is still built into the gate pillar next to the Lodge at the riverside entrance. Does anyone still have a key? It certainly does not have the appearance of having been opened for many years.

Advice on layout was sought from friends both in London and Edinburgh before it was decided how the rooms should be arranged. 'On the ground floor were accommodation for staff, kitchen, medicine shop, clerk's room, and two smaller rooms, one for cold and the other for a warm bath; the first floor contained Directors' room, Surgeons' room and two Wards 30 feet by 16 feet and other accommodation; on the second floor there were an Operation Room 32 by 14½ and two Wards as on the first floor. At each end of the House there were wings of two storeys, on the ground floor of each of which there were four vaulted cells for lunatics, 8 feet square, with a keeper's room in each wing 8 feet by 10 feet 9 inches'.

The first patient, Elspet Munro from the Parish of Urquhart, was admitted on 3 July 1804. Treatment was not always welcomed, either by patient or patient's family, and in April 1806 Dr Kennedy was extremely sorry to be obliged to state in the strongest terms his disapprobation of the unwarrantable conduct of a patient who 'on Saturday evening took advantage of the gates being open, and clandestinely left the Hospital, being assisted in his escape by his wife who had privately got admittance. Dr Kennedy recommended the committee to adopt such measures as to them seem proper for preventing such disorderly practices in future'. Two months earlier Dr Forbes had reported that a male convalescent patient had been ordered to work in the garden when the weather is favourable, as garden labour will most likely promote the cure of his complaint. Infectious diseases were a constant problem; the first was of typhus only five months after the first patient, whilst the first death had been only ten days after Elspet had been admitted.

In September 1806 it was reported that 'Independent of 4 lunatics there are at present 14 patients in the house, vizt. Eight Male & Six Female, & the cook who is threatened with Consumptive Complaints. Of these, One gets 8 glasses of Port Wine, one 3 and another 4 every day, and Two have each a Bottle of Porter'. In July of the following year however there were no patients at all. About this time the Matron received a half-year's wage of £5, the gardener £7 10s, the cook, chambermaid and nurse £2 each. A patient admitted with a fever in December 1811 was later found to have smallpox and hence was not admissible by the laws of the Institution; he was, however, allowed to stay, but in a ward 'quite distinct by himself'.

An outstanding servant of the Infirmary and the Burgh is first mentioned in 1814 when Dr John Inglis Nicol 'made representation of Alexander Bremner's case, and in consideration of his utility, docility and uniformly good behaviour, have ordered a shilling's worth of tobacco for him weekly'. It fully accords with this good Doctor's character that he should thus first appear in a humanitarian role. Some years later he was to be co-opted to the Town Council and elected Provost on the same day, a most outstanding honour at a time after reformation of local government had removed the nepotism of earlier days. His death in 1849 was also in character — a victim of cholera contracted whilst attending to his patients.

Visiting hours were apparently causing difficulties, and in 1837 the Committee recommended 'that the hours at which friends of the patients should have access to the House be from 10 to 11 o'clock a.m. and from 3 to 6 p.m. and directed the House Surgeon that this arrangement be strictly attended to'. As early as 1822 the desirability of a separate institution for the care of the mentally afflicted was being argued but it was only with the erection of Craig Dunain Hospital in 1864 that the Infirmary was relieved of this type of patient. Like the Infirmary itself Craig Dunain drew its patients from the whole Highland area including the Western Isles.

The Tweedmouth Memorial Chapel, gifted by Lady Tweedmouth in memory of her husband, was dedicated on 18 September 1898.

In 1929 the Duke and Duchess of York visited the Infirmary and opened the York Ward for children, part of the re-construction and extension being undertaken at that time, on the completion of which in 1930 it was given the right to add 'Royal' to its title. The same royal couple again visited it in 1948, then as King George VI and his Queen, but that year was to mark the end of the institution as a Voluntary Hospital; with others throughout Britain, it passed into State control.

Chapter 2 — Streets

General; Castle Street; High Street with Eastgate and Bridge Street; Church Street; Academy Street; Chapel Street and Shore Street; 'Bewest the Waters of the Ness'.

General

In the fifteenth and sixteenth centuries the streets of Inverness, in common with those of most burghs and villages throughout Scotland, were still unpaved so that they were often deep in mud and ordure. In the middle of each street was a line of flat stones, the 'crown of the causey', and only by walking on this could the pedestrian hope to pass with but moderate contamination. In 1565 Regent Moray ordered the chief of Clan Gunn to be executed in Inverness for, according to Sir Robert Gordon, no greater crime than that of taking the 'crown of the causey' from the Regent.[1] Not until 1679 were Inverness streets levelled and paved and it was the Duke of Cumberland during his stay in the town after Culloden who first ordered that they be swept at public expense.[2]

Off the main streets, especially off Castle Street, were closes, wynds or vennels leading to courts lined by houses, access seldom being easy because of middens and rubbish-heaps barring the way in spite of repeated regulations ordained against them. The houses were not built according to any co-ordinated plan, often being set at varying angles to their neighbours. Most were of wood, some of rubble and very, very few of dressed stone. Almost invariably they had thatched roofs. Usually the ground-floor would be a shop, often one or two steps below street level, the upper floors being the dwellings approached by an outside stair protected by upright boards. Glass windows were a rarity and rat-infestation common. Extensions in the form of booths, especially in High Street, often fronted the shops to give yet more selling space.

Street lighting was unknown and it was dangerous to move at night without the aid of a lantern or a guiding link-boy; uncovered lights were prohibited because of the risk of fire amongst so many timber buildings. A curfew was rung every night, as it still is, and one male from each house would report for possible duty as the watch. Some would be detailed to patrol the streets and others to join the parties going to Ballifeary or Clachnaharry to keep watch lest any marauders should approach under cover of darkness. Those not required for these duties would then, especially during the winter months when darkness came early, repair to one of the many taverns to hold high revelry until a reasonable hour for sleep.[3]

Wallace quotes Macaulay as saying,

> Though the buildings covered but a small part of the
> space over which they now extend; though the arrival
> of a brig at the port was a rare event; though the
> Exchange was in the middle of a mirey street in
> which stood a market cross much resembling a
> broken milestone; though the sittings of the
> Municipal Council were held in a filthy den with a
> roughcast wall; though the best houses were such as
> would now be called hovels; though the best roofs
> were of thatch; though the best ceilings were of bare
> rafters; though the best windows were in bad weather
> closed with shutters for want of glass; though the
> humbler dwellings were mere heaps of turf in which
> barrels with the bottom knocked out served the
> purpose of chimneys — yet to the mountaineer of the
> Grampians this city was a Babylon or a Tyre.[4]

In fact the buildings in Inverness were of better quality at the start of the fifteenth century than at its end. At its start they were substantial and reasonably comfortable, but the burning of the town in 1411 and again in 1429 by the Lord of the Isles caused the building of less permanent erections of wood and rubble,[5] a circumstance confirmed by archaeologists of the

Burgh Museum who excavated a site at the north end of Castle Street in 1979 and 1980.

Castle Street

Excavations during 1979 and 1980 have provided evidence of human habitation at the lower end of Castle Street as long ago as 7000 BC, although not proving that it has been continuous. The once swampy nature of the surrounding area may well have caused a break between this ancient period and recorded times. As far back as records go, and as recently as the eighteenth century, there were only three streets in Inverness after it had moved from the Crown area to its present site — Church Street, High Street with its continuations of Eastgate and Bridge Street and Castle Street. Long before the last assumed its name however it was variously mentioned in charters as 'Dymingisdale', 'Damisdaille' and 'Doomsdale'. In ancient times the town's gallows was at Muirfield so that condemned felons would pass along what is now Castle Street on their way to execution, to their doom, and this could explain the old name. The word 'doom' is not necessarily to be associated with death however; it can mean judgment, verdict, sentence, fate or destiny (as in Doomsday Book for example), and had a statistical connotation. Since there was once a mote-hill (court-hill) at Muirfield, a court was held at Le Balloch's Hill, now Viewmount, at the top of Castle Street in 1376; thus the name may mean 'the way to the meeting place where justice was dispensed'.

The fosse established by William the Lion and the inner paling maintained by the Burgesses ran along the ridge to the east of the street which was cut out of the gravel hill, the glacial moraine. John Anderson in the *Archaelogia Scotia* says 'The western portion called the Crown was cut through by the approach to Fort Augustus now called Castle Street'[6] whilst Sir Aenas MacKintosh says 'Castle Street being cut out of the hill looks very dark'.[7] It was then much higher at its southern end and considerably steeper than today, having been lowered and given a more even gradient in 1697.

At an early period Highland Lairds began to seek the more sophisticated society of the town, and several built or hired dwellings in Inverness. Bridge Street and Church Street appear to have been the more popular, but Castle Street had a share, the Robertsons of Inshes being mentioned as owning land in it was early as 1488. The Laird of Culclachy (the old name for Nairnside) was there soon after, and not only had a residence but also a brewery kiln alongside, an amenity then almost as essential as a scullery or pantry since the only way to obtain water was to carry it from the river. Not until 1829 was water supplied in any other way, a reservoir being then built within the fork of Old Edinburgh and Culduthel Roads opposite Viewmount. This reservoir was filled by pumping from the river although consent to draw water from Leys had received Parliamentary approval in 1808. Both the Robertson and Culclachy residences would be part of the redevelopment of the street after the burnings of 1411 and 1429. An indication of the type of building then being undertaken is given by a special mention, in 1508, of a stone house existing in Castle Street — surely pointing to the rarity of such a building in Inverness at the time. As so often happens, even today, different trades tended to congregate in particular areas and Castle Street became the centre for armourers and glovers.

In 1564 there were 'four brewers of aquavite' in Inverness and one of them, Martin Waus, was in Damisdale. At that time the word 'aquavite' was applied indiscriminately to any alcoholic liquid produced by distillation, but its conjugation with 'brewers' sounds curious to modern ears. It appears that the modern distinction between brewing and distilling was not then observed, both being called brewing. An example of this, although strictly outwith the scope of this history, is the famous whisky 'Ferintosh' which was the product of the 'ancient brewery of aquavitae in Cromarty' destroyed by the Jacobites in 1689 in revenge against Duncan Forbes of Culloden who owned it. By way of compensation he was allowed to distil free of duty, a privilege not rescinded until 1784 by which time it had achieved national renown, even John Knox writing that it was 'the social practice of

Highlandmen in all ages to seal, ratify, and wash down every compact or bargain in good old ferintosh', whilst Burns gave it an epitaph when it lost its privilege:—

Thee Ferintosh! O sadly lost!
Scotland lament frae coast to coast!
Now colic grips an' barking hoast
May kill us a';
For loyal Forbes' charter'd boast
Is ta'en awa.[8]

The fount of this whisky was never described as anything other than a brewery. After strong protests the limit of four brewers in Inverness was raised to a maximum of eight pots in 1567.

Little is recorded of Castle Street for almost eighty years, until Sir James Fraser of Brae, Commander of the Covenanting forces then in possession of the Castle, is said to have 'surrounded the town by a ditch, cut down a number of beautiful trees in Greyfriars and Chapel Yards and erected a strong gate at the top of Castle Street' in 1644.[9]

Master James Fraser, Minister at Wardlaw, has an interesting tale to tell of an event in 1668.

Uppon the hill south of the castell the horse mercat stands, and there being some women uppon the edge of the breay selling of cheese and bread, readdy for such as could not go farr to fetch it, one Finlay Dow, a townes man, takeing up a cheese in his hand, asked what rate it was. This being told him, whither designedly or by negligence, he let the cheese drop out of his hand, and down it runns into the river. The woman told him she would oblidge him to pay. He (a crabbed fellow) gave her cross language of defyance. One that stood by, espouseing the quarrel, held him fast, and tooke off his bonnet in pledge untill he should pay the woman. A relation of Finlayes challenged this man as non of his concerns. Yes, said he, I am concerned as a witness to see just things. To threatning words and as goods, they goe from wordes to blowes, till at length most of the hill market is ingaged to a confusion. This allarms the

72

whole town. The guards are called, who come in arms, and John Reed, a pretty man, their captain, in betwixt the parties to seperate them. Several other gentlemen present offer mediation; no hearing, but swords drawn, guns presented, some wounds given. Provost Alexander Cuthbert is told that his guards are not regarded, puts on steel cap, sword, and targe, caust ring the alarm bell, comes up straight to the hill, and many pretty fellows with him. The people cry for justice. The guard, being opposed and abused, let off some shot. Two are killed outright, and above ten wounded.[10]

Fraser was alive at the time of this affray so that his account is likely to be more accurate than another somewhat different one written by one who probably spoke to eye-witnesses in his youth but only recorded his story some eighty years later. MacLean says that the dairymaid herself dropped the cheese which rolled into the river from whence it was recovered by some town-boys. Seeing this she called on some country-boys to try to regain it and so the fight started, lasting for over three hours.[11]

The first bank in town, a branch of the Bank of Scotland, was established in Castle Street in 1775 and the locally owned Caledonian Bank had its first office here in 1838 until the present handsome building in High Street opposite Castle Street was erected in 1849. This latter bank was eventually absorbed into the former. In 1790 the Post Office was at 32 Castle Street. A number of old buildings at the High Street/Castle Street corner were demolished in 1867 to allow the building of the YMCA which was itself taken down in 1955. This same corner saw the first automatic traffic signals erected in Inverness.

The unstable nature of the escarpment through which the street is cut has caused many minor land-slides, but a serious one took place at 3.30 a.m. on Saturday 8 October 1932 when the retaining wall between the Castle and the houses on the west side of the street collapsed. About a month earlier a police inspector had reported cracks in the wall and just the day before the fall a local technical expert had made an examination as a result of which it had been decided to call in an even more highly qualified engineer on the Saturday. Meantime the residents had not received any warning. Fortunately nobody was killed although several were suffering from shock, their homes seriously damaged. A new Mission Hall of St Columba Church which had only been opened several months earlier was totally destroyed and the Castle itself endangered. The edge of the slide was only seven feet from the corner of that building. The collapsed wall had been built by General Wade as part of the repairs he carried out from 1724 onwards to make a very elaborate fort and barracks named Fort George after the King.[11a]

High Street with Eastgate and Bridge Street

Eastgate, High Street and Bridge Street are really one continuous road today and formed one of the three roads of the town after its establishment at the present location on deserting the old centre on the crest of the hill. It appears that the old approach from the east was further south than it is now, being roughly along the line of Culcabock Road, Kingsmills Road and down Stephen's Brae to our present-day High Street.[12] From there travellers to the north and west would turn down what is now Church Street and across the river by a ford at about Friars' Shott, whilst those for the south-west would turn up our Castle Street and along the south-east side of Loch Ness to Saidhe Chuimein (Fort Augustus).

Originally the whole length from Stephen's Brae to the top of Bridge Street appears to have been called Eastgate but later the western end became High Street and the remainder, with as much of Millburn Road as then existed, Petty Street. This name, which lasted until the second half of the nineteenth century, did not arise because it led to the neighbouring parish of Petty but because it was here that the petty customs, those on internal trade which had been given to the Burgesses by William the Lion, were exacted. Nor does 'gate' signify that there once was a gate here that could be opened and closed as it does in walled towns; in Scotland it derives from 'gait', a way or a street, and is linked with the English word for a particular manner of walking.

John Wood's map of 1822 shows, by a pecked line, a 'projected road' from near the foot of what is now Victoria Drive in a nearly straight line to the southern end of Inglis Street — north of the existing road which took a bowed route. In 1971 the north side of Eastgate was demolished and eight years later a new road was laid out so that, after over 150 years, the 'proposed road', or rather something near it, became a reality; the municipal machine certainly grinds slowly. This new road did not take the whole of the line that had originally been suggested, but turned sharply south before its intended end to give access to Crown Road. So disappeared a length of road that had been the main highway for upwards of six hundred years leaving the small portion that dates 'from time immemorial'. With it Hamilton Street, once Castle Raat (Castle Road) and then Theatre Lane, almost disappeared. From being a vehicular road with substantial business premises fronting it, it now became a short pedestrian way virtually only serving a single large store.

The area north of this new road had long been marshy road, often flooded at high tides and containing a stagnant pool known as Loch Gorm (gorm meaning bluish green), a circumstance that probably accounts for the higher route taken by the ancient eastern approach to the town. Not until 1738 when an embankment was built at the Longman was this zone made suitable for building. The cattle markets, which were to use a large portion of this reclaimed land, continued at the top of Stephen's Brae long after the land had been drained. At the foot of the Brae was a flesh market, and just a little way along Petty Street, a fish market. At the point where Eastgate now becomes High Street a footway runs up the slope, variously called 'Market Brae' and 'The Post Office Steps', both derived from the land at its foot in High Street; the Post Office erected in 1844 being on the site of the former fish market and of an old building whose lower portion had been a meal market. When, in 1888, the Post Office moved to

Queensgate this became the Customs House so that now the 'great' customs were collected near where the 'petty' ones used to be. At the time of writing the Royal Arms (Scottish quarterings) still adorn this building, no longer a Customs House but still a taxation office.

Throughout its history High Street has been a street of merchants, of tradesmen who bought and sold rather than who manufactured. Its buildings were usually dwelling houses with booths that opened onto the street for the occupants to display their wares; and often there would be a further line of display in front of the booths for the country people to expose their produce. The whole street, and especially the open flagged area at its western end known as 'The Exchange', was one long market. By 1847 it had become somewhat formally organised as described in a book published that year:

> A market, principally for dairy produce, is held on the Exchange on the mornings of Tuesday and Friday every week to which the country farmers send in milk, butter, eggs, poultry etc. sufficient for the town consumption. The fruit and vegetable market is held on the same mornings at the head of Academy Street where the street is wide enough to accommodate the fruiterers with cart-room — selling from off the cart being the mode of doing business.
>
> The butcher market is situated at the east end of Petty Street, but being too far out of the way, it is now chiefly used as a slaughter-house — the fleshers having shops in different parts of the town.
>
> The fish market, which was formerly held on the site of the present post-office, was considered too much in the centre of the town, and consequently transferred to the butcher market.
>
> The feeing markets, or trysts for hiring servants, are held on the last Fridays of April and October.[13]

In addition to these frequent markets all held in, or in the immediate vicinity of, High Street, there were five annual fairs each proclaimed on the Exchange on a Wednesday and held on the two succeeding days. To these the country folk brought their coarse home-made cloths, worsteds and farm and dairy produce but, by this time, because the town shops were now well supplied with such goods, little business was done compared with previous years. On these same days a cattle market was held at the southern end of Waterloo Bridge but a new horse and cattle market was being discussed. (From the Ordnance Survey map of 1868 it appears to have been found at the Capel Inch). The somewhat complicated way of fixing the dates for the proclamation of these fairs is vaguely reminiscent of the formula for determining Easter Day: Candlemas Fair on the first Wednesday after 11 February, Old Style* or on 11 February if that happend to be a Wednesday. Whitsuntide Market on the Wednesday following 25 May (whether Old or New Style is not stated). St Andrews Fair on the first Wednesday after 18 July, New Style. Marymas Fair on the first Wednesday after 15 August, Old Style or the 20 August New Style of that was a Wednesday. Martinmas Fair on the first Wednesday after 11 November, Old Style.[14] By this time however a newer and greater fair had arrived as a result of the Highland Clearances, the annual Wool Fair on the second Thursday in July and the two following days. So great was the trade (about 100,000 stones of wool and the same number of sheep changing hands each year) that it was accepted as the gauge for sheep prices throughout Scotland. Although it is still held annually its former glory has sadly diminished.

The Exchange, until 1961 measuring some 66 feet long by about 30 feet broad, was always a focal point for proclamation, demonstration and celebration. In 1642 it was the scene of a lavish spread for the entertainment of the Master of Lovat on his way home with his new bride, Ann Leslie, daughter of the Covenanter General the Earl of Leven. Doubtless the tables then spread were the same ones used only eight years later to welcome the great Marquis of Montrose on his sad journey from betrayal in Assynt to execution in Edinburgh.

*Prior to 1752 the calendar got out of synchronisation with the sun through lack of leap years. In that year eleven days were 'lost' and September 3rd became 14th. 'Old Style' refers to the date ignoring these lost days, 'New Style' to the date after taking them into account.

But now I set down that which I myself was
eyewitness of. The 7th of May at Lovat, he sat upon
a little shelty horse without a sude, but a quilt of rags
and straw, and pieces of rope for stirrups, his feet
fastened under the horses belly, with a leather tether
and a bit halter for bridle, a ragged old dark reddish
plaid and a Montier cap called Magirky on his head,
a musketeer on each side and his fellow prisoners on
foot after him . . . At the end of the bridge, stepping
forward an old woman, Margaret nin George,
exclaimed and brawled saying 'Montrose, look above,
view these ruinous houses of mine which you
occasioned to be burnt down when you beseiged
Inverness' yet he never altered his countenance but
with a majesty and state beseeming him, kept a
countenance high. At the cross, a table covered, the
magistrates treat him with wines which he would not
touch until allayed with water; the stately prisoners,
his officers, stood under a forestair, and drank
heartily. I remarked Colonel Hurry, a robust, tall,
stately fellow with a long cut in his cheek. All the
way through the streets he never lowered his aspect.
The Provost, Duncan Forbes, taking leave of him at
the town's end said 'My Lord, I am sorry for your
circumstance'. He replied 'I am sorry for being the
object of your pity'. The Marquis was convoyed that
night to Castle Stuart where he lodged.[15]

The next year the Presbytery of Inverness was concerned to
hear that there was, in the parish of Dunlichity, 'ane
idolatrous image called St Finane keepit in a private house
obscurely'. A deputation was duly sent to investigate and if
possible find this image and bring it to the next meeting; this
having been done, the meeting duly ordered that it should be
burned on the Exchange on 21 December. It was here also
that Duncan MacRae of Kintail, suspected of being a spy, was
hanged from an apple tree growing in front of the Town Hall
in 1746 on orders from the Duke of Cumberland. According
to local legend the tree immediately withered and died.[16]

More recently the Exchange was the assembly point for citizens joining together to welcome the New Year; a report in the Inverness Courier of 1 January 1907 gives a good example of the festivities with which the opening year was greeted early this century:

The New Year was welcomed in time honoured fashion in Inverness. Shortly before midnight hundreds gathered on the Exchange and in the vicinity and as soon as the clock in the Old Steeple had struck the hour of midnight loud cheers were raised and fireworks were set off. There was hand-shaking on every side and good wishes were expressed. The gathering, composed mostly of young men and maidens, was orderly and great good humour prevailed. The Town Band, under the leadership of Mr H.T. Tuff, made its appearance in the streets playing with great vigour 'A guid new year to ane and a''. The band paraded the principle streets followed by a large crowd which, although somewhat boisterous in behaviour, did not go too far in their demonstrations. The crowds in the streets soon dispersed many going on 'first-footing' expeditions. Watch-night services were held. There was a large congregation in the Wesleyan Methodist Church. The Rev. Howard May delivered an appropriate address.[17]

Next to the Town House stood the Horns Hotel and both buildings were used by the Duke of Cumberland as administrative offices in the aftermath of Culloden. It was to the hotel that Provost Hossack went to protest about the treatment the citizens were receiving from the Army, only to be answered by General Hawley 'damn you puppy, do you pretend to dictate here?' ordering him to be kicked out, an instruction literally obeyed. The poor Provost was manhandled to the head of the stairs where he received from Sir Robert Adair such a kick that it is said he never touched a stair until he was at the foot of the first flat. Oddly, the said provost was a convinced Whig and Hanoverian.[18] He was for ever afterwards known as 'The Kicked Provost'; he was rather more successful when requesting that Fort George be re-sited at Ardersier (see page 55).

On market days it was not uncommon for the town boys to taunt, and even lightly assault by throwing shot, the country boys accompanying their families displaying their wares on the Exchange. One day in 1738 a lad MacLean from the braes of Glenurquhart retaliated and rendered four of his tormentors *hors de combat* before their cries rallied reinforcements who far outnumbered him. In his predicament he called 'Is there not a son of Clan Gillean here today', an appeal which the Provost of the day, also a MacLean, found too compulsive a claim on his clan loyalty to resist. Accordingly he joined the affray, knocking several of his fellow citizens to left and right; only when he reached its centre was he recognised and the trouble quelled. William Inglis, one of the town's most worthy Provosts, was descended on the female side from this Provost MacLean.

The Town Cross, now standing on the Exchange (or what is left of it) once stood in the middle of High Street about half-way between Eastgate and Bridge Street and was moved to its present position on 17 August 1768.[19] 'Clachnacuddin', the stone embedded at the foot of the Cross also once stood in the middle of High Street but nearer to its present site than where the Cross had been. Its name 'the stone of the tubs' comes from the practice of the housewives resting their baskets of washed clothes on it whilst they had a breather and a 'wee blether' after ascending the brae from the river. It became the fetish of Invernessians who proudly proclaimed themselves to be 'Clachnacuddiners' or 'Sons of Clachnacuddin'. Those leaving the town to live in the far places of the world often chipped off a small portion of this stone to keep as a talisman to such an extent that, after being moved to its present position in 1796, it was lowered and given its protective covering in 1900 lest it disappear altogether in small portions. Proclamations used to be made from this unusual platform but now, as occasion demands, they are made from the steps of the Town House. Until less than twenty years ago it was the custom at midnight each Hogmanay for the Provost in his robes, supported by the Magistrates and Town

Councillors, to appear from the front door of the Town House and wish a happy new year to the many citizens assembled on the Exchange before retiring inside to have a celebratory dram with his colleagues, who would then disperse to their own family celebrations. About the time that this custom lapsed the Forbes Fountain, a drinking water dispenser, was moved from the centre of the Exchange and re-erected in Cavell Gardens in a somewhat truncated form.

On 6 March 1839 the *Inverness Courier* reported that, 'On Monday last the workmen engaged in the erection of the new inn, High Street, adjoining the British Linen Company's banking office, found part of a deer's horn, 36 inches in length, about ten feet below the surface of the street. Part of the horn was covered with sea-shells', an indication that even as near the centre of the town as this the tides had once encroached. The new inn was to be the Union Hotel, situated on the north side of the street about midway along just about opposite the old site of the Cross. It was under the same management as the Caledonian Hotel in Church Street and the two were the termini for coaches then operating at what now seem to be decidely unsociable hours. In 1847 the Royal Mail Coach from Edinburgh by way of Perth and Badenoch arrived at half past midnight and left for the return journey an hour and a quarter later. To take passengers onwards the one for Tain left at a quarter past one in the morning whilst the one coming in from that town arrived at 1.26 a.m. to let its passengers catch the Edinburgh and Aberdeen coaches. There was a choice for passengers going to Aberdeen; they could take the Mail at 2 a.m. and go by Campbelltown (Ardersier) and Nairn, or they could take *The Defiance* at 6 a.m. which went direct to Nairn and onwards. The fare by either route was £2 inside or one guinea outside and passengers could join at either of the two hotels. Even in those days tourists, or more probably sportsmen arriving for the shooting, were catered for, the *Duke of Wellington* leaving 'every lawful morning' at 6 a.m. for Perth during the summer and autumn months, having arrived the previous evening at 8 p.m. Another coach, bearing the same name, left for Strathpeffer during the summer season at 3 p.m. 'every lawful day'.[20] The Union Hotel was purchased in 1870 to become the Highland Club, a social and residential establishment much frequented by local business men for lunch and by County Councillors staying during the meetings of their Council — usually held over three or four successive days each month except January and August. The Club closed in 1977, soon after the demise of the County Council.

'The front elevation of the Caledonian Bank in High Street looking up Castle Street is unquestionably the best piece of architectural ornamentation in the place and is deserving of notice. Above the basement, which contains two finely carved archways, is a large portico with four fluted columns having beautifully carved Corinthian capitals which support a massive pediment within which are arranged a group of allegorical figures, from the classic chisel of Mr H. Ritchie of Edinburgh'.[21] The central figure is Caledonia, holding in her hand the Roman fasces, emblematical of power. On the right is a figure representing the Ness, from whose side rises another female form, symbolic of a tributary stream. On the extreme right are two small figures rowing a bark, representing Commerce. On the left is Plenty pouring out the contents of her cornucopia, a reaper with an armful of cut corn, a shepherd and sheep, emblematical of the rural interests of the country.

In 1815 an Atheneum was established opposite the Town House on land said previously to have belonged to the Knights of St John of Jerusalem, 'The Hospitalers'. Carved on the frontage were, and at this time still are, a number of biblical texts, and new Councillors were warned that, after civic receptions, they might be asked to read these texts whilst standing at the Town House door as a test of sobriety. During my lengthy period as a Councillor I never knew of anyone failing this test; but come to think of it neither did I ever hear of anyone actually being submitted to such a trial! There was a fire in the basement of this building in 1846 and although there was a copious supply of water 'the fire engines were in wretched order the principal engine having been sent to Glasgow for repair'. The fire was subdued after two hours but later that same year another fire, this time behind Academy

Street, 'gave another proof of the necessity for a regular brigade'. For once the Council acted promptly and within a fortnight had made arrangements for the equipment of a brigade and appointed a superintendent.[22]

In 1901 a letter appeared in the Courier complaining about the speed of a car which had been involved in a minor accident with a cyclist near the Exchange. The driver of the car was not named, but the fact that Dr Kerr replied to this attempt to damage his character proves that there were few, if any, cars other than his in the town at that time. It was at this point that, in 1932, the first traffic lights in Inverness were erected.

Buildings in Bridge Street are almost wholly of recent construction, only the dominating steeple and the facade running west from it are earlier than mid-twentieth century. In 'Ye charter of ye tolbooth' of 1436 Cristina Makferry feued to the Burgesses and the community of Inverness the land on which the steeple now stands for 'two pence of usual money in name of Blench Farm if asked and to our Lord the King five pence annually'.[23] Just when the steeple was erected is not known but the earliest recorded reference is in 1569 when the Council ordered that the charters and public records should be put into the 'stepill' for safe-keeping. In 1593 mention is made of the 'house and fortalice called the steeple of Inverness'. A demand was sent to the Provost: 'Forasmuch as Lachlan MacKintosh of Dunachton one of the Commissioners granted to Andrew Lord Ochiltrie and John Earl of Athol for the prosecution of George Earl of Huntly and his accomplices for the slaughter of the Earl of Moray . . . being truly informed that the said Earl of Huntly is assembling to prosecute the said Lachlan MacKintosh, his friends and partakers also the House of Inverness . . . MacKintosh charges the Provost, Bailies, Council and community to surrender and deliver the House and Fortalice called the Steeple of Inverness into his hands'. The Magistrates duly assured the MacKintosh that they intended to 'keep the aforesaid steeple and fortalice thereof from the said Earl of Huntly to their own use and utility'.[29]

The earliest known picture of Inverness, by Slezer in about 1680, shows the Steeple, but too vaguely to give much information about its appearance. One of 1725, however, shows it to have a square tower with a castellated top above which a plain slim spire rose to carry a weather-vane in the shape of a cock which gave rise to the local expression for being in prison, 'neath the cock'. Near the top of the tower is shown a clock, presumably with four faces. 'In 1690 a stone spire was built upon the tower on the battlements of which the spikes for fixing the heads of criminals were placed and long ago, says Nonagenarian,* I remember seeing part of a skull on one of the spikes. This old building was well supplied with all the instruments of torture: thumbkins, bootkins, branks, cuckstool, stocks and pillory'.[25] Another description of Inverness in the year 1725 includes the words 'and had a steeple with bells and clock'. The official records show that about that time the Council were paying £40 Scots to the official responsible for maintaining the clock. In 1758 the bell was taken down, weighed and given to the care of Captain Reid to transport to London and the next year £172 7s 6d. Scots was paid 'for adding to the casting the old bell' which had by then been brought back from London and re-hung.[26]

Thirty years later the adjoining jail was re-built but, on account of the expense involved, it was decided to leave the steeple unaltered. During the demolition, however, it was realised that the steeple was in a dangerous condition and so, mainly through the drive and initiative of Dean of Guild William Inglis, later to be Provost, funds were raised and a more artistic and dignified substitute agreed. The foundation stone was laid on 22 August 1789 with great ceremony and full Masonic honours. At this time Masons were in the process of changing from "operative to free and accepted masons" and appear to have been invited to many official stone-laying ceremonies. Thus it was that brethren of the two Lodges, St John Kilwinning and St Andrew's Kilwinning, paraded in black coats, vests and breeches with white stockings and gloves the ubiquitous William Inglis appearing in the dual

*Referring to the *Reminiscences of a Clachnacuddin Nonagenarian*, McDonald, Inverness, 1886.

5 *The Town House today*

6 *The Exchange and High Street showing the Forbes
Fountain now re-erected in Cavell Gardens and "Faith, Hope
and Charity" above the Clan Tartan Warehouse*

7 *The Town Centre with Queen Mary's House occupying part of the site now filled by the Highlands and Islands Development Board building*

8   *The Suspension Bridge about 1890*

9   *Before the second Castle Tolmie was built, about 1890*

capacity of Dean of Guild and Right Worshipful Master of Lodge St Andrew's Kilwinning. The new erection cost £1600 towards which Sir Hector Munro of Novar, Member of Parliament for Inverness Burghs,[27] contributed £200 and presented a new clock.

According to the *Courier* article mentioned above[26] the architect was Alexander Laing but most other writers credit William Sibbald who designed a very similar spire for St Andrew's Church in Edinburgh. William Inglis certainly took a very keen interest in the design and also accepted personal responsibility for payments required before donations were received. Towering 155 feet it comprises three decorated square towers on top of each other slightly reducing in ascent surmounted by two similarly embellished octagonal towers on top of which is a slender spire carrying a long rod piercing first an onion-shaped globe and then two balls and topped by a weather vane. The lower, and larger, ball contains coins, newspapers, photographs and a pint of Millburn whisky. In the angles formed by the lower octagon and the higher rectangle towers, are four stone urns. The clock, with a dial on each side of the top rectangular tower near its apex, gives purpose to what is otherwise of no practical use although of very considerable aesthetic value. *The Statistical Account of Scotland* says of this steeple, 'The spire was built by the architect of St Andrew's Spire in Edinburgh and is said to surpass it in beauty; the slender appearance of St Andrew's spire, arising from a defect in proportion, renders it less agreeable.'[28]

The clock, with two others maintained by the Council, was converted to electrical drive in 1979 — the others being in the Old High Church and in Grant Street.

The old bell, repaired in 1758, was again cracked when being rung to celebrate the victory at Waterloo, but was not repaired until 1844. An earthquake, felt over most of Scotland, on 13 August 1816 damaged the spire, twisting it out of true alignment and causing it to become an object of considerable curiosity, compared by some even with Pisa's leaning tower, so that there was considerable adverse comment when it was repaired in 1828. Disputes and troubles continued to surround the steeple, especially after the adjoining jail and courthouse had been demolished and, in 1853, plans were produced for their replacement with shops and offices. The *Courier* of 26 May that year commented, 'The only objection to the scheme, if it proves a paying one, which can possibly be urged, is strongly brought out by Mr Batchen's lithograph — namely the absurdity of attaching a steeple to a row of drapers' or grocers' shops. It seems droll enough to raise a lofty steeple on a jail, but by the new arrangement, the only conceivable purpose of our elegant spire will be to support the weather-cock and amuse the jack-daws.' About a hundred years later, when re-development of that side of Bridge Street was again being considered, fierce argument raged as to whether it should be demolished or left on an 'island' site with Church Street traffic passing on either side. A new traffic system including the prevention of any vehicles turning into Church Street from High Street, introduced in 1976, has given at least a temporary reprieve.

The jail and courthouse were probably erected before the first steeple, almost certainly only a few years after the feuing of the site, but history tells us little of this early building. Here, in the mid-sixteenth century, the Provost and Bailies sat as the Burgh Court and 'all manner of men came before them and all manner of questions were disposed of'. The court was always opened with formality — it was 'lawfully fenced and affirmed and suits called' and then the business began. In addition to the Provost and Bailies, who constituted the Court, there were present four officers of Court and Dempster, all of whom were appointed yearly. The duty of the officers was to serve writs coming from the Court and to execute its warrants; that of the Dempster was to repeat to the accused the sentence of the Court which was first read by the Clerk. It may also have been part of his duty to carry out death sentences when pronounced by the higher Courts of the Realm but this is not certain so far as Inverness was concerned.

One curious feature in the proceedings of the Burgh Court is the comparative rarity of a suit for the recovery of money. A man sues his neighbour for a boll, or a number of bolls, a victual; for a barrel of salmon, or a dozen barrels; for a dozen hides, or for any other article of traffic in the district, but he rarely sues him for its value. When money is sued for it is usually lent money, and when a suit of that sort does appear the pursuer is generally a man from a distance. No Inverness burgess seems to have been able, or willing, to lend money to his neighbour. As a rule justice was fairly administered, although doubtless lapses of burgesses from burghal decorum were less severely dealt with than those of 'outlandish men'. When a Celt named MacHenrick charged against Gilbert Gollan that 'he dang me with his naiffs, and drew a great quantity of my blood in the away taking of my weapons frae me' the jury were probably right in acquitting Gollan . . . but one may speculate whether the result of the trial would have been quite the same had the half-drunken Highlander been in the dock and Gilbert Gollan, a member of the Saxon colony and official taster of ale for the Burgh, in the witness box.[29]

"The Church had not long before been disestablished but the unemployed priests found employment as pleaders in the Burgh Courts . . . Occasionally a priest-lawyer who appeared for the defender took exception to the constitution of the Court . . . Thomas Cuthbert was charged at the instance of the Burgh Treasurer with keeping the half of the Stell Fishing belonging to the town for five years without paying rent. The very obvious objection was taken that as the town was the pursuer it was improper for the Provost and Bailies to act as judges, but that was over-ruled. It was then objected that the Provost, the Bailies and the Clerk were all so nearly related by blood or marriage to the Treasurer, who was the pursuer that, leaving the interests of the town out of the question, the judges ought not to try a case in which the Treasurer was the pursuer. In support of this objection the priest-lawyer, whose knowledge of local genealogies must have been exact and extensive, narrated the family connections of Provost, Bailies, Treasurer and Town Clerk for several generations, and traced a not remote cousinship between every member of the Bench, the Clerk of the Court and the Prosecutor.[30]

The litigation ended when the Treasurer turned upon his opponent and asked if he did not admit the debt — which he did.

Records of Inverness published by the New Spalding Club in 1911 contain this interesting reference: 'Donald Yet, having taken six salmon from the cruives, was sentenced to have his ear nailed to the Trone and to remain there for nine hours'. Dr John MacDonald, Medical Officer of Health, read a paper at the Inverness Field Club meeting in February 1919 in which he gave a description of the jail, which must have been in a very bad state at one time, much needing the attention of a John Howard or an Elizabeth Fry. It was for many years too small, admitted of little or no classification, was situated in the principal thoroughfare, and had no open courts on facilities of any kind for air or exercise. The sanitary arrangements, as in other prisons in Scotland, were of the most primitive. 'Squalor Carceria' was indeed the order of the day. On the 29 September 1709 the Town Clerk paid an officer 4s 6d Scots to buy peats to be burned in it to remove the bad scent, and in December 1737 the Magistrates ordered the Town Clerk to purchase a spade to be given to the hangman for cleaning it.

An official document of 1786 states that the jail consisted of two small cells for criminals and one miserable room for debtors. It was often so crowded as to make their condition most deplorable. There were often thirty people confined in those holes, none of which measured more than 13 feet square. Bad as these conditions undoubtedly were they were far better than those in the cell already described as having been built into the Ness Bridge. One unexpected benefit to those subjected to these conditions is brought to light in 1731: 'The prison is a bleak old building and the town is not in a condition to keep it in repair. The greatest part of the murderers and other notorious villains that have been committed since I have been here have made their escape.'[31] Burt goes on to suggest that clan loyalties were mainly responsible for these escapes. A notable escapee was

Roderick MacKay, imprisoned for trying to rescue a con-
signment of illicitly-distilled whisky from the excise officers
who had seized it. He managed to entice a warder into his
cell, took his key and locked him up instead. Roderick then
walked out of the jail, fled to the west coast and, in July 1773,
sailed from Loch Broom for Halifax, Nova Scotia. The key to
his cell in Inverness is still preserved in the Public Archives in
that Canadian city.[32]

A new order of things was coming and, in 1788 as is shown
on the commemorative stone now in the Museum, a new jail
and court-house were built on the same site — but the escapes
continued. In an early side-effect of the Highland Clearances
five men, Hugh Breac MacKenzie, Malcolm Ross, Donald
Munro, Alexander MacKay and William Cunningham, were
sentenced at the Circuit Court for driving away sheep from
areas of Ross-shire. The first was sentenced to transportation, two others to jail and the remaining two to banishment
from Scotland for life. Before these penalties could be carried
out the jail doors were opened one night and all five
disappeared, never to be heard of again — at least not by the
authorities. Since the chief sufferer at their hands had been
Sir Hector Munro MP some doubt is cast on the disinter-
estedness of his contribution to the erection of the new jail
and steeple.

Even the new building was far from satisfactory, as is
shown by a comment in the *Inverness Courier* on 12
November 1818:

> A correspondent of the 'Times' gave a very
> unpleasant account of the gaol in Inverness, 'a corner
> building at the junction of two main streets', namely
> Bridge Street and Church Street. 'The outer door of
> the prison opens into the main street, and
> immediately on entering you perceive a flight of steps
> on either hand; that on the left leads to the
> court-room where prisoners are tried; the deal boards
> with which the court is fitted up have never been
> painted, and the dirt on them and on the walls gave
> to both a rather miserable appearance'. At the top of
> the opposite flight of steps a door opened into a

stone gallery facing the cells. This gallery was the appointed place for airing and recreation 'and as often as the prisoners avail themselves of it' says the writer 'they are exposed like wild beasts in a cage to every passenger below'. At the time of his visit there was only one criminal prisoner, who had been tried for an attempt to assassinate and sentenced to confinement on account of derangement. This poor man's cell is described as horribly loathsome. He had been in it for six years.

'There were no other prisoners at the time I am speaking of, except seven debtors; one of these was by himself in a room sufficiently commodious but very dirty; the other six were in a room very much smaller, but still very dirty; they all looked very sickly'.

The *Courier* devoted an article to this report which it claimed to be exaggerated. It agrees that the prison ought not to be in the centre of the town but claims that its construction was better in many respects than that of most Scottish prisons. 'The grated gallery or arcade which extends along the whole front of the prison, whatever it may appear to chance visitors, affords the prisoners the liveliest amusement. It overlooks the busiest part of the town and gives them an opportunity of seeing and hearing all that is going forward. There may be some objection to this too familiar intercourse with the street, but the charge of exposing them like wild beasts in a cage must be laughed at by every one who knows anything about the real condition of the persons said to be exhibited.' As for the poor prisoner, the writer says, he had since his commitment become furiously mad and annoyed the whole town with his nocturnal bellowings. He was, however, confined under a warrant of the Justiciary Court until bail could be found and the town in the meantime was obliged to submit to the infliction. If six debtors were found in one room it must have been from their own choice, and in daytime only.[33]

Proof of the inadequacy of the Courthouse was shown in the General Election of 1826 when the electors met there as usual, but too many attended and they had to move to the High Church. Since only fifty-nine votes were cast we have some ideas of the size of the room. In 1831 the Castlehill was bought from the Duke of Gordon to provide a site for a new courthouse and prison, the former to be built by the County, the latter by the town. It was to be fifteen years before the foundation stone of the jail was laid and 1848 before it was occupied. The old one in Bridge Street was then purchased by the town and demolished in 1853.

Originally Bridge Street was a narrow wynd leading to a dead-end at the river and even after a bridge was provided it was still not of major importance. Only a narrow path led to the riverside to the north, a building known as Castle Tolmie blocking most of the access, whilst to the south the lands of the Castle stretched right to the river. In neither direction was there anything approaching a roadway along the riverside until 1794 when the banks were extended and strengthened. Behind Castle Tolmie stood a house where, it was said, Mary Queen of Scots found shelter when denied admission to her own Castle by the Earl of Huntly's Lieutenant-Governor in 1562. After many alterations, additions and subtractions this building, long known as Queen Mary's House, was demolished in 1968. Its vaults, probably all that remained of the house as she had known it, were incorporated into the entrance vestibule of the new development, the offices of the Highlands and Islands Development Board. Castle Tolmie, which had been erected in 1678 was demolished when the new bridge was being built after the flood in 1849, and the name transferred to the tenements on the opposite corner of Bridge Street. These in turn were demolished when the next bridge was built in 1961. The appearance of this part of the town in his day was well described by John MacLean, 'the Inverness Nonagenarian' who was born in 1756:

> One building (the original Castle Tolmie) contains an ancient structure with elaborately carved coat of arms in the stone-work to the attic windows, and bearing at the gable ends the date 1678. The building was occupied as a town residence by Forbes of Culloden. It is now divided into several domiciles, being occupied by a saddler, grocer and vintner. Although the stone turn-pike stairs were removed the house

now projects so far into the street as to allow of no pavement or footpath whatsoever before it, and when the ancient pile of building on the opposite side, known formerly as the town residence of the Robertsons of Inshes and which also contested the claims of having Queen Mary as a visitor under its roof, projected to the same extent on the street, and when to this is superadded the still greater projection of the stone stairs belonging to these venerable buildings the reader will conceive the lane-like appearance which the neighbourhood presented in my early days.[34]

It was widened in 1817 to a width of 34 feet between buildings. Further widening took place in 1961 when the whole of the south side of the street was demolished. Efforts by some enlightened citizens, including the Chamber of Commerce, to have the site left vacant to form a park-like foreground to the Castle, failed because of the loss of rateable value. In 1967 the other side, except for the Steeple and the facade of the building erected to replace the old jail, met a similar fate.

On 3 October 1692 a group of tradesmen left their businesses for six months (on pain of fine or imprisonment if they refused) to become the town's first police force. George Anderson, wig-maker and Thomas Ritchie, glover, patrolled Duff Street whilst John Munro and Alexander Fraser, smiths, watched over Kirk Street. Two others were given Bridge Street, and a Mr Johnson and a Mr Wilson were allocated 'bewest the waters of the Ness'. Eventually a police force was created and a police office erected next to the jail; in front of this building the body of the last person publicly executed (in fact the last person to be executed) in Inverness was buried. When the office moved to Castle Wynd the body was moved too, to lie beneath the steps at the entrance. In 1975 this office was demolished after the police had removed to new headquarters at Culcabock but John Adam was left in peace.

Church Street

In old charters known as 'The King's Highway to the North' Church Street is first referred to by that name in 1240, and evidently led to a ford over the river near Friars' Shott.[35] Once a bridge was provided it assumed names associating it with the Town's Church — Kirkgate, Kirk Street and now Church Street.

The steeple has already been described and, it apart, there is now nothing to show how the south end of the street appeared even a very few years ago. Gone is the old Caledonian Hotel replaced by a modern namesake and gone too is the Northern Meeting Rooms building which probably saw more glamour during its existence than any other establishment in the town and, although retained in a reduced and almost un-noticed form, gone is the typical vennel which ran at number 11 to join with one from Bridge Street to give access to the ancient hostelry now Gellion's Hotel.

Founded in 1788, the Northern Meeting Society first met in the Town Hall and its members dined in various hotels until their own Rooms were built in 1790. Here they held their Annual Ball which, for nearly two centuries, was the highlight of 'the season', several times graced by the attendance of members of the Royal Family. Soon after its opening it was damaged by an explosion and was then reduced from three storeys to two. Just behind it, in Baron Taylor Street, stood a building containing a soup kitchen and the premises of a candle-maker and it was above such establishments that the Council chose to locate their powder magazine! One day Robin Goodwin the candle-maker, commonly known as 'Robin Goodfellow', left his tallow-kettle to boil whilst he went for a convivial dram. It proved too convivial, he lingered too long, the pot boiled over, the premises caught fire and the powder exploded. Several people were killed and many others injured. Robert immediately fled the town and the next record of him is a report in the *Inverness Courier* of 4 June 1818 saying that an Aberdeen paper had recorded the finding in the River Clyde the dead body of Robert Gooden or Goodwin, a soap-boiler and native of Forres.

We observe from the description and the name of the person alluded to that he was the same individual who, on the 12 March 1801 while employed in his usual occupation of candle-making in Inverness left his tallow kettle to boil over, by which the house was set on fire, and before the accident was discovered, the fire had communicated to a quantity of gunpowder (not less than 8½ barrels) which exploded; 14 persons lost their lives and the shock and destruction thus occasioned will ever be remembered in Inverness by all who experience the sad effects of it.[36]

The candle-makers premises were in the Black or Back Vennel, the old name for Baron Taylor Street whose present name is of uncertain derivation. Probably the most accepted one is that it comes from a John Taylor, a merchant who once had premises in the Vennel, who earned the sobriquet 'The Baron'. Another possible derivation is from a Mr Barron who was once a tailor in the street. A former provost, Provost Wotherspoon used to insist that it was the 'Bar on Taylor Street' but he never accounted for the word 'Taylor'.

Not long before the Northern Meeting Rooms were built there had been another near-disaster at the site. When the Lords of Justiciary visited Inverness they were always very hospitably entertained in the Islands (see page 184) with salmon caught fresh from the river as a main feature. Evidently this fare did not always suit the tastes of these gentlemen and they usually brought their own cook with them. About 1779 the lodging house in which they par-simoniously stayed in preference to the nearby Horns Hotel or the new Mason's Hotel caught fire during the night and the cook was burned to death. Lord Gardenstone, the judge, was rescued by the assistant cook, an Inverness woman, who rushed into his room, rolled him in his blankets and carried him to the street. A grateful Lord bestowed a life pension on her for thus saving his life. The Rooms were built over the site of this lodging house.[37]

A peripatetic Post Office occupied the position across the road on the north corner of Bank Lane for a few years after

1820 to be followed by the *Inverness Courier* in 1838 prior to moving to its present site at the foot of the Lane. The south corner was occupied by the National Bank and gave the Lane its name. Beyond the Post Office stood a hotel built in 1776 by the two Masonic Lodges and was hence known as the Mason's Hotel or the Mason Lodge Hotel until about 1825 when its present name of Caledonian Hotel first appeared. The Masons continued to meet in the hotel even after they had sold it and until it was demolished for re-building in 1966. The first tenant was John Ettles who later owned hotels of his own in one of which Robert Burns stayed when visiting the town in 1787.

In 1824 Robert Wilson became tenant, and it is he who is said to have brought to Inverness the sport of curling.

> Last week the curling-stones, brooms, and other accompaniments were brought forward, and Loch-na-Sanais[38] on the road to Dochfour, with the picturesque hills of Tomnahurich and Torvain, echoed for the first time to the shouts and noise of the 'roaring play'. A bonspiel was played on Saturday between a team of married men on one side and bachelors on the other. Grave Magistrates, Councillors, lawyers and other citizens mingled in the pastime and were as eager and animated as ever they were at the Council Board . . . The novelty of the game drew forth a number of ladies and gentlemen, and there were several hundreds of spectators on the ice and in its neighbourhood. The public are indebted to Mr Wilson, of the Caledonian Hotel, for the introduction of this pastime. He provided the curling stones and has very handsomely given the use of a coach and horses to convey the parties to and from the scene of action.[39]

In 1829 several hundred people assembled at Lochgorm with an effigy of Charles Grant MP, who supported emancipation, in a 'No Popery' demonstration. After burning the effigy at the Exchange they moved to the Caledonian Hotel, demanded the appearance of the MP and, on his refusal, proceeded to smash all the front windows. They then moved on to wreck the Roman Catholic Chapel in Margaret Street. The hotel again suffered similar damage in 1846 during a protest against the shipment of potatoes from Inverness when, due to blight, there was a severe shortage at home and a veritable famine in Ireland. A claim for £300 was made for replacement and the Town and the County each paid £140 leaving the hotel to bear the remainder.

Opposite the hotel now is Union Street, opened only in 1863. There had previously been a vennel at about this position running from Church Street to what was still called New Street. Two notable fires occured in Union Street, both in the same building. Half-way along the north side, opposite Drummond Street, there was a Music Hall (not a vaudeville theatre) over ground-floor shops until it was destroyed in 1898 and then renovated the following year. Later, this was purchased by the Wesleyan Methodists and became their church in 1922. In 1961 this also was destroyed by fire and the space remained empty until 1980 when a restaurant was built over the shops which had been saved in the conflagration. The Methodists used the Town Hall for a very few Sundays, and then the cinema in Academy Street until their new building in Huntly Street was ready.

Queensgate, the next road linking Church and Academy Streets, was not completely developed until 1900.

At number 45, a little north of the hotel, lived Lady Drummuir in 1746. She was the widow of Alexander Duff and their elder daughter, Anne, had married Lachlan MacKintosh of MacKintosh who had died in 1731. Anne survived him and their daughter-in-law, another Anne but this time a Farquharson of Invercauld, was to become the 'Colonel Anne' of the 'Rout of Moy'. Although minor details are disputed the generally accepted version of this notable affray is that news of the presence of Prince Charles at Moy reached the Hanoverians in Inverness, who then planned a foray under Lord Loudon to take him captive. News of this plan, in turn, reached the Prince's sympathisers in the town and one, probably Lady Drummuir but possibly even the MacKintosh who was serving in the Royal Army under Loudon, sent a boy to Moy to warn Colonel Anne.

96

With the benefit of this warning Colonel Anne posted the smith at Moy, Donald Fraser, and four assistants all with loaded muskets on either side of the road Loudon would be using. On the approach of Loudon with some 1500 men these five stalwarts shouted to quite imaginary regiments of Clanranald, Keppoch, Locheil and so on to charge, at the same time opening fire on the government troops who promptly panicked and fled. The Prince was saved and Loudon and his army thoroughly demoralised so that they deserted Inverness and moved into Ross-shire leaving Charles a free entry into the town.

Lady Drummuir's house was said to be the only house in the town with a parlour not having a bed in it, and this was the Prince's base until the Battle of Culloden. After the battle Cumberland used the same accommodation and Lady Drummuir is said to have remarked, 'I had twa king's bairns living with me in my time and may I never see another'. Although strictly outwith the scope of this book, a short description of the Battle of Culloden might be given since it profoundly affected the town in so many ways.

About eleven o'clock notice was given that the royal army was in motion whereupon the Prince, placing himself at the head of his forces gave orders to fire a cannon as a signal for the gathering of those who had strayed. When his troops were assembled it was found that they amounted to about 5000 men but from the exhaustion and fatigue they had already undergone they were in no fighting condition. The royal army on the other hand numbered 8811, were well disciplined, properly accoutred for the field, and were in no wise suffering from the privations to which the others were exposed, having rested and fared well on the previous day at Nairn. With these odds against him, it would be thought that the Prince would endeavour to shun an engagement but he perceived that if he lost the present opportunity his troops, especially those who showed symptoms of dissatisfaction with their condition, and the hardships to which they were exposed, would fall off, and that matters were not likely to be afterwards brought to a more promising issue. Thus, then, were two armies approaching each other, upon whose procedure for one short hour, depended the welfare of Great Britain. The contending parties, aware of this, were brought to a state of desperation. The highlanders, eager for the onset, commenced the action by cannon-firing, without receiving any return from the royalists. The shots, however, were ill-served and did little execution. A few minutes after one o'clock the royal artillery was opened upon the rebels and a few well-directed shots cut down their ranks with great slaughter. In this attack the Prince himself narrowly escaped the destruction occasioned by two pieces fired amongst a body of cavalry.

After cannonading for nearly half-an-hour, during which the rebel ranks were greatly thinned, while scarcely a man of the royal army fell, Charles made a charge upon the latter which was met by repeated volleys of musketry and grape-shot from the cannon. The first line who advanced to the attack was speedily swept away but still the assailants advanced and a second line encountered as deadly a reception as the first — chiefs and vassals fell in the same heap. So well directed was the fire from the side of the royalists that in little more than half-an-hour from the time the action commenced the rebel army was very much reduced and many of them fled notwithstanding the entreaties of the Prince and his officers who, in expectation of further aid, urged them to keep their ground. Charles would still linger on the field in the hope that the day was not yet lost, but pursuit obliged him and his few remaining followers to fly, and in their flight one party took the road to Inverness while another proceeded to the south-west, crossed the river Nairn and took refuge among the hills. Those who fled towards the town were closely pursued by the Duke's army who cut them down most unmercifully. Many of the inhabitants of Inverness who, either from curiosity or anxiety for the fate of their relations, had been attracted to the battle-field became victims to the fury of the soldiery, who slaughtered every one they overtook wearing the highland garb; the road from the moor to within a mile of the cross of Inverness was literally paved with dead bodies. The Prince left the field along with those who took the other direction and with them reached the hills in safety. The loss of the royal army amounted only to 310 while that on the Prince's side was upwards of 1200. The conquerors also captured 30 pieces of cannon, 2320 firelocks, 109 broadswords, 37 barrels of gunpowder and 22 carts of ammunition. The whole engagement occupied only forty minutes.[40]

Lady Drummuir was a very thrifty lady but much given to charity. Whenever she went to church she always carried over her arm a bag containing two or three shillings in copper which she handed out to the needy and so created a vogue of poor people on 'creepy stools' sitting along the street in the vicinity of the gateway to the High Church waiting for the pittance of the congregation. When her house was demolished in 1843 two muskets, a jewelled gold ring and a jewel-handled knife and fork were found in one of the vents. These articles were placed in a box for safety but, when it was opened the treasure trove had disappeared and was never recovered.[41]

Almost opposite the site of Lady Drummuir's house was St John's Episcopal Church, still standing at the time of writing, and used as auction rooms. It was built in 1800 as the successor of a church almost at the northern end of Church Street on the same side, which in its turn replaced a small chapel at the Maggot. The current church is in Southside Road.

Further down is Bow Court, recently restored by the generosity of a local builder Mr James Campbell, to something like its original form. It was erected in 1830 as the Trades Hall, home for the six Incorporated Trades of Inverness whose armorial bearings are depicted in six of the windows in the Town Hall. Immediately beyond, across School Lane, is Dunbar's Hospital and on the other side of Church Street the gateway to the Old High Church (pages 23/

25). On either side of the gateway stand two houses typical of the traders' houses that once graced the three original streets of the town but, unfortunately, the crow-step gabling has been removed to be replaced with concrete slabs. Just beyond these, to the north, is the building that was once St Mary's (Gaelic) Church, the Third Charge of Inverness, whose congregation but not its commitment to the Gaelic language, was transferred to St Mary's Dalneigh. It was in this church that evening services, in English, were first regularly held, a result of gas-lighting having been installed in 1827.

Higher up Church Street, and still on its western side, stands Abertarff House, the oldest example of domestic architecture remaining in Inverness. It was built in 1593 and occupied by the Frasers of Lovat. Hidden for years by houses fronting the street it was in a dilapidated condition when purchased, as part of a larger area, by the Commercial Bank who built their premises between it and Fraser Street, a building presently used as the North of Scotland Hydro-Electricity Board's showroom. The house was handed to the National Trust by the bank in 1963 together with funds to help in its restoration and when that had been completed it was let to An Commun Gaidhealach, the society dedicated to the preservation and extension of the Gaelic language and culture.

At one time this part of Church Street had an open drain running from the 'Foul Pool', the remnant of the old fosse of King William the Lion, at that time much contaminated by waste from the malt-kilns and barns covering the land east of Church Street to well beyond what is now Academy Street. In 1916 Dr Alexander Ross read a paper at the Inverness Field Club in whch he gave a description of Church Street, partly from reports and records he had read and partly from his own memories. It provides a fitting close to this account of the street:

> In a report, by Joseph Mitchell in 1826, a full
> description of the streets is given, and there is
> evidence to show that there was a hollow or
> depression about the middle of Church Street,
> between the Caledonian Hotel and Church Lane; in

fact Church Street there was an undulating surface, high
at the Exchange or old Town House, with a considerable
depression or hollow from what is now Queen's Gate to
Old School Lane and rising to a considerable height
opposite the Gaelic Church, as evidenced by the present
level of the High Church Burying-ground and the
exposures of the foundations of the Gaelic Church and
the houses opposite. The old outside turn-pike stairs and
projecting gables had then to be swept away, interior
stairs made to the houses, and I can recollect the old
stairs projecting into the streets at each door.

On 11 June 1818 I observe a note in the *Courier* to the
following effect — 'We are glad to observe that the
Magistrates have employed workmen to make a covered
drain to convey the water which runs down Church
Street from the Old Grammar School Lane across the
street and through the opposite lane to the river.
Independently of the comfort that will be derived from
having the water conveyed underground instead of on
the surface of the street, this will really be a
considerable improvement, by doing away with the
hollow in the street at that place, which was very
dangerous and annoying for carriages and carts'. In
former times, though the main outlet from the Foul Pool
was by the Harbour or at the Maggot, this depression
down near School Lane to the river probably also
formed an outlet from the Foul Pool, and to a certain
extent separated and excluded the Maggot and the
Ecclesiastical Buildings from the town fortified lands.

When clearing the foundation for the original Free
Church in 1843, which was from plans made by my
father, the builders came on the remains of an old
conduit or ditch, some five feet diameter, and at another
point, what is now the east end of Queen's Gate, in my
father's garden which then extended from Church Street
to Academy Street, a similar tunnel or ditch was
discovered, roughly arched, and which the old folk said
was a passage for smuggling, and which they alleged
extended out toward the Longman. May it not have

been an old ditch or outlet of the Foul Pool towards the river? The same hollow was used by Joseph Mitchell in 1826 as the outfall from Church Street. Some relics were found at the east end of the tunnel, and one copper plate bore the date of the formation of the street, 1778, or thereabout, as if thrown out amongst the rubbish used in levelling the pool.[42]

Academy Street

The defensive ditch created on William the Lion's orders that circled the town until the mid-fifteenth century, deteriorated thereafter until the north-eastern portion became a virtual cess-pool. Its name, too, gradually changed, from 'The Auld Ditch' to 'The Foul Pool'. Eventually it was filled in and its line, in 1765, used for building New Street. Twenty-seven years later the Academy was built fronting this thoroughfare and its name was changed to Academy Street with the southern end becoming Inglis Street in honour of Bailie William Inglis, later to be Provost and already a notably far-sighted administrator.

From its start in Inverness until 1965 the Methodist Church was to be centred in or near these streets. John Wesley first came to Inverness in 1764 when, at half-past-five in the evening he preached to a full High Church at a service arranged only that afternoon. 'Were it only for this day I should not have regretted the riding of a hundred miles,' he wrote, words which are now incorporated in the present in Church the large window recalling his visit. Six years later he was here again, and once more preached in the High Church as well as in a 'commodious room' in Dunbar's Hospital at seven in the morning. That same year the Methodist Society rented from a Mr Cornish a disused malt-kiln in 'Kiln's Close' off New Street at its northern end at an annual rent of £4. The caretaker received twenty-five shillings a year 'to clean the kiln and keep the boys away from the door'.

The year 1777 saw the appointment of the first Methodist Minister in the town, and when Wesley returned in 1779 the

Society had over fifty members and held three services every Sunday, the first at 7 a.m. His final visit was in 1784 when he preached in their new chapel, fronting New Street and opposite what is now Rose Street. Even these new premises did not meet their needs for long, and in 1797 the Methodists moved to a site at the junction of Inglis and Academy Streets where they remained for well over a century. In 1922 they moved into Union Street, into what had been a Concert Hall, and even when these premises were burned in 1961 they still remained in the vicinity, using the La Scala Cinema at the corner of Academy Street and Strother's Lane. Only when their new church was built in Huntly Street and opened in 1965 did the Methodists leave the neighbourhood of Academy Street, after being there for two hundred years.

The first building on the east side of Academy Street with a short flight of steps leading to its front door was built as the town house of the MacKintoshes of Aberarder of which family John was to be Provost in 1794/97 and 1800/03, William Inglis occupying that Chair in the interval. Next is the Station Hotel and then the railway station itself, originally opened in 1855 for the Inverness and Nairn Railway Company who operated a line linking those two towns without any connection whatsoever with any other rail system. Other lines soon followed, however, the extension from Nairn to Keith giving access to the line from Forres to Perth in 1858, a line to Dingwall in 1862 which created a need for further platforms and, in 1898, a line south by Carrbridge avoiding the detour through Forres.

A little further down, at the corner of Strother's Lane is the building which gave the street its name. Now a large food store, it was the first Academy, successor to the Grammar School in Dunbar's Hospital and of the 'scule' attached to the Friary. In 1847 it was described as, 'A plain but large and commodious building, erected by subscription, and incorporated by royal charter in 1792, with a large and spacious play-ground behind. It contains class-rooms for five masters and a fine large hall . . . The Academy is provided with a rector and able teachers who give instructions in all departments of a commercial and classical education and in the elements of mathematics and philosophy.'[43]

Across the road is the covered market with a fine arched entrance adorned by sculptured heads of sheep and cattle. It was planned and the ground bought in 1842, and although building soon followed, the open-air markets and fairs survived for years before gradually fading to extinction. The nostalgia for these ancient amenities is well expressed by John Noble:

> It was with a feeling akin to that of missing an old friend removed by death from his usual haunts that we attempted, in November 1892, the search for some evidence of the old fair. Gone were the 'sweetie' stalls that crowded the south side of the High Street in the years that are past; we saw only one table spread with the syruppy 'gundie' or candy that formed part of the main purchases of the 'Clach' boys. Gone the gingerbread tables which were wont to be spread with the birds and animals so wonderfully and fearfully designed in the peppery stuff. Gone all the 'fairins' of cheap jewellery that used to form the staple purchases of the 'scallags' when treating their lasses. Gone the old ballad stall of the quiet, placid 'Sandie Smith' who for years at all the fairs occupied the site on the edge of the pavement nearly opposite the old Post Office, and who possessed a stock of 'The Ram of Derby' and ballads and songs of a similar school, with 24-page histories that would be a fortune now to the old fellow if he were still in the flesh.
>
> On the north side of the High Street no longer were to be found a single stall with the ready-made leather constructions from Fortrose, Rosemarkie, and Campbeltown, where were manufactured the chief displays on the stands devoted to what were called boot and shoes. Once we heard a maiden declare, when it was proposed that a purchase be made for her at the fair of a pair of shoes 'that she was not going to wear any of those "boxies"'.

Inglis Street had no longer its crowded corner where a foreigner held a monopoly of the disposal of 'Fancy Baskets'. Across the way were laid out the washing-tubs, pails etc, of the 'timmer trade' while further down the 'Cheap Jacks' and the sellers of 'duffing' watches and purses of half-crowns had their stands and bellowed their loudest to secure victims. The occupation of the latter is gone. The country lads are no longer to be imposed on, and the purse fakers we hope have taken to more honest callings. It was this point of the street that itinerant ballad- singers mostly haunted, and the discordant, raucous babel was loudest as each tried to draw most attention to their wares.

But butter and cheese was the staple of the fair, and from the top of Academy Street, near Baron Taylor's Lane, to Rose Street, we have seen the country carts closely packed together on both sides of the street laden with butter in kegs and jars and kebbocks or cheeses, the produce from their crofts and small farms. The market lasted for three days. As early as Wednesday afternoon might be seen signs of the approaching fair — the arrivals of country carts in town with their loads of produce. On the Exchange or Plainstones in front of the old Town Hall, and crowded round Clachnacuddin stone, were seated old women with rolls of plaiding, bundles of stockings, and homespun thread, while crowds of thrifty housewives discussed the quality and the price. Friday was the chief day of the fair, and the attendance largest.[44]

Back to the eastern side of the street and the East Church at the corner of Margaret Street. The main part was built in 1798 as a 'Chapel of Ease' for the High Church, but it became a separate Parish Church in 1834. At the 'Disruption' in 1843 it became a Free Church. It was very considerably enlarged ten years later to designs by Dr Alexander Ross, and then, with the union of churches in 1929, it again became a Parish Church. On the site now occupied by its halls adjacent to it in

Margaret Street was a chapel erected by the Seceder Congregation in 1803, which later became the Roman Catholic Church until it moved to Huntly Street in 1837.

Margaret Steet leads to Farraline Park, now a bus station, originally an open space where, in 1845, a temporary pavilion was erected to accommodate the Assembly of the Free Church formed only two years previously. Its local members had met for a few weeks in the Wesleyan Church in Inglis Street until they could build their own premises. First they considered, and even feued, a part of Farraline Park but eventually they built at the corner of Bank Street and Church Lane. The church was ready for opening on 31 December 1843 — only seven months after their break from the Established Church. Services were in English, the East and North Churches, which had also broken away, catering for the Gaels. The Assembly continued from 21 to 27 August and the *Inverness Courier* which then normally only published weekly had three issues within six days to cover the deliberations. 'Notwithstanding the unfavourable state of the weather the attendance has been unprecedently large. The pavilion is constructed to contain about 3300 persons and there has seldom been less than apparently 2500 present. Nearly half of these are strangers from the south. . . The Gaelic singing was an interesting novelty to part of the audience. It is at once simple and solemn and the melodies are characteristic of the antique solitary grandeur of our hills and glens. . . The position of the Church in the Highlands, and the refusal in some places of sites, occupied one long sederunt.'[45]

At this time the park was known as Bell's Park and was owned by the trustees responsible for the school overlooking it — Bell's Institution. 'This handsome edifice, erected in 1841, is supported by the munificent bequest of Dr Andrew Bell of Westminster, author of the Madras System of Education, who left £10,000 3% Consols, under the trusteeship of the Magistrates and Town Council. Two able teachers officiate — one in the English and the other in the commercial department. The class-rooms are large and there is sufficient space for out-door exercise. The institution, in short, possesses every comfort and convenience that could be desired.'[46] This school continued until 1937 when it was purchased by the town council and the building used for a wide variety of purposes. In recent times one half was a 'Little Theatre' and the other for a time the Police Station and Burgh Court-house until new police headquarters were built at Culcabock in 1975, and the court transferred to the Castle in December 1977. At the time of writing it is intended to transfer the Public Library to this site, an object fulfilled with the official opening of the converted building on 31 January 1981. On 8 July 1840 the Courier reported that the previous week 'the workmen who were engaged in the new buildings in Farraline Park (Bell's School) dug up nine entire skeletons at a depth of from eighteen to twenty-four inches. The bodies did not seem to have been regularly interred and they were probably the remains of men who had fallen in fight.'[47]

Back to Academy Street, there is little to be told of the northern end. Outstanding is the story of Rose Street Foundry, now A.I. Welders, but that will more properly be dealt with later. Rose Street itself was once named Scatgate, a name which could be derived from the old 'scat' or tax, or could mean 'herring way' since it was the route by which catches landed at Longman Point were brought into town. Almost the last building on the eastern side used to be Anderson's Bakery and next door was 'Catch-my-pal Hall', a social establishment based on total abstinence from strong drink. Part of a larger organisation operating in other towns, the Inverness branch was founded by Mr Anderson soon after the first World War and, with little competition for interest of young men since there was little other social activity for them, it was for years a flourishing concern.

Chapel Street and Shore Street

As early as 1248 we read that the vicar was bound to see that divine service was held not only in the church, but in the chapels too. By the time of the Reformation over a dozen different dedications are mentioned, sometimes called chapels, often just altars. Many were probably altars within the church and were endowed with parcels of land by which they were designated, the income from this land maintaining them and supporting the chaplain responsible for them. Others may possibly, though it is unlikely, have been wayside shrines of the type often encountered on the Continent today; but this particular style of religious observance does not appear ever to have been common in Scotland. Some were buildings that we would to-day recognize as having been chapels and amongst these was undoubtedly one dedicated to the Blessed Virgin Mary of the Green, usually known as 'The Chapel of the Green'.

The Green, later to be the Minister's glebe, covered most of the area now occupied by Shore Street south of the Railway, Chapel Street, Friars Street and Glebe Street. There was another green, the 'Big Green', which lay on the other side of the river between Young and Abban Streets. From this Chapel, mentioned in 1371[48] but not in 1248, the Street and Burial Ground take their names. The Parish Church, also dedicated to the Virgin Mary, had been starved of funds after its endowments had been given to the Abbot of Arbroath (see page 22), and it was to prevent similar fates that later chapels were built away from the town church. Such was the origin of the Chapel of the Green. In 1359 David II gave a peck of land at the Carse 'to God and the Chapel of the Blessed Virgin Mary at Inverness', a gift most likely to have been to the Chapel but possibly to the Parish Church, the similarity of the dedications frequently making positive identification difficult. Then, 'on 1 August 1361 John, Bishop of Moray, with the consent of the Dean and Chapter, and of Master Eustacius, perpetual Vicar at Inverness, feued to John Scott, burgess of Inverness, a number of acres, roods and annual rents, gifted by King David, Allan Freskyn,

Susanna and Edoua of the Auldcastle, Marjory called Dyll, Stephen Skynner, Alexander Ironpurs, William Traverne, William Earl of Ross, and Matilda called Defe to the said chapel. The reddendo payable to the said chapel is 100 shillings, with 12 pence for illuminating of St Catherine's.' Just a week later the said John Scott not only 'obliges himself to Sir Ade de Nairne, the chaplain, to pay the 100 shillings annually, but also to build him a sufficient dwelling-house upon the two roods of land contiguous to the burying-ground of the chapel. He further obliges himself to furnish a fit and suitable robe adorned with fur at the feast of St Andrew yearly; as also, but for Sir Ade's life only, assigns him an acre of his land at the Ship Flat.'[49] Confusion arises in 1447 when in one deed there is a reference to 'land of the Blessed Virgin Mary lying in the Lordship of Auldcastle' which is apparently the land mentioned in 1361 as having been given by Susanna and Edoua of Auldcastle, and in the same year but in another deed to the 'land of St Mary the Virgin of the great altar of the Parish Church of Inverness" also being at Auldcastle — from which it would appear that both Church and Chapel had land there.

The existence of the Chapel did not prevent the use of the Green for wholly secular purposes as is shown by a story in the Wardlaw Manuscript. The Hero is Hugh Fraser, 9th of Lovat, who died at the early age of 29 on New Year's Day 1576.

> At solemn meetings and conventions of the shire at Inverness, the Lord Lovat frequently tristed with the nobles and gentry, diverting themselves with manly exercises of arching, football, putting of the stone, throwing the barr. In all such he was singular, and never wanted 10 or 12 of his young kinsmen with him, each more expert than another, for so he had trained them at home. The Chapell yard at Inverness was their gameing place. If it was football be sure he had the first and last hale over the roap; if arching he carried the arrow; at races he often road horse, tint and wan the prize; for he was wonderful nimble, and the onely rider in the north. One day at tilting Lovat

dismounted the Laird of Grant and Sherref Murray successively, two very stout men, laying them flatt upon the spott. The affront was so notar that in revenge they persued him, being supernumary, for Lord Hugh but a single horseman with him, and at the edge of Clachniharry he jumpt with his horse over the edge of a rock, and outrunn them; for they stopt and durst not follow. There a print and impression of his horse shoes was noticed and kept clean by a certain man for a yearly pension, and severals cam to view the feat; it was so very rare. I knew an old man that saw it kept visibly clear till the Lord Hughes time 1636 years.[50]

When Cromwell's army took possession of the town the chapel was destoyed and its stones, with those of many other ecclesiastical buildings in the area, used to build the Citadel,[50a] although local tradition has it that some went to the building of part of the harbour. In 1563 Andrew Sutherland was tried before the Magistrates for carrying away the bell of the Chapel of the Green and for selling a stone that lay at the east end of the Chapel wall; he was fined, ordered to return the stone and deliver the bell to the town.[51] On this incident Mr Kenneth MacDonald, Town Clerk of Inverness at the turn of the century, makes the wry comment that there is no record of the Parish Church ever having a stone worth stealing! Wallace also comments that, until this time, it had been the custom of the Magistrates to meet in this Chapel, not the Parish Church as might have been expected, to elect their Provost each year.

Fraser-Mackintosh records a deed of 1462 which delineated property as 'lying on one side betwixt the structure of the cemetery and the Chapel of St Mary the Virgin of the Green.'[52] There is no trace now of such a cemetery but the Chapel Yard continues as a burial ground containing the tombs, burial monuments and enclosures of many notable families of the town and its environs — Forbes of Culloden, MacKintosh of Holm, Fraser of Fairfield and Inglis of Kingsmills amongst them. It was given to the town to be used as a burial yard in 1680 by Margaret Cuthbert of the Castlehill family,[53] and was enclosed in 1784.[54]

The military connection was not confined to Cromwell's destruction and removal of materials; just prior to this public worship had taken place in the Chapel Yard over some time to accommodate a Highland and an Irish regiment then stationed in the town. Apparently there was no room for them in the Parish Church and the Chapel was either too small or too ruinous. In 1643 a minister was appointed temporarily to preach to them. The Jacobite Army too, after destroying the Castle, demolished some of the tombs because their proprietors refused to declare for the Prince. After the Battle of Culloden the Yard became a fold for the cattle of Lord Lovat's estate, it having been forfeited to the Crown because of his connection with the rebellion. Sir Aeneas MacKintosh says that 'all the men of the Royal Army who were wounded at Culloden or who died during their stay in Inverness lie buried in regular order two deep, having their officers at their heads',[55] but this hardly conforms with the Yard being a cattle-fold unless that was only a very temporary use. Early in the nineteenth century the Gaelic congregation assembled here on sacramental occasions because their church was too small to hold them.[56] In 1815 the town's Common Good Fund exposed to auction various assets including 'the handbell and grass of the Chapel Yard' which that year yielded £57.[57]

Apart from the Yard there is little on record about Chapel Street, or even its vicinity. In 1675 what appears to have been the first quay in the harbour was built, the quay on which tradition claims stones from the Chapel were used. Until this improvement boats simply lay on the sand at Longman Point or close to the river banks in what is now the harbour, fishing boats even as late as the end of the eighteenth century passing beyond the quay and reaching the end of Chapel Street to discharge their catches.[58] This first quay was built with the income from the Shore Dues, a tax granted to the Burgesses in the Great Charter of 1591 and paid even today by the Harbour Trustees to the District Council by an annual levy of £332, a figure agreed 'in perpetuity' when the Trust was created in 1847 as compensation for the loss of this particular revenue. Both Suter[59] and Wallace[60] describe the new erection as a pier but neither were mariners and both Ross[61] and Cameron[62] are likely to be correct in calling it a quay. The Ordnance Map of 1868 shows a quay running due east from the end of the 'Black Bridge', along what is now Portland Place, to the present Shore Street where it turns almost due north to the railway briidge and gives the name 'Old Quay' to both portions. A passage, it could hardly be called a road, from Church Street to the Citadel site passed through what was later to be the site of the gas works and Chapel Street simply did not exist, the Yard sloping down right to the banks of the river. In 1567 a John Irrwall of Elgin delivered to John Ross two millstones for the Mill at Culloden 'at the stone of Inverness' and eight years later Alister Gordon agreed to deliver to Alister McThomas Roy 'sufficient Sutherland victuals at the stone of Inverness where the ships and boats lie'.[63] Wherever or whatever 'the stone of Inverness' was it certainly was neither the Broadstone in Midmills Road nor Clachnacuddin in High Street; no ships or boats ever lay in the vicinity of either!

On 19 September 1819 the *Inverness Courier* reported, 'The inhabitants of the town will be glad to learn that the repair of the road from Church Street to the Shore, so long in contemplation, has been contracted for, and will commence immediately. There will be a foot-path of considerable width along its whole extent'. Yet James Suter, listing desirable improvements at the time of the publication of his book in 1822 still included the extension of Church Street through the Glebe to the Black Bridge; apparently the 'immediate commencement' had failed to materialise. Continued improvements at the harbour must have been considerably stultified by this failure to provide suitable access.

In 1718 Alderman Sir John Barnard MP., Lord Mayor of London, whose portrait still hangs in the Town House as a result, helped the Council to obtain a Parliamentary Act allowing them to levy a tax of one-sixth of a penny on every pint of ale or beer sold within the Burgh, the income to be used for the building of a church and harbour.[64] This Act was originally only to apply for twenty-one years but was later extended by a further nineteen. In its first years it raised around £445 each year but by 1744 this had fallen to £128 'owing to the excessive use of "rum-tea and brandy" which the people could buy so cheap'. How the church fared I do not know but a new quay, the Citadel, was built in 1738 which could 'with high tides, receive loaded vessels of 150 tons'.[65] Further development followed at Thornbush, across the river, and in 1978 a further new quay, virtually an extension of the Citadel, was added. For many years there was a dock, due east of Lotland Place, and just north of it was the Cherry Shot, a name said to derive from the Gaelic 'curach' — a skiff. At the point where the river bank merges with the shore of the firth was the Cherry Flat or 'Scalp na Curach', the place where the smaller boats used to beach. Just a little further round into the firth was the Ship Flat.

The railway bridge, north of and almost parallel with the Black Bridge, was built in 1862, Joseph Mitchell, the noted engineer whose 'Reminiscences' provide so much insight into the conditions of his times, being responsible for its construction.

In 1530 James V granted a charter to the Blackfriars in which the Maggot was still described as an island[66] and thirty-seven years later Mary, Queen of Scots, gave all the lands, chapels and churches 'formerly pertaining to the Dominican or Preaching Friars of our said Burgh to the Provost, Bailies, Council and Community of Inverness'.[67] Included in this classification was, of course, the Maggot by then called 'The Maggot Green'. Nearly two centuries later John MacLean, the Inverness Nonagenarian, tells us that high tides uncovered the dead in the burial ground of the Maggot. Could this possibly be the burial ground mentioned in the 1462 deed and could it have been the burial ground for the Friary?

"Bewest the Waters of the Ness"

Although extensive, the part of the Burgh west of the river has figured but little in the history of the town and had few buildings until quite recently. On the first Ordnance Map to be published, a little over a century ago, there were few pockets of habitation. Merkinch, around Grant Street, was developed and little is shown north of it until the ferry where there was a public house and three cottages; Muirtown Green had another group of houses, a tannery and Well's foundry which was to give its name to a street there. From that street a strip of housing along the river-side as far as the bridge completes the zones of concentrated development — over the remainder only a few scattered buildings are shown except for one terrace of houses, which still stand in Telford Street, erected for the families of men working on the construction of the Caledonian Canal. Kenneth Street is shown but only bears the name for the short stretch from Ardross Street to Tomnahurich Street, now often called 'Little Kenneth Street' to distinguish it from the much longer portion then un-named. Bruce Gardens is shown but also not named, and Tomnahurich Street continues in a straight line, without the present kink, leading to the cemetery entrance. In fact about that time it was often referred to as 'Cemetery Road'.

The old road to the south-west on this side of Loch Ness is clearly shown although now blocked by the Canal. It ran along what are now Greig Street, Fairfield Road, Montague Row, Rangemore Road and Caledonian Road to the canal bank; from the other side it ran up the brae to the Leachkin and along the ridge to Abriachan.

Sporadic building apart the first real development west of the river was at Merkinch, feued for building in 1803 and said to have a population of over 1000 by 1822.[68] In 1807 the foundation stone of a new bridge was laid leading to 'the new village of Merkinch', to become the 'Black Bridge' opened as a toll bridge in 1808, the year the village was incorporated into the Burgh.[69] Prior to this the only access had been through King Street and, because the estuary of the Ness then had several outlets, the area had often been an island as its name 'Horse Island' indicates. A charter of Alexander II in 1236 had confirmed to the Burgesses the lands of Merkinch for the support of the Burgh to cultivate if they chose or deal with it in any other way, for a feu duty of one pound of pepper, payable on the Feast of St Michael annually. This charter was subscribed 'at Inverness' so the King must have been here in person.[70] In 1331 we find that 17 shillings was paid to the Crown in respect of the pepper due to the King that year and for the preceding sixteen, and in 1451 the sum of £2 7s 6d was paid for 19 pounds of pepper valued at 2/6d a pound.[71] By 1640, however, the Councillors had managed to acquire various properties of the town for their own use and benefit and James Ross, elected Provost that year, was described as 'of Merkinch'. Ross subscribed 300 merks to the cost of the Ness Bridge — might this have beeen conscience money?

In 1861 the Free Church Presbytery, after some hesitation, declared 'That there is a part of the town of Inverness, on the western side of the River Ness, containing a population estimated at more than 4000 souls, and composed in a great proportion of the poorer labouring classes; that it is ascertained that many hundreds of these are living in neglect in the house of God . . . Divine service will be conducted next Lord's Day, in both the Gaelic and English languages. The use of the former is found to be indispensable in dealing with the lower classes of this population but it is intended to make English the preferred and predominant language of the mission.'[72] This mission, sponsored by the Free High (later St Columba High) Church, held its first service on 17 February in the Central School, then in Queen Street, at 2 p.m. for Gaelic speakers followed by an English service at 6.30 p.m. in Merkinch School which was then in Madras Street.

The following year a site was feued 'close to the tan works' and the present church was built, its first use being for Harvest Festival Thanksgiving on Thursday 18 November 1863. Four years later it had its own Minister and had become a full church, able to have communion dispensed in it, under the name 'Free West Church'. In 1929 it became St Mark's West Church and just ten years later, having built and opened its own mission or 'Hall Church' in Lower Kessock Street, its name was changed again to Merkinch (St Mark's) Church. The morning services were held in the old building, the evening ones in the Hall Church but in spite of strenuous efforts the new extension charge never really became accepted and the building was eventually sold for commercial usage. Soon afterwards the old church was also closed and its congregation joined with that of Queen Street Church but, in 1977, it was re-furbished and the combined congregations moved to it under the name of Trinity Church, the Queen Street premises being sold.

North of Merkinch lies 'The Ferry', a name denoting a district not just the crossing of the Firth but, of course, it is that service that gave it importance. There does not appear to be any record of its start but it certainly has a long, if somewhat erratic, history relying on sail. Granted to the Burgh in the Great Charter of 1591 it, like so many other assets, was somehow diverted into private ownership until in 1825 it was sold, along with the estate of Redcastle on the Black Isle, to Sir William Fettes for £135,000 and to him must go much of the credit for its modernisation. Within six months he was proposing conversion to steam and by 1828 had not only achieved this but had built new piers and an inn at the northern terminal.

In 1837 *The Inverness Courier* recorded, 'The increased communication between Inverness and the other Northern Counties is strikingly illustrated by the fact that the Ferry at Kessock, near this town, which about twenty-five years ago used to let for £150 per annum, now draws a rent of £800 a year'.[73] It was also said about this time to be run 'about a dozen times daily'. The phrase 'near this town' is worth noting and on 27 August 1844 a 'new omnibus between the Inverness Exchange and Kessock Ferry began running' having received a subsidy of £10 from the Burgh Council, the first public bus service in Inverness. The ferry was later purchased jointly by the Town and Ross and Cromarty County Council and operated by them until it passed into the ownership of the Highland Regional Council in 1975 at the re-organisation of local government. With the present

10 The second Castle Tolmie and the temporary bridge built for use during the building of Ness Bridge

11 Saint Andrew's Cathedral

12   The Castle endangered by the landslide of 1932

13   The Castle Street landslide of 1932

14 The Steeple today

15   The south side of Bridge Street

16   Interior of St. John's Church when in Church Street, now an auction sale room

building of a bridge across the Firth at the Longman, due to be completed in 1982, the long history of the Kessock Ferry seems to be nearing its end. The last improvement before its demise was the provision of a new boat, *The Rosehaugh* in 1967, enabling cars to drive on and off without manoeuvring.

A map of Inverness published in 1830 by John Thomson and reprinted in Sinclair[74] shows an 'Old Fort' at Carnarc Point immediately beyond the ferry jetty. The windmill which stood at the junction of the present Kessock Avenue with Kessock Road, is said by John Fraser to have been in operation in 1845.[75] It was still shown on the Ordnance Survey Map of 1868. The map also shows 'Stone marking the site of Thorn Bush' somewhere about the present fishing boat quay at the northern end of Thornbush Road, and half-way between the windmill and the Thornbush Brewery and Inn. On 17 May 1849 a schooner, the *Lady Ann* was launched from the slipway at about this point.[76]

On 11 September 1851 the Inverness Courier reported that the Mackintosh Trustees had accepted an offer of £890 for the construction of an embankment and roadway from Kessock towards the Canal. 'The proposed embankment is to begin at the roadway at Kessock Pier, and proceed towards the Canal, to the bank of which the road will be joined; should Mr Duff of Muirtown proceed with the embankment of that portion of the ground which belongs to his estate'.[77] The embankment may have been built but no roadway appears ever to have existed, doubtless because the said Mr Duff sold almost all of his estates at Muirtown to Alexander Matheson MP the following year.

The history of the Duff family is well documented, starting with David Duff who was born about 1375 and from whom, through seven generations, came Adam Duff of Clunybeg, father of William (1632-1715) who was four times Provost of Inverness, 1692-95, 1699-1701, 1703-1706 and 1709-12. His elder son, Alexander (1657-1726) of Drummuir was also Provost alternating with his father, 1706-1709 and 1712-15. It was his widow who owned the house in Church Street where both Prince Charles Edward Stuart and the Duke of Cumberland slept, whose daughter in law was the 'Colonel

Anne' of the 'Rout of Moy', and whose second son William (1707-1782) purchased the estates of Muirtown in 1741 from the Laird of Grant.[78] Next in line was Lt. Col. Alexander (1737-1778) who married a Christian Baillie of Dochfour but who died before his father so that the estates passed to his son Major Hugh Robert (1771-1832). He married a Sarah Forbes of Culloden and also built the memorial cairn that still stands above Clachnaharry. Their eleventh child and eldest surviving son was Huntly George Gordon Duff (1822-1856), so named because of his father's friendship with the Marquis of Huntly, George Gordon. It is for him that Duff Street, Huntly Street and Place and Muirtown Street are named although they were developed after he had sold the land 'between the canal and the river'.[79]

The cairn built by Major Hugh at Clachnaharry is to commemorate a clan battle between the Munroes and the MacKintoshes the date of which, to put it very mildly, is much in dispute. Suter[80] has it 1333, Fraser[81] in saying 1378 even gives the exact day, 27 June, whilst the Ordnance Map of 1868 dates it as 1434. Finally Shaw, in his *History of the Clan MacKintosh and Clan Chattan*, and Fraser-MacKintosh, who doubtless took his date from Shaw, both say 1454. Thus there is a range of over a hundred years between the dates given; but the origins and outcome are not disputed. The Munroes from Easter Ross had been on a cattle-raiding expedition and returned home with their booty through the MacKintosh lands. It was well-established custom in such circumstances for the passengers to pay a tax on any plunder thus transported to the clan through whose lands they passed, but this the Munroes refused to do. The slighted MacKintoshes accordingly pursued them and, after taking a shorter route to get ahead, laid ambush at Clachnaharry. In the battle the MacKintosh Chief was killed but, according to Fraser, their leader in the fight, Malcolm, eventually married Janet, sister of John who had led the Munroes.

A subject recorded in the Inverness Courier on 26 October 1846 is beset by similar ambiguities: 'The Parochial Board of Inverness had a long meeting to consider the question of poor-house accommodation.' Dunbar's Hospital was in use for the purpose, and a place which is called 'Muirtown Hospital'. Muir*field* Hospital was still sixteen years away so the name could hardly be a mistake for that institution, but no other trace appears to exist of a poor-house at Muirtown.

The Muirtown wharf in the Canal Basin was built in 1809,[82] and in 1801 a nursery garden, which still exists a hundred and eighty years later, had been started in Telford Street alongside the present Caledonian Football Park which was then known as 'Polla' Criadh', the clay-pit, hardly a propitious name for a successful garden centre.

Muirtown Green has also been involved in some confusion, being often mistaken for the Chapel Green. Both had chapels, the Muirtown one being dedicated to St Catherine according to Provost Inglis, although Dr Alexander Ross believed that there was an altar in the Parish Church sustained by land at Muirtown, rather than an actual chapel there.[83] Meanwhile the Chapel of the Green appears to have held land at Muirtown also. There is a strong local tradition that James IV worshipped in a chapel at Muirtown, and hence gave a name to King Street. This supports the argument that St Catherine had a chapel, not just land, on the west of the river. It was somewhere on this green too that, in 1720, Donald Forbes set up a school in competition with the Grammar School in Dunbar's Hospital, to the distress of George Steele, Master of the older establishment.[84]

What is now Muirtown Street was once known as Beauly Street and formed part of the main route to the Aird until Telford Street was laid out as part of the development of the Abban area, only then made possible by the building of the Canal and the consequential prevention of flooding. Until the embankment for the Canal was built the Abban area was regularly covered by the tides; in 1818 houses were built in Huntly Place as a result of the reclamation. Flooding, however, still continued nearby as is recalled by Dr Ross:

> When I took charge of Sir Alexander Matheson's estate in Inverness in 1867, the tide used to come up by the Canal from the Carse to Huntly Place, and the ground from there to the sea was a foul marsh. On the development of the streets and roads on the west

side of the river in 1870 I had all the surplus earth and soil removed by the making of the streets deposited in the Abban and Carse hollow, and the ground thus levelled up is now cultivated and built over. I also had the roadway raised at Huntly Place, and the river outlet over the roadway at Huntly Place to the Abban raised, and the river stopped from passing to the sea by this route.[85]

What is now called Abban Street was, until then, actually one of the channels of the river mouth, running out through the present Muirtown Basin. All etymologists assure us that this is the derivation of the word — from the Gaelic for such a feature, 'Abhuinn', but it is a curious fact that the Ordnance Map of 1868 shows it as 'Abbey Street' with, just about where the corner of Dunabban Street and Lochalsh Road is now, an Abbey Cottage. Are both of these names the result of English cartographers mis-understanding local pronunciation? Most likely, but if not where was the Abbey?

Mugging is usually accepted as a twentieth-century malaise but according to James Barron in 1827, 'The town of Inverness is declared to be at this time in a state of immorality and disorder, scarcely ever remembered. There were many thefts and what are called riots. Such is the disorderly state of the town that none but a brave man may dare venture to be out after nightfall, liable as he is to be insulted or to have his pocket picked. The want of an efficient police force encouraged this state of things'. On the 4 July the *Inverness Courier* again records, 'A gang of thieves who had long infested the town of Inverness attacked a man in the Green of Muirtown and robbed him of a pocket-book containing a deposit receipt of £70. It is stated that seven persons were implicated and three young men were soon apprehended. The state of the town loudly calls for the establishment of an efficient police, and a power to inflict summary punishments on such characters.[86]

Yet another cause for concern is reported in 1832 when, at a public meeting in January, organised by Inverness Board of Health, to consider the health and housing of the poor:

No less than 840 persons were represented as being in a state of great poverty, of whom 140 resided in the Green of Muirtown. The reports stated that the practice of keeping offensive manure in the close neighbourhood of dwellings was almost universal amongst the poor; that in some districts pigs were as numerous as dunghills and a greater nuisance . . . It was resolved to raise a public subscription to provide means for manure stances, for lime-washing and medicine, for food, clothing and straw for bedding, flannel belts and a soup kitchen; and also, if necessary, for securing a cholera hospital.[87]

The latter proved all too necessary, for cholera reached the town on 23 August, and by the end of the epidemic in the last days of October there had been 553 cases and 175 deaths.

Alexander Matheson had bought most of the Muirtown estates on the death of Huntly Duff with the intention of developing them, and he wasted no time in starting, nor did he fail to leave his memorial in the names given to the streets he formed. His own residence was at Ardross in Ross-shire, his father's at Attadale; Tanner's Lane became Alexander Place and other members of his family received perpetuity in Kenneth Street, Maryann Court, May Court and the like, even Perceval Road, carrying the name of the only Prime Minister ever to be assassinated in the Palace of Westminster, commemorates the politician's daughter who had married Sir James Matheson, member of Parliament for the Ross-shire division. Alexander was Member for Inverness Burghs from 1847 until 1868 when he moved to succeed his uncle in Ross-shire. He was created a baronet in 1822. To him must go the main credit for the extension of railways in the North, especially the Highland Railway, but his lasting memorial is his perspicacity in selecting Dr Alexander Ross to be the architect for his housing developments.

The eighteenth century Balnain House, which used commonly to be called 'The Blue House', was built by a Mr Munro, retired indigo planter, and was the first house in Inverness to be roofed with the blue slates from Ballachulish. The sobriquet may have come from this external feature or from its builder's former occupation, we cannot be sure. The Nonagenarian says, 'Starting from our bothy I remember the time when, including it, there were over fifteen smokes and only eight small windows, with the exception of Phopachy House, to be seen between the Blue House, now occupied by Aberarder, and Kessock Ferry'.[88] Dr Ross also states that Balnain House was used as a hospital by Royalist troops after the Battle of Culloden, and also by the Royal Engineers when engaged in the survey work for the Ordnance Map of 1868. Later it was divided into flats which, having no other facility, used the front grass as a common drying green — a cause of constant disputes amongst the different occupiers. This grass had, at one time and in common with the gardens of other houses along both banks of the river, extended right to the water's edge. Eventually the tenants were re-housed in the 1960s and the building taken over by a Trust, sponsored by the Inverness Civic Trust, which is presently engaged in the full restoration of this interesting edifice for as yet undecided use.

Reference has already been made to the Kirk Session and to the fact that the West was one of the three members of it. In 1624 a second Minister was appointed in Inverness but there was still only the Parish Church, now the Old High, for their use. This second pastor was given 'the second charge' which was ultimately to be the West. In 1706 a Gaelic Church was built almost alongside the Parish Church and this became the Third Charge although there were still only two buildings. Then, in March 1835, the Session met to consider the propriety of petitioning Parliament in favour of additional Church accommodation throughout Scotland and in Inverness in particular. This was agreed and a petition, signed by nearly 1900 people was duly presented. Eventually the new church was consecrated in May 1840 having cost about £2000 and having seating for 1800 which was somewhat reduced at a later date when an organ was installed. A notable Minister of a later date, notable in his own right but even more so because of the fame of his relative, was Rev. Gavin Lang who served from 1882 to 1917. Himself a 'son of the Manse' he doubtless had hoped that his son would follow in his steps; instead

Matheson became one of the greatest actors of his day to his father's horror, for this was at a time when 'the stage' and all connected with it were frowned upon by upright people.

The Catholic Chapel, also in Huntly Street, was opened in 1837 having previously been in Margaret Street just behind the East Church.

Greig Street owes its name to the Agent for the City of Glasgow Bank in Inglis Street, Mr J.K. Greig, and the bridge, first considered in 1875 and opened in 1881, takes its name from the street. The City of Glasgow Bank had not long been established, its prospectus having only been issued in 1839 and was considered somewhat of a parvenu in banking circles, 'following procedures which were, as far as one can see, rather at variance with the practice and procedures of more orthodox firms. So much so that in 1857 it had to suspend all payments for over a month till its affairs could be sorted out. One would have thought that this sort of thing would have given warning to the public but, oddly enough, the activities of the City Bank seem to have been almost a source of pride in douce Glaswegian business circles'.[89] By 1878 it had 133 branches throughout Scotland, more than any of its competitors. Then disaster struck and on 1 October that year it closed its doors, never to re-open — except in Inverness. Telegrams were sent to all branches on the evening of 1 October, telling them not to open next morning but, for some unexplained reason, the one to Inverness did not arrive until mid-day on the 2nd, by which time some £15,000 had been withdrawn by the prudent depositors who had doubtless received warning of the disaster. The Bank's accumulated debt was over £5 million, a quite staggering sum in those days, and all eight of its directors, hitherto highly respected business men and pillars of the Church, were jailed for issuing false balance sheets. Throughout Scotland thousands faced financial ruin and the Inverness-based Caledonian Bank had to close for seven weeks, help from the Bank of Scotland saving it from liquidation only at the expense of yielding some of its branches to its saviour.[90] In 1907 the Caledonian Bank in its entirety was absorbed into the Bank of Scotland. One of the jailed Directors was Henry

Inglis, Writer to the Signet, who, amongst other public offices, held that of Deputy Lieutenant for Moray. Although possibly a distant relation he does not appear to have been closely connected with the prominent Inverness family of the same name. He was struck off the Rolls on 15 April 1879.

In 1899 the Sanitary Inspector, Alexander Knowles, reported that there were still 144 houses with thatched roofs in the town accommodating 824 people, and of these 28 had clay floors. According to Wallace one of these, built 'of clay and straw' was in King Street.[91]

The lane running from Young Street to Ardross Street originally extended along the river-side to the end of Bishop's Road and was called Tanner's Lane. Here in 1853 'a ragged school was opened' situated in a school-house where Mr MacKay, who was appointed teacher, 'had previously instructed 170 children in the elements of education'.[92]

The name Ballifeary is one which could cause some doubts as to its origin but the history of the area makes it clear.

In 1398 'Alastair Currach' MacDonald, first of Keppoch, divided the church lands of Kinmylies, including Ballifeary, between Reginald Macalyshander and John de Chisholm, though he does not seem to have had any substantial right to them, as appears in a 'warning' issued against him by the Bishop of Moray, on 20 November in the same year. The MacDonalds of Keppoch continued, however, their attentions to Inverness down to the end of the seventeenth century — on one occasion, at least, taking the magistrates prisoners, and keeping them in durance until released on payment of a very heavy ransom. An outpost was in consequence erected for watchers or sentinels at Ballifeary, to give notice of the approach of the Macdonalds or any of the other western tribes; and from this the place was called 'Baile-na-faire', or the town of watching, now transformed into Ballifeary. In a charter of the lands of Kinmylies, by the Bishop of Moray, dated 13 May 1544, the name of the place is given as 'Balnafare'. This, in my opinion, is conclusive. The village of Clachnaharry takes its name from a large stone in its immediate neighbourhood, used for similar outpost duty to the erection at 'Baile-na-faire'. Probably it was originally 'Clach-na-fhaire' — the stone of watching.[93]

Dalneigh (Dail-an-Eich, horse's field or portion) is but slightly altered from its original, and it is purely coincidental that it was to be the scene of the earliest organised horse-racing in Inverness, races restored in 1662 after having been suspended during the Commonwealth. There is a tradition that it was here that the Frasers and the Chisholms bivouacked on their way to the Battle of Culloden. Land was feued here in 1932 for the building of a Technical School, now the High School, and four years later the lands of Dalneigh Farm were offered to the Town for housing at a feu of £15 per acre, a development interrupted by the Second World War.

In 1645, at the Battle of Auldearn, an order by Urry, the Parliamentary General, to a Captain Drummond was wrongly interpreted or wrongly given so that the Captain 'wheels his horse to the left for right hand and confuses the foot'. After the battle Captain Drummond faced a court-martial in Inverness and, having been found guilty, was 'shot at the post upon the high road as you go to Tomnahurich. Here died a gallant gentleman and stout soldier, not for any bad conduct of his own but the false word of command which Col. Hurry had given him to mar the whole battle'.[94] Of this same road to Tomnahurich a story is told which I have always regarded as apocryphal but which a correspondent to the *Inverness Courier* on 18 July 1980 claimed to have been within his own memory.

> I remember an incident before the 1914 war. It happened on Tomnahurich Street, when a scaffie's horse was turning from King Street on to Tomnahurich Street it fell on the ice and damaged its legs. It was at 4 p.m. just as the children from the Central School were coming home. They gathered around the fallen horse and cart and in the centre stood a red-faced policeman making a report. He asked the children to spell Tomnahurich Street and he got six different spellings, as he stood wondering which one was correct, a smart lad said 'We can all spell King Street' so the policeman and about a

hundred children pulled and slid the horse and cart for
five yards into King Street.

The writer was not imputing any lack of knowledge to the
school-children but was arguing the difficulties of correctly
spelling names only properly given in the Gaelic.

Not only does the spelling of Gaelic names cause difficulties, often the true meaning and derivation is even more
difficult and Tomnahurich is an example. Most picturesque is
the suggested 'Hill of the fairies' from a story of a sort of Pied
Piper of Hamelin who led fairies into the hill instead of
children. Another is 'Hill of the yew trees', the Gaelic for yew
being 'iubhar' or 'iubrach' but probably the most likely is
'boat hill' from its shape which is not unlike that of an
up-turned boat. In passing it should be noted that Gaelic
names are almost invariably purely descriptive.

One legend associated with the hill is that here the Feinn,
three giants of ancient Scotland, were buried with a bugle
beside them which, if blown three times, would cause them to
rise and free Scotland from her oppressors. One day, it is
said, a wandering shepherd boy came upon an opening in the
hillside and on entering discovered a bugle which he blew. At
his second blast three huge figures stirred in the darkness and
rose to their elbows. Terrified he fled leaving the bugle
behind where it remains with the Feinn rising on their elbows
awaiting the third call which has never been given because
nobody has since been able to re-discover the opening. So
Scotland awaits her deliverance from her oppressors, real or
imagined. Another legend concerns the Scottish poet and
seer Thomas the Rhymer of Earlston in Berwickshire. He
lived around the middle of the 13th century but his mainly
gloomy prophecies were only published some four hundred
years later. To this day enthusiasts attempt to unravel his
often obscure predictions and to fit them to historical events.
His gift of prophecy, so legend asserts, was bestowed upon
him by a fairy queen who had chosen him as her lover and had
caused him to be transported to Elfland where he remained
for three earthly years before being allowed to return to his
normal environment only on the promise that he would
return to her whenever she called him back. His re-entry to

Elfland was to be by way of Tomnahurich. From this time he wandered the whole country making his gloomy predictions in verse, the death of Alexander III, the Battle of Bannockburn and the inheritance of the English throne by James VI being amongst the more notable historical forecasts with which he is credited. In 1297 the summons came, naturally in cryptic form, and leaving the friends he was entertaining in his Earlston home he followed a stag and a hind into the forest to disappear for all time from the sight of men and to live with his mistress beneath the hill of Tomnahurich — without, it is hoped, disturbing the repose of the Feinn.[94a]

According to Suter, who is generally reliable on facts but a little dubious on dates, there was a battle at Tomnahurich in 1187 between Islanders under Donald Bane and a party from Inverness Castle under Duncan MacKintosh, son of Shaw the Governor of the Castle, in which Duncan was killed. He also relates the story of another battle the same year 'in the environs of Inverness' in which Donald MacWilliam, a chief related to the King, who had invaded Moray was killed by the Lord of Galloway.[95] Barron, however, says that these two battles were in fact one and he makes no mention of MacKintosh, only of Roland of Galloway. Donald MacWilliam, more commonly known as Donald Bane MacWilliam, or just as Donald Bane, had claimed the throne as lineal heir of Duncan, eldest son of Malcolm Canmore.[96] In his 'Invernessiana' Dr Fraser-MacKintosh dates this battle as 1190 and says that the Duncan who was killed was a younger brother of Shaw, not his son. Wallace even claims that nearby Torvean is named for Donald Bane although the more usually accepted origin is the 6th-century Celtic missionary St Bhean who was Columba's successor.[97]

On 15 July 1544 a particularly bloody clan battle took place at the head of Loch Lochy between the Frasers and Clanranald in which both Lord Lovat and the Master of Lovat, together with virtually all their clansmen, were killed. It is claimed that as a result of this battle 80 pregnant widows were left, each of whom produced a son to replenish the clan, and that all these men mustered at Tomnahurich in 1574 under the new Lord Lovat when he had been instructed by Regent Moray to secure the castle and hold it against Huntly.

Writing of the year 1623 Fraser says:

> Every year there was an annual race run about the promontory of Tomnahurich, the cup and silver spur still provided by Earl George of Huntly . . . Except one of the seven years my Lord of Lovat and his family carried the race . . . The Marquis of Huntly being Protestant and the other Lords of Murray, Seaforth and Lovat of the same persuasion, made them more unite'.[98]

Wallace points out that the winning post was set up 'at the end of the reeds upon the edge of the marsh close upon the road' showing the nature of the low-lying ground in the town and its environs.

Forty-one years later a great congress was held in Inverness to settle an old dispute between the MacKintosh and Locheil about their lands in Lochaber, an unusual procedure in those days, when the MacKintosh lay at the Haugh with a number of gentlemen and some 500 rank and file whilst Locheil camped at Tomnahurich with his friends and 300 men. The Lord Bishop of Moray and the Laird of Alter (Altyre?) reached a settlement on the third day.[99]

'The most remarkable hill in this parish is Tom-na-Heurich, near the town, on the west side of the river. It is a beautiful insulated mount, nearly resembling a ship with her keel uppermost. This hill, in the year 1753, was inclosed and planted, chiefly with Scotch fir. The hill is composed of sand and gravel and before it was planted yielded but a short thin heath and was of no advantage to the proprietor'.[100] It is part of the moraine, remnant of the Ice Age, along with Torvean and, on the opposite side of the river, the Drummond. In 1856 a public meeting was held to decide on a site for the new cemetery which the Town Council had decided was essential and Tomnahurich appeared to be the favourite with most of those present. A decision was, however, delayed until a further meeting a month later when a resolution was carried that a new one was not needed. The *Courier* editor remarked that only fear of an assessment had caused such a conclusion and it would soon be realised that a new cemetery really was essential. He was quickly proved right and the present necropolis was opened shortly afterwards. The main entrance was off what is now Bruce Gardens alongside (according to the 1868 Ordnance Map) a small lochan which was probably artificial.

In 1961 Hugh Barron wrote:

> The present road from Inverness to Dochgarroch dates only from about 1818 when the Canal was opened to shipping . . . The old road, on leaving Tomnahurich, wound its way between the slopes of Torvean and the Ness until Little Loch Ness (later to be Loch Dochfour) was reached. Beside this road there were inns or alehouses to the east of Tomnahurich Bridge and at Dochgarroch and until fairly recently there was one at Lochend. The usual way to Urquhart was by the old road which climbed over the Leachkin (there was a branch here towards Bunchrew) and which kept to the high ground through Caiplich. Between the Leachkin and the heights of Dochfour this road is still quite easily followed as it is bounded by stone dykes. Further south it can be traced between Abriachan and Gartallie in Glenurquhart.[101]

Although created as a route early last century the present road did not become the main road to Lochaber until after the First World War.

In 1823 a new race course was opened at Dunaincroy and races were held there in conjunction with the Northern Meeting. Pony races were still taking place there in 1900 and in that same year mention is again made of curling on Loch-na-sanais, 'the Loch of Whispering'. This lochan was formed by the extraction of clay for the building of the Caledonian Canal and curling appears first to have been played there in 1838, a club being established in 1841.[102] This club later moved to a specially built rink and hut at Kingsmills where the sport is still enjoyed when the weather is suitable.

Meantime several indoor clubs have been formed to play within the covered Ice Rink at the Bught. Horse racing continued at Dunaincroy until about 1915.[21][20][5]

The nearby Whin Island was opened as a play and adventure area in 1980; before then, as its name indicates, it was merely a stretch of rough and overgrown land. It became an island only by the construction of a mill-lade which operated the first electricity generating station in Inverness. This building is now used as a shop and booking office for the boating pond.

Chapter 3 —
Names and Institutions

Earl of Inverness; Baillie of Dochfour; Cuthbert; Forbes of Culloden; Gordon; Grant; Inglis; Eden Court; Inverness Courier; Inverness Scientific Society and Field Club; Northern Meeting; Post Office; Sett; Stent.

Earl of Inverness

To many it must appear strange that a town of such antiquity, so strategically important and exercising such influence and even control over so wide an area should for many centuries have failed to be a territorial designation for nobility. Not until 1684 was there a peer 'of Inverness', doubtless the result of the town being a Royal Burgh and location of a Royal Castle. By a patent dated at Whitehall on First November 1684 George, 9th Earl and 4th Marquis of Huntly, became Duke of Gordon, Marquess of Huntly, Earl of Huntly and Enzie, Viscount of Inverness, Lord Badenoch, Lochaber, Strathaven, Balmore, Auchindoun, Garthie and Kincardine. He duly made his submission to William — but kept his options open by visiting the exiled Court at St Germains. He died in 1716.

Alexander, second Duke of Gordon and Viscount of Inverness, was 'out' in 1715 and fought at Sheriffmuir, after which he returned home and surrendered to the Earl of Sutherland. He was imprisoned in Edinburgh Castle for a time but then, on the intercession of Sutherland, was pardoned and had his estates restored. He died in 1728.

The 3rd Duke and Viscount appears to have been a little more prudent and died peacefully in 1752 to be succeeded by another Alexander who lived until 1827 when he died at the age of 83. His son George, 5th Duke and Viscount, died nine years later without issue and the titles became extinct.

Meantime John Hay of Cromlix, third son of the Earl of Kinnoull, had also been 'out' with his brother-in-law the Earl of Mar in the 1715 rebellion and had taken possession of Perth in the name of the exiled James. On the collapse of the rising he retired to St Germains where on 8 October 1718 James created him Earl of Inverness and then, on 4 April 1727, Duke of Inverness. Neither title was, of course, accepted in the United Kingdom, and at his death on 24 September 1740 these titular honours became extinct. For twenty-two years there had, therefore, been two nobles claiming 'of Inverness' — Gordon with a Viscountcy recognised in the United Kingdom, and Hay with an Earldom and then a Dukedom which none but a Jacobite would acknowledge.

In 1801, whilst the Dukes of Gordon were still also Viscounts of Inverness, Prince Augustus Frederick was created Duke of Sussex and Earl of Inverness and the distinctive Inverness Tartan previously associated with the Jacobite title was adopted by the Royal Duke. He is said to have married Cecilia Letitia Underwood, daughter of the second Earl of Arran, ecclesiastically but not legally (which would have required the consent of Parliament) about 1831, and at his request she was created Duchess of Inverness on 10 April 1840. Her title became extinct when she died in 1873, as had his on his death thirty years earlier, seven years after the Gordon's Viscountcy had ended. Thus from 1801 to 1836 there had been a Gordon Viscount and a Royal Earl both of Inverness and then from 1840 to 1843 a Royal Earl and a Duchess in her own right.

Not until 1892 was there another Earl of Inverness, George Frederick Ernest Albert, later to be King George V, receiving that title with that of the Duke of York on his marriage on 24 May.

In 1923 another Duke of York, later King George VI, was created Earl of Inverness on his marriage. As such he wore the Inverness Tartan; so, too, did his daughter, and it came to be popularly known as 'Princess Elizabeth Tartan'.

At present there is no Earl of Inverness but the Burgh took special interest and pleasure in the birth of Prince Andrew in 1960 in the anticipation that the precedent would be followed and that, one day, he would be not only Duke of York but also Earl of Inverness.

Baillie of Dochfour

Now holding the title of Baron Burton and owners of the most extensive estates in the vicinity of Inverness the Baillie family have been prominent in the area since the middle of the fifteenth century. Alexander, son of Sir William Baillie of Lamington in Lanark, appears to have moved north to support the Earl of Huntly against the Earl of Crawford and, for bravery in the Battle of Brechin, was granted lands at Dunain and Torbreck and made Constable of the Castle of Inverness under Huntly in 1452.[1] For once Dr Fraser-MacKintosh is undoubtedly wrong when he states that Alexander was grand-uncle to the puppet King John Baliol and uncle of the founder of Balliol College,[2] since Baliol's reign was over a century and a half earlier and the college was founded in 1269 by the King's mother in memory of his father. However, Alexander may well have been related. He married a daughter of the Laird of Grant and from them descended the Baillies of Dochfour, of Dunain and of Leys; comparatively small estates which remained virtually unchanged until the early nineteenth century when the wealth accumulated by Evan, second son of the Laird of Dochfour, enabled the family to extend their territorial possessions dramatically.

Born in 1740, Evan entered the Army at the early age of fifteen and after serving 'with credit and distinction' as a lieutenant in the West Indies and on the American mainland, he retired on half-pay in 1760 at the age of twenty. Since he lived for another seventy-five years he must surely hold the record for having drawn half-pay for longer than any other officer in the history of the British Army.[3]

In 1764 he was induced to enter the mercantile business and

returned to the West Indies for some years before establishing a business in Bristol in 1775. In this he was immensely successful and became one of the most eminent merchants of his time. In 1779, on the death of his elder brother, he succeeded to the Dochfour estate, but for a time continued to be an 'absentee landlord', entering Parliament as representative for Bristol in 1802. Thirteen years later, at the venerable age of 75, he retired from Parliament and from active business in Bristol, and returned to Dochfour to spend the remaining twenty years of his life in unostentatious retirement. The *Inverness Journal* had carried a report on the death of Peter Baillie of Dochfour, MP for Inverness Burghs, in 1811 and 'Through some mistake the name of Evan Baillie Esq., MP for Bristol, was inserted in the obituary of most of our contemporary prints, but we have the pleasure to state that, though at an advanced age, that gentleman is in perfect health, except in so far as it may be affected by so severe an affliction as the death of a beloved son'.[4] Mitchell recalls seeing him, 'a perfect model of a gentleman of the old school, his hair powdered and terminating in a queue. He was very polished in his manners but he was held during his residence at Dochfour to be penurious considering his great wealth and it was said that every Friday he used to drive in to Inverness to the British Linen Company's bank where he kept a large deposit and on which he had interest calculated every week and the money re-deposited'.[5]

He bought Kinmylies but was too old when he settled in the north to take any active part in public affairs in Scotland. Of his three sons the youngest, Colonel Baillie, purchased Redcastle and Tarradale which then passed to his son the Right Honourable Henry Baillie, MP for the County of Inverness; the first has already been mentioned and the second, James Evan who succeeded his father as MP for Bristol, purchased Kingussie, Glenroy, Glenelg and Glenshiel before he died in 1863. These estates he left, together with Dochfour, to the heirs of his older brother. 'Whether it is from their long habit of accumulating wealth, as mercantile men, or from long residence in the South, the Baillies of Dochfour differ from most Highland proprietors in

increasing instead of diminishing their territorial possessions'. (Mitchell)[44]

The Laird of Dunain, another Colonel Baillie, died in 1797
leaving a son 'weak in intellect' who died a bachelor, and that
estate passed to two ladies who sold it 'to the present Mr
Baillie of Dochfour' at about the same time that he purchased
Ness Castle.[6]

Colonel John Baillie, Laird of Leys, went to India about
1790 leaving behind his two sisters who for many years
occupied Ness House in Inverness, on the site of the present
Palace Hotel. He returned about 1816 and ten years later was
elected MP for the borough of Hedon in Yorkshire. He
moved to the Inverness Burghs in 1830 at the request of the
magistrates of the town, as an anti-Reform candidate. When
the vital vote on reform was taken, and carried by only eight
votes, he was absent, as were the members for Banff, Ross-
shire and Dumfries,[7] but was returned in the subsequent
election only to die six years later. He had married a lady of
the Court of Oude by whom he had a daughter who inherited
the estate and castle which he had been building and which
was still unfinished at the time of his death. She bought
Torbreck and Castlehill and married a brother of Dochfour
by whom she had two sons, the eldest of whom inherited her
estates on her death when he was only twenty-one. The
younger joined the Army but retired whilst still a youth.
'Unfortunately neither of the sons took any useful occupation', quickly ran through all the available money and
'Leys Castle lands were lately in the market'.[8] Later they
were to be purchased by Mr Walker, later Sir Francis Walker,
Convenor of Inverness-shire County Council, and are still
owned by his family.

Meantime a successful brewer in England, Michael Arthur
Bass MP was, in 1886, created first Baron Burton of
Rangemore and Burton-upon-Trent, with succession to his
male heirs. He had none. In 1897 the then unusual provision
was added that the succession should pass to his male heirs
whom failing to his daughter — who did in fact succeed twelve
years later. Commonly known as Nellie Bass she is quoted as
having said that she was 'Beer de Beer, not Vere de Vere'.

She married James E.B. Baillie of Dochfour who died in 1931 and their son, who had married a daughter of the Duke of Devonshire, was killed in the Second World War so that, on her death in 1962, her grandson Michael E.V. Baillie succeeded to the title. Until this time it was the practice for the Factor or his assistants to hire a room in the Caledonian Hotel each half-year to collect the feu duties payable by feuers of lands within the Burgh owned by the Baillies — lands which included Rangemore Road, named for the Burton estate in Staffordshire. These dues were later collected by post until legislation enabled them to be redeemed by single payment.

Mitchell,[8] writing of the family up to his time, had commented that they 'had taken no interest in the business or progress of public improvements in the North', but this certainly was not true from his days onwards. In 1896 a company was formed under the name of the Invergarry and Fort Augustus Railway to build a line from Spean Bridge to Fort Augustus and the following year no less than three proposals came forward for extending this line to Inverness. The first scheme was completed, largely financed by Lord Burton. Lady Maud Baillie will long be remembered in both town and county for the extensive charitable work she undertook, especially in connection with the Red Cross, and her son, the present Lord Burton, was a County Councillor for many years and Chairman of the Roads Committee for the five years prior to Local Government re-organisation in 1975. He was also Right Worshipful Master of St John's No. 6 Lodge of Freemasons in their Tercententary Year.

The Dochfour family and its offshoots are not the only ones of the name to have earned a place in the history of the town. As early as 1568 Alexander Baillie was elected Provost and, unusually, not at the Head Court but at the Burgh one.[9] Then, in 1638, Bailie Robert Baillie made his mark at the General Assembly of the Church of Scotland. It was an important meeting mainly because it was the first the King had allowed since the five Articles of Perth were enacted in 1618. These were the last in a series of Articles in which the rights and liberties of the Kirk had been filched from it. The Assembly met and the pent up indignation burst into full blast; the King's prerogative was defied, every vestige of Episcopacy was eradicated, the Acts of the last six meetings were repealed as 'unfree, unlawful and null and never to have had nor hereafter to have any ecclesiastical authority, and their conclusions to have been and to be of no force or efficacie'. The bishops were all deposed and some excommunicated.

At the Inverness Presbytery meeting following the Assembly the battle was joined again, 'James Fraser of Brey, Thomas Fraser of Struy and Robert Bailzie, burgess of Inverness, urging the changing of the moderation of the Presbytery, they being ruling elders according to the Acts of the General Assembly holden in Glasgow'. William Clogie of the First Charge of Inverness had held the position of Moderator for several years and had become a sort of minor bishop, and it was his 'moderation' which the Commissioners named now wished to end. It took nearly a year to achieve this objective, and victory then really came because Clogie wisely decided voluntarily to leave his charge in Inverness. With only one dissentient the Presbytery then decided to give full support, and ordained an announcement to this effect from every pulpit, to the Solemn League and Covenant.[10]

In 1701 a Robert Baillie was appointed to the Second Charge and it is interesting to theorise, in view of the similarity of names, that he was descended from the Bailie Baillie who had fought for the rights of the Kirk, but it can only be conjecture. Thirty years later a William Baillie was appointed to the Third Charge, and in 1748 St Andrew's Lodge of Freemasons was meeting in 'John Baillie's House' which from other evidence appears to have been the Horns Hotel.[11] This meeting, on 6 January 1748, is of special interest:

> The distress and confusion which have happened in
> the country having interrupted any meeting of this
> Lodge since St John's Day 1745 when the said Daniel
> Barbour was chosen Master, the members did
> enquire at their Treasurer for their Charter, records,
> jewels, utensils and cash; and he reported to them
> that the Duke of Cumberland and the Army came to

this place, the room of his house, which was our ordinary Lodge, became the Guard Room of the Orderley Serjeant and that all particulars mentioned were destroyed or carried off except the Charter which he had saved by accident.[12]

From that record it would appear that John Baillie not only owned the hotel but was also Treasurer of the Lodge. A later minute discloses doubts about the truth of his assertions but enquiries were just dropped.

Cuthbert

In its day one of the most powerful families in Inverness was Cuthbert of Castlehill and Drakies, but it is now almost extinct in the town, only one living descendant of the name being known. At one time the influence of the family extended well beyond the bounds of the Burgh and even outside Scotland for Colbert, famous Minister of Louis XIV of France, not only claimed descent but actually obtained an Act of the Scottish Parliament testifying to the fact. The Act not only shows his asserted lineage but the very wide ramifications the family had established throughout Scotland.

The first known Cuthbert in Inverness married one of the ladies of 'the Auld Castle' and through her he inherited, around 1368, the lands that were to remain in the possession of his family for three centuries. One of his descendants, son or grandson, fought at Harlaw in 1411.[13] At this early period the Cuthberts appear to have been more concerned with consolidation and modest expansion than with the rapid acquisitions and public aggrandisements that were to follow in the sixteenth and seventeenth centuries, although a cadet branch managed to acquire the lands of Drakies which had been granted to the Burgh in the Great Charter of 1591. As early as 1620 Provost James Cuthbert is designated as 'of Easter Drakies'.

In 1547 George Cuthbert was killed in the Battle of Pinkie,[14] and it was possibly in recognition of this loyal sacrifice that the Queen granted a charter to another George, presumably son of the slain, which gave to him,

Twelve acres of land lying continuous between the lands of St Michael and the lands of heirs of the late Robert Vaus, the Queen Street and the sea. Four acres upon the Castlehill, viz in Milnfield, between the lands of the heirs of James Cuthbert, the lands of the Chaplains of the Holy Rood, the road that leads to the Mill and the rig that leads to the Broomtown; the other in the field between the lands of John Cuthbert and the rig leading to Drakies; the third between the lands of the late John Cuthbert and the street leading to the Drakies; and the fourth lying between the lands of the late Robert Vaus, the land of the Chaplins of the Blessed Virgin Mary's High Altar and the way leading to the Drakies which the said John Cuthbert of Auld Castle Hill resigned.[15]

This George became Provost in 1556-59, the first of his family to occupy that office. He was far from the last. Over the next one hundred and thirty years we have no record of who held the post for twenty-four but we do know that one or other Cuthbert was Provost for sixty of the other one hundred and six, often with a kinsman as Town Clerk and even in one instance Deputy Town Clerk also. In the year 1660 there were Provost Alexander, Bailie John, Councillor James, Councillor John and Town Clerk James.[16]

It was to this first Cuthbert Provost that the Dominican Friars entrusted their valuables and records when Reformation was imminent, only for them to disappear without trace. He also managed to acquire many of the lands once owned by the Friars as well as the Friary itself, thus diverting to his own use and profit lands which had been specifically given to the town for the relief of the poor. Drakies had also been given for the same charitable purposes.

In 1644 news was received of Irish landings in support of Montrose and all inhabitants of the town were ordered 'to convene with their best weapons' when it was decided that 'eighty of the most resolute and best framed musketeers be presently sent from the Burgh to the heights of Stratherrick,

John Cuthbert of Castlehill to be captain and prime commander, and to follow the said Irish rebels into Badenoch'.[17] About thirty years later Margaret Cuthbert of the Castlehill family presented Chapel Yard to the town to be a burial ground,[18] after, it is said, seeing bodies in the Maggot burial ground exposed by the tides.[19]

The last Provost Cuthbert was John 'of Drakies' who reigned from 1683 to 1689, but soon afterwards the Drakies line died out and possessions passed to the main branch 'of Castlehill' whose own prominent position was soon also to suffer serious decline.

> It was upon the small croft at the eastern extremity of Aultmuniack vale [now the Perth Road from Culcabock to Millburn] that the last witch was burnt in the commencement of the 18th century. George Cuthbert of Castlehill, sheriff-depute of Inverness-shire, under the too renowned Lord Lovat, a notorious persecutor of these victims to a degraded belief, met his death in the year 1748 at the western extremity of Aultmuniack, by a fall from his horse. A smiddy now stands upon the spot; remarkable also as being, in the traditionary belief of the country people, the pit or grave of King Duncan and so named 'Slochd Dunache'. With the characteristic weakness of popular superstition, Mr Cuthbert's death was, and is, looked upon as the retributive act of those weird sisters whose companions had suffered by his command.[20]

To these supernatural causes for his misfortune Wallace adds, 'along with the seizure of Ecclesiastical property' and then says 'the estate had to be disposed of to clear him of his liabilities'.[21] Certain it is that, from about this time, the power and prestige of the Cuthberts rapidly waned.

Lewis Cuthbert, Provost Marshall of Jamaica who had lived at Cradlehall, eventually entered into possession of Castlehill, 'and had every prospect of raising the position of the family', but although he raised considerable sums of money in Jamaica for Inverness Royal Academy, when he died he left 'but a few small properties in Inverness'.[22] The

141

glory had departed but the family lived on, albeit in more modest circumstances. There is a portrait in the Town House of 'Provost Cuthbert' dated 1730, but there was no Provost of that name after 1689 (see pages 43/4).

In 1716 'the lands of Broadstone, having been advertised by placard at the Cross, were let by public roup to Doctor George Cuthbert MD at a yearly rental of 120 merks'.[23] The Freemasons had a George Cuthbert as Right Worshipful Master of St John's (Kilwinning) Lodge in 1737, and twenty-two years later James Cuthbert of Milcraig wrote to the Deacon of the Inverness Incorporation of Hammermen, 'Importing that Murdoch MacKenzie, younger of Ardross, had agreed to contract with the Corporate Trades of Inverness, or with any one or two of them for one hundred of white corn oatmeal at one mark per stone deliverable at the shore of Inverness'.[24] It would appear that he was an office-bearer in the Corporate Trades organisation. In 1783 Alexander, still 'of Castlehill', was admitted a freeman of the Burgh before the days when this was but an honour without rights, the last of the line to receive public notice. Many families of note still living in the area are descended from the Cuthberts, but none in the male line.

Abroad the strain continued in strength, and the Inverness Nonagenarian records, 'Colbert, Marquis de Seignelay, Minister to Louis XIV, applied for and obtained a warrant of 'Bore Brieve' from the Scottish Parliament, attesting his descent from the Colberts or Cuthberts of Castlehill. This document being Act 47 of the Scottish Parliament 1685 is in itself interesting by making early mention of many noble families of the North'.[25]

Speaking of the Cuthbert family, the First Statistical Account of Scotland has a postscript; 'Colbert, the Prime Minister of Louis XIV was a cadet of it, that his illustrious descendents recognised, and still recognise, their origin in the family, that sons of it rank high in the church and armies of France, and that the Bishop of Rodez is brother to Lewis Cuthbert Esq., Provost Marshall of Jamaica, the representative of the family'.[26]

Forbes of Culloden

Alexander de Bois, founder of this ancient clan, is said to have killed a wild boar single-handed and so earned from the Bruce the appellation 'Fear Bois', the origin of the name. The location of this feat is usually said to have been in the Aberdeenshire parish now called Forbes where the Chief still resides but as early as 1303 an Alexander de Bois, probably the same person, was Governor of Urquhart Castle, which he was killed defending.[27] It would appear that this was but a transitory connection with the Inverness locality, since it is over three hundred years before we hear of the name again.

In 1607 John Forbes attended the Convention of Royal Burghs as a Commissioner for Inverness,[28] and eighteen years later Duncan Forbes of the Bught, an Inverness merchant, became Provost[29] and purchased the estate of Culloden,[30] although seven years later he was still designated 'of Bught'. He did not have to seek trouble, it immersed him almost as soon as he took office. The previous year the Earl of Moray had threatened to turn the Mackintoshes out of their possessions in Petty, so the Clan rose and ravaged the Earl's own lands. Moray then managed to procure a Royal Commission of Lieutenancy over the whole of the North, punished the Mackintoshes and fined the Burgh a large sum for 'aiding and comforting' them.[31] In 1626 the new Provost was sent as Commissioner to the King to petition against this fine and to say that the Earl 'sought utterlie to subvert to the desolation thereof, in all ages hereafter, that anciente Burgh, whose foundation was long before the birth of Christ'.[32] Again, in 1643, another Duncan Forbes, now 'of Culloden', was elected Provost and like his predecessor sent away as Commissioner after only one year in office but this time to meet Argyle at Turray. Inverness, in common with most of Scotland, had joined the Marquis of Argyll in his opposition to Montrose's support of Charles I. For this journey Forbes was given 40 merks to cover his outlays.[33]

Always staunch Presbyterians, the Forbes found the restoration of Charles II in 1660 not at all to their liking and were quickly at odds with the Town Council which, as was its wont, supported the crown no matter who wore it. At the time of the Restoration John Forbes of Culloden was Provost, but he was replaced the following year by Alexander Cuthbert. In 1665,

A party of the town's people having met at Dunhill (the hill above the town, now known as Viewmount) with a body of the Macdonalds, a dispute and conflict took place in which the Macdonalds were defeated and some of their men killed, in consequence of which the Clan Donald threatened to take ample vengeance on the Burgh. The threats and boastings of the Lord Macdonald's friends having been reported to the Council they wrote certain noblemen and gentlemen for advice and concurrence; and the inhabitants were ordered to provide for able bodied men to be brought in for their defence from the country. Thereafter the Clan Donald proposed the following articles as the basis of a treaty of peace:—

1   A convenant or bond to pass for entertaining offensive and defensive leagues by which if the town be invaded the Macdonalds should come to assist and per contra the town to send 100 men to assist them.

2   The town to become liable presently in 100,000 merks Scots to them.

3   The town to quit their superiority of Drakies and to require no stent taxations.

4   The Council to swear upon oath what persons did draw the Macdonald's blood to be delivered up to their mercy.

5   What arms, money, clothes, goods, cattle etc. were lost should be repaid to the Macdonalds as they should depone upon the worth.

6   When any Inverness man shall meet Lord Macdonald's friends or followers or any one of them, that the Inverness men shall immediately lay down their arms on the ground in token of obedience.

7   The town to pay what sums the Macdonalds and their people shall have spent from the time they became a body until they disbanded.

> To which articles the Council replied that upon the
> Clan Donald disbanding they were willing to give
> hearing to indifferent friends, being conscientious and
> indifferent men, to speak of such overtures as they
> found necessary and expedient to make use of, for
> removing hostilities and making a right understanding
> betwixt them.[39]

(Since the Macdonalds of Sleat did not at this time have the
title 'Lord' whilst Glengarry, then living at Drakies, was Lord
Macdonell and Aross it is presumably to him that these
articles refer).

The affair with Clan Donald was submitted to the Privy
Council who decreed that the town should pay the Clan £4800
Scots as damages together with the fees due to the surgeon
who attended the wounded Macdonalds.

The Commissioners who had been sent to act for the town
before the Privy Council reported to the Town Council, 'That
they had been greatly prejudiced, hindered and crost, by
supplications and cross petitions tendered to the Privy
Council by some ill affected and malicious neighbours
whereby they pretended and protested to be free of all
personal and pecuniary fines to be imposed upon this Burgh
for that unhappy tumult raised in August last with the
Macdonalds', whereupon the Town Council resolves: 'That
the persons, protestors and complainers to the Privy Council,
viz., John Forbes of Culloden; Duncan Forbes his brother;
William Robertson of Inshes; T. Watson, A. Forbes, A.
Chisholm and W. Cumming, being ill-affected burgesses,
should not in time to come be received as Councillors of this
Burgh'. The act of Council here mentioned was expunged in
1675.[35] It is interesting to note that the first named 'ill-
affected burgess' had been Provost only five years earlier.

About 1670 John Forbes purchased both Ferintosh (see
pages 71/2) and Bunchrew where the most famous member
of the family, Lord President Duncan Forbes, was born. This
latter estate had originally been the first settlement of Fraser
of Reelig, but had then passed into the ownership of the
Frasers of Lovat from whom John bought it. The Culloden
estate had previously belonged to the Mackintoshes.[36] It is

worth noting that the town house of Forbes of Culloden for many years, the original 'Castle Tolmie' erected in 1678, had apparently also been first owned by a Fraser since the windows had elaborate stone carvings around them showing the 'fraises' or strawberry flowers from that family's arms.[37]

In 1691 a Presbyterian was appointed to the vacant Parish Church but the Magistrates, who favoured Episcopacy, prevented him from being placed for some time. Duncan Forbes attempted to force his way into the church along with the new minister on a day fixed for placing him but was driven back from the doors by armed men guarding them. The government then sent a regiment to the town to support the Presbyterians.[38] Ten years later John, elder brother of the President to be, was elected Member of Parliament for the County of Inverness and continued in that representation through the Union of Parliaments until 1727.

Reference to witchcraft has already been made with regard to the decline in the fortunes of the Cuthberts; the Forbes were at least more fortunate after their brush with superstition. In 1704 two men were in durance at Inverness 'alleged guilty of the horrid crimes of mischievous charms by witchcraft and malefice, sorcery or necromancy' and a commission consisting of Forbes of Culloden, Rose of Kilravock and some others was ordered to take them on trial. Both men were afterwards executed 'under the care of the magistrates of Inverness'.[39] Burt, writing somewhat later, mentions the hospitality of the Forbes of Culloden at this time:

> It is said that the custom of the house was to remove the top of each successive cask of claret and place it in the corner of the hall to be emptied in pailfuls.
> The massive hall table which bore so many carouses is still preserved as a venerated relic, and the deep saturation it has received from old libations of claret prevent one from distinguishing the description of wood of which it was constructed.[40]

The election of the Town Council in 1715 'having taken place under the influence of the Pretender's friends' the Burgh was disenfranchised the next year and a new election by poll was ordered.[41] After the new election John Forbes of

Culloden became Provost, Suter says by election but the
Burgh records themselves seem to indicate an appointment
by Royal Commission. At the same time his younger brother
Duncan was appointed Town's lawyer at an annual salary of
20 merks. He became Member of Parliament for the Inverness Burghs in 1722 at the age of thirty seven and only three
years later was appointed Lord Advocate. On the death of his
brother in 1734 he became Laird of Culloden and of the other
family estates. In 1737 he was appointed to the post with
which he is always associated, the highest office to which any
Scottish lawyer can aspire, Lord President of the Court of
Session, a position he filled with great dignity and ability.[42] It
was, however, the Rising of 1745 that developed in a striking
degree the talents and patriotism of this distinguished
statesman:

> No man did more for the successful suppression of
> the Rebellion than Lord President Forbes. His
> estates were situated in the neighbourhood of two
> important Highland clans, the Frasers and the
> Mackintoshes. He was intimately acquainted with all
> the neighbouring chiefs, and his talents and eminent
> position as the chief judge of the kingdom gave him
> weight and influence even among the turbulent
> adherents of the Pretender. Indeed had it not been
> for his active interference, the Rising would have
> been augmented by many additional adherents and
> clans in the Highlands.
>
> In Ross-shire all were kept loyal to the
> Government except the Earl of Cromartie and his
> son Lord MacLeod who, it is said, were seduced by
> the crafty Lord Lovat. Even Lord Lovat's efforts
> were in a great measure neutralised, although not
> wholly defeated by the Lord President's vigilance . . .
> In the disturbed state of the country it was impossible
> to obtain remittances from the Government and the
> Lord President had to raise funds on his own
> responsibility amounting, it is said, to three years
> rental of his property . . . For these pecuniary
> sacrifices no repayment seems to have been made,

and no gratitude was expressed for his indomitable and energetic efforts.[43]

It was, however, his behaviour after the defeat of the Jacobites that earned him undying affection throughout the Highlands. Whilst Cumberland was earning his nickname of 'Butcher', ably abetted by General Hawley, the Lord President exercised his considerable influence in the highest circles to alleviate their barbarities — as he had indeed done after the '15 although from a less exalted position.

On a different plane, Duncan Forbes was a heavy drinker, a very sociable man and yet a most diligent student who read the Bible eight times in the original Hebrew during his holidays at Bunchrew. There is also a tradition that the first hats ever worn in the Town Council of Inverness, in place of the old blue bonnets, were presented to them by the Lord President after a dinner at Bunchrew. He had brought them from Edinburgh and they were so prized that they were only worn on Council days, at all other times they were carefully locked away. Before this presentation there were only four hats in the town, those of the two ministers, the Provost and the Sheriff.[44] Duncan Forbes died on 10 December 1747, exactly one month after reaching the age of 62.

He was succeeded by his son John who had fought both at Fontenoy and Culloden, and who died in 1772 when his son Arthur was only twelve. Seven years later this heir married Sarah Stratton, a name still familiar in Inverness if only for the dairy of that name. Through her he inherited an immense fortune with part of which he built the present Culloden House on the site of the old castle built by the Mackintoshes about the year 1620. It cost £30,000. He also purchased the Drakies estate. John Forbes was only 48 when he died; he left an heir of 22, Duncan George, whose extravagance quickly dissipated his fortune so that he was eventually reduced to absolute want. He left three sons, the youngest of whom emigrated to Australia, whilst the other two stayed on at Culloden, although not in the fine house their grandfather had built. By frugal living they did eventually move into the mansion where the Laird hoped to re-establish the family through his son and his daughter. It was not to be. The son

17 Station Square in 1883

18 The Market Arcade

19 The Academy built in 1792 in the street to which it gave its name

20 The original Black Bridge

21 *Highland Region Headquarters and Eden Court before the theatre was built*

22   Chisholm's Close off Duff Street about the turn of the century

23   Greig Street and the Free North Church

died in 1873 at the age of 22 and the daughter, who was betrothed to Duff of Muirtown, died in 1877. The estate passed to the second brother, a bachelor, who built the memorial cairn on the burial ground at the battle-field. The Forbes connection with Culloden ended in 1897 when the estate was sold.[45]

Gordon/Huntly

One of Bruce's supporters in his struggle for Scottish independence was Sir Adam Gordon, a lowland laird, who fought with him at the Battle of Inverurie for which service he was, in 1314, granted the estate of Strathbogie in Aberdeenshire.[46] There the family prospered and in 1449 Alexander Seton, Lord of Gordon, was created Earl of Huntly. Three years later, 'The Earl of Huntly granted the estate of Denain, part of the Castle lands, to Baillie of Hoprigg and Lamington for bravery at the Battle of Brechin'. In fact, since 1268 the MacKintosh Chiefs had been hereditary Constables of the Castle, an inheritance confirmed to them as recently as 1428.[47] Their rights appear to have received but scant consideration, and were finally erased in 1466 when the Earl's son George, soon to be the 2nd Earl and who had married Annabella the daughter of James I, was appointed Constable of Inverness Castle. Thus was formed a connection between town and family that was to last for four centuries.

In 1508 Alexander, the 3rd Earl, was appointed Heritable Sheriff of Inverness and Governor of the Castle, and was instructed to add a hall, chapel and enclosing wall. These instructions appear to have been completely ignored by him, but observed years later by his grandson and immediate successor, to whom they were repeated with more explicit details. This 4th Earl was only ten years old when his grandfather died in 1524, and was not granted the Sheriffdom until twenty years later when he was also made Lieutenant-General of all the Highlands and ordered to build, at his own expense, a hall of stone and lime upon vaults, 100 feet long, 30 wide and 30 high with a slated roof and with a kitchen and chapel attached.[48] That same year the Earl of Moray died without heir so that the title reverted to the Crown; four years later it, too, was added to those already held by Huntly.[49]

Probably as a legacy of the usurption of the MacKintosh rights, fierce enmity between the two families continued resulting in William, Laird of MacKintosh and Captain of Clan Chattan, being beheaded in Strathbogie after a mock trial in 1550. For this murder the Earl was later compelled to make over to the MacKintosh family a large part of the Castle lands of Inverness, especially in the Essich area.[50] On the national stage, too, the Earl found a part to play in any trouble brewing, until both Earldom and Sheriffdom were taken from him in 1554. This deprivation did not halt his rebellious activities, and in 1562 he openly opposed his Queen and caused the Lieutenant-General in Inverness Castle to refuse her admission to her own fortalice when she visited the town that year. She was accompanied by Regent Moray, who had been given his forfeited Earldom. As their feudal superior he called on the MacKintosh Clan to join him, but they were intercepted on their way by their Chief who called on them to fight for their Queen instead. They obeyed their Chief,[51] and joined the Frasers and Monroes to capture the Castle and hang the Lieutenant-General. The Earl himself was killed that same year in a fight at Corrichie near Aberdeen.

His son, George, was restored to the forfeited Earldom of Huntly, but soon he too was at odds with authority, and in 1574 Regent Moray was sending urgent instructions to Lord Lovat to secure the Castle of Inverness against him.[52] He died in 1576, to be succeeded by the even more turbulent George Gordon, 6th Earl of Huntly. Brought up in France as a Roman Catholic, he signed the Protestant confession of faith in 1588 but continued to plot a Spanish invasion of Scotland. His machinations were discovered, but he was pardoned. The following year he raised a rebellion in the North but was eventually forced to submit and was again pardoned after a short imprisonment in Borthwick Castle. Then he began to attack the lands of the MacKintoshes because they had given aid to his enemy, Moray. In 1592, the 6th Earl of Huntly stabbed Moray to death with his own hands, the origin of the ballad 'The Bonnie Earl of Moray'. Once again he was charged with treason, and once again allowed to go free, but ordered either to renounce Romanism or leave Scotland. He refused to do either and was consequently attainted.

In 1593 a demand was made on Inverness, 'Forasmuch as Lachlan MacKintosh of Dunachton, one of the Commissioners granted to Andrew Lord Ochiltrie and John Earl of Athol for prosecuting of George Earl of Huntly and his accomplices for the slaughter of the Earl of Moray . . . being truly informed that the said Earl of Huntly is assembling to persecute the said Lachlan MacKintosh his friends and partakers also the house of Inverness . . . MacKintosh has charged the Provost, Bailies, Council and Community of Inverness to surrender and deliver the house and fortalice called the Steeple of Inverness into his hands . . .' To this the Provost and his colleagues gave the somewhat curt answer that they were quite capable of defending their own Steeple, and intended to do so.[53]

Huntly eventually left Scotland in 1595 but then returned secretly, submitted to the Kirk and was restored to his estates. Four years later he was created first Marquess of Huntly. Yet his intrigues continued, he was excommunicated in 1608, imprisoned in 1616 and for the last time in 1635. He died a natural death in 1636 after declaring himself still to be a Roman Catholic.

In 1605 a reference was made to the Marquess living in the Castle,[54] and as repairing and strengthening it two years later.[55] The Earl of Moray had, in 1624, procured a Royal Commission of Lieutenancy over the whole of the North, causing Huntly to resign his heritable Sheriffdom five years later — for which deprivation he received £2500 in compensation.

George Gordon, 2nd Marquess, was a Protestant but he supported the Royalists in the Civil War, and was beheaded in Edinburgh by order of the Scottish Parliament just two months after Charles I had suffered the same fate in Whitehall. The attainder that had accompanied the sentence was, however, reversed by Parliament in 1661.

At last the lesson seems to have been learnt, and little is heard of the family in national affairs from then onwards. The circumspect 4th Marquess was created Duke of Gordon and Viscount of Inverness in 1684 for no obvious reason, and his prudence was continued by his successors. In 1773 a kinsman, Lord George Gordon — the chief participator in the 'Gordon Riots' seven years later — decided to oppose the sitting Member of Parliament in the Inverness-shire Constituency, General Fraser, heir to the forfeited title of Lovat and was ably supported by the Duke who visited Inverness with his 'charming' wife (the famous 'Recruiting Duchess'). Together they indulged in most lavish hospitality to potential voters. General Fraser to whom the Lovat estates, but not yet the title, had recently been restored hurried home from Portugal to defend his seat, and then bought an English seat for Lord Gordon to ensure his own unopposed return.

One lasting memorial to the tenure of the Castle by the Gordons still remains. Speaking of the destruction of the Castle by the Jacobites in 1746, Noble records, 'In 1776 a Mr Godsman, factor to the Duke of Gordon at Inverness, completed the work of destruction which the Highlanders had begun, by removing the walls to build dykes. He took away, much to the chagrin of the gentlemen of the town (as a venerable lady resident there has informed me) a carved stone bearing an inscription commemorative of the era when the Castle was erected. My informant, when a little girl at school, was often promised a reward by her father if she could discover this stone in any of the dykes; and many were the anxious and fruitless researches she made in consequence. She never learnt that it was found'.[56] These particular stones were mainly used to delineate the Factor's path from his home at Aultnaskiach, now known as Godsman's Walk. The *Inverness Courier* of 16 August 1855 continued the story of Godsman's Walk:

> The Town Council was interested in the right of way in Godsman's Walk. Bailie Dallas gave an interesting history of the lands of Aultnaskiach and the footpath. Some fifty or sixty years before the lands had belonged to the Duke of Gordon. They were

comparatively valueless but were occupied, with
Aultnaskiach Cottage, by his factor an Englishman
named Captain Godsman. At the time, and 'from time
immemorial before it' there was a right of way for the
citizens to pass through the moorland, covered with
whin and broom, to the lands of Campfield and
Drummond.

To get rid of many footpaths Captain Godsman made a walk
and fenced it with a stone dyke gathered from the fields (and
from the Castle according to some reports). When he died, he
was succeeded in occupancy of lands and cottage by Dr
Robertson who subsequently purchased the property. At that
time the path was open, but Dr Robertson, in concert with a
solicitor, set about shutting it up: 'They built a dyke and
placed a gate upon it without a lock, then the gate came to
have a lock and ultimately the gate was converted into a dead
stone wall'. Bailie Dallas was right in most of his story but his
dates are not too accurate and according to Dr Fraser-
MacKintosh, Captain Godsman was a native of Banffshire,
not an Englishman.

In May 1831 a meeting of the Inverness-shire County
Council was informed that the Duke of Gordon had agreed to
sell the Castlehill for the erection of a new jail and
court-house, the price to be thirty year's purchase at £11 per
annum. The meeting agreed to the terms and thanked the
Duke.[57] Five years later the Duke died without issue and the
title became extinct. Although the Earl of Aboyne, a very
distant relative, inherited the title of Marquis of Huntly whilst
Gordon Castle passed to the late Duke's elder sister, the
Duchess-Dowager of Richmond, the connection of the family
with Inverness virtually ceased.

Grant

The Grants may have first settled in Stratherrick about 1214, having acquired the area through marriage to the heiress, a daughter of Lovat[58] (though that designation does not appear to have been in use at the time). In 1211 an Anglo-Norman named John Bisset was granted the district of Aird, together with other lands in the Counties of Ross and Nairn, by William the Lion as reward for his support against the sons of Donald Bane in 1210. This grant certainly included Lovat, and it is from these lands that the present Lord Lovat takes his title; but Bisset was using the title 'Lord of the Aird' in 1221, and probably earlier. The list of lands included in the grant does not make any mention of Stratherrick or its neighbourhood.[59] That does not, however, mean that Suter is wrong; it is possible that Bisset owned land in Stratherrick before he was granted the Aird. Dr Fraser-MacKinoosh mentions a Lawrence de Grant, Sheriff of Inverness, who in 1263 married the heiress of Glencharnich and so obtained a foothold in Speyside which his descendants retain to the present day. Once established in Speyside, the Clan expanded and affected the Highlands in many areas; but our concern here is with the Town, and so is mainly concerned with two families of the name.

First there is the family of Charles Grant, born at Aldourie in 1746, not, as sometimes claimed, on the day of the Battle of Culloden in which his father fought and his uncle was killed, but probably in March of that year.[60] Grant's father, Alexander, was a brother of Shewglie, and until the uprising was a tenant of a small farm Balbeg near that property in Glenurquhart. No longer able to farm there after Culloden, he eventually joined a Regiment of the Government he had opposed and spent much of the remainder of his life serving abroad. He left his wife, aided by Shewglie, to bring up their children in her father's home. Charles became an assistant to a William Forsyth, merchant and shipowner in Cromarty, who assisted him to widen his knowledge, and encouraged him with advice and financial aid. After about five years in Cromarty, Charles moved to London where he entered the counting house of his father's cousin, Alexander Grant of Shewglie, who was now an East India Merchant and had served in India under Clive. Two years later Charles, now twenty-one years old, set out for Bengal where he found employment with Richard Becher, a member of the India Council. In 1769 he became immersed in relief work during the Great Famine, to such an extent that his health broke down and he returned to London towards the end of 1770. During his convalescence he married Jane Fraser of Balnain and together they returned to India in 1773. There they were to remain until 1790, when her health caused them to return to Britain.

During these seventeen years he had become established as outstandingly trustworthy in an era when such an attribute was not particularly commonplace. He had risen steadily in the Indian Service until, it is suggested, he would have become Governor-General had he not been forced to leave the sub-continent. In 1793 he was elected a Director of the East India Company, of which he was later to become Chairman, and in 1802 Member of Parliament for the County of Inverness. Through the Company he fought to improve conditions in India by introducing the mechanical skills of the West, modernising methods of agriculture and introducing Christianity. Deeply religious, he personally helped to finance several churches — and not only in India; in the Highlands his assistance was repeated and he is credited by Suter with having established the first Sunday School in Inverness. He remained Member of Parliament for sixteen years, during which time he strongly supported Catholic Emancipation and promoted many schemes for the benefit of the Highlands, mainly in the extension and improvement of transport, the Caledonian Canal being the most notable.

He had three sons, all born in India, but only two engaged themselves prominently in public affairs — Charles born in 1778 and Robert born a year later. Having returned home with their parents, both boys entered Magdalene College, Cambridge, in 1795, and both achieved exceptional academic distinction there before being called to the Bar, again together, in 1807. Charles did not practice but entered

Parliament in 1811, representing Inverness Burghs and becoming a Lord of the Treasury two years later. He still held that office when, in 1818, he moved to the representation of the County of Inverness on his father's retiral. A year later he was appointed Chief Secretary for Ireland and became a Privy Councillor. In 1823 he became Vice-President of the Board of Trade, and in 1827 President as well as Treasurer of the Navy. The following year he resigned office, but returned in 1830 as Colonial Secretary and was raised to the Peerage as Lord Glenelg. Just the year before he had experienced the fickleness of popular opinion; a mob had burned his effigy on the Exchange and had smashed the windows of the Caledonian Hotel where he was staying in a 'No Popery' demonstration and then, only a few months later, had 'chaired' him through the town with music and banners because of his support for Reform. He finally retired from office in 1839.

Robert Grant did not enter Parliament until 1818, the year his father retired from it. He became member for the Elgin Burghs, and continued to be their representative until 1826 when he moved to the Inverness Burghs. Reform was very much the 'question of the day' and the Inverness Magistrates, not unnaturally since they were self-appointed did not approve of it. Robert Grant did. In the General Election of 1830, caused by the death of King George IV, the Magistrates decided to nominate Colonel John Baillie of Leys instead of Grant, a decision that made his defeat almost certain, so he transferred to Norwich where he was returned with a large majority. Two years later he again moved, this time to Finsbury, and then resigned in 1834 on his appointment as Governor of Bombay when he also received a knighthood. Robert was a poet of some considerable merit and his best known composition 'O Worship the King, all-glorious above' was often called 'The Inverness Hymn'.

The other family worthy of note is that 'of Bught' mentioned in 1791 when Duncan Grant of Bught was a member of the Kirk Session of Inverness, according to their Minutes of 20 June. He was also Cashier and Boxmaster to the six Incorporated Trades of Inverness, offices he held for

54 years before resigning at the end of 1810 to be succeeded by his son James, presumably the James Grant who became Provost in 1804. This James held office as Provost for three years from his first appointment and then in 1810-13, 1814-16, 1823-24 and 1827-29. On 4 May 1847 the *Courier* records that 'Mr Grant of Bught' was elected Convener of Inverness County, just possibly the ex-Provost but more likely his son. Again the same paper records, in its issue of 25 March 1875, the deliberations of a meeting of the Town Council and Grant's Trustees to arrange for the building of a new Town House, Duncan Grant of Bught having left £5000 for this purpose. The new building (the present one) cost £13,500 before it was opened in 1882, and the Grant Crest of a burning rock together with that of MacRae, Duncan's wife's clan, adorn the centre windows of the main hall as a result of his bequest (see page 42). He also had instructed that his estate should be sold to the town at what was really a nominal price, with a restriction on the area that could be built over, the remainder to be used for sport — the present Bught Park and its surroundings.

Other members of the Clan deserve a mention; the Laird of Grant who, in 1741, sold the Muirtown Estate to Duff; Reverend John Grant, whose ordination into the Parish of Petty was objected to on account of his deficiency in Gaelic (in which language he was in fact quite fluent); and the Messrs. Grant, merchants in Manchester, natives of Strathspey and patterns from whom Dickens drew the Brothers Cheeryble in *Nicholas Nickleby*. In 1841 the Messrs. Grant gave £100 towards the Northern Infirmary, part of £2000 they gave to various charities in Inverness-shire over a period of three years. Although not directly involved in the affairs of Inverness, Colonel Grant deserves a mention since he was Provost of Elgin from 1816-18, and at the same time was Provost of Forres from 1816-17, and a member of Nairn Burgh Council from 1812 to at least 1820 and member of Parliament for the county of Elgin from 1812 to 1840.[61] Finally, a notice of an article in the *Inverness Journal* of 14 March 1817 reads:

This issue contains a paragraph condemning the flogging of a woman named Grant through the streets of Inverness. The punishment was inflicted three times within a fortnight. The writer of the paragraph admits that example was necessary and was made in this case with the best of intention, but he urges rightly that the public flagellation of a woman is repugnant to feelings of respect and delicacy. . . . A few months afterwards, mainly as a result of this case, an Act was passed abolishing the power to whip women publicly, and some years later the sex was exempted from the private infliction of such punishment.[62]

As a postscript it may be added that Grant Street is named for Major Alpin Grant, owner of a factory at the Citadel and maternal great-grandfather of Isabel Harriet Anderson, author of *Inverness before the Railways* in which she records this information, along with the fact that Anderson Street nearby is named for her grandfather who had a rival factory at Thornbush.

Inglis

Inverness, like any other ancient town, has had its share of famous and infamous civic heads, but it has been fortunate in that the former have heavily out-numbered the latter. Names which are spoken of with justifiable pride include Burgess Pilche and Provosts William Inglis, Dr Nicol, Sir Alexander MacEwen and William (Bobo) MacKay; and of these notables William Inglis of Kingsmills surely stands supreme.

A merchant and banker, he was Honorary Treasurer of the Burgh in 1775 and then, except for a short break to become Dean of Guild, was a Bailie continuously until elected Provost in 1797; an exceptionally long time to have served as a magistrate before reaching the highest civic office. It is not, however, the length of his service but its quality that makes him outstanding. Mainly remembered for having entertained Robert Burns, Scotland's National Bard, to supper in his home at Kingsmills House in 1787, his most meritorious achievement was the founding of the Northern Infirmary. He died three years before it opened, but he was the driving force behind the project from its inception shortly after he became Provost. During his short term as Dean of Guild he organised the raising of finance to erect the present steeple, and it was he who raised the finance and convinced the Council of the need for the erection of a retaining wall along the foot of the Castlehill. Without this wall it is doubtful whether the Castle itself would have survived the flood that swept away the Ness Bridge in 1849.

Of his death in 1801 James Suter wrote, 'In this year died William Inglis of Kingsmills, merchant and banker, a native of the town and Provost of the Burgh, the ablest and most useful Magistrate it had ever possessed, the founder of its finest public buildings and of some of its most valuable institutions, and for 30 years the chief promoter of all its improvements'.[63] Another obituary stated that the Infirmary and the Steeple were 'two lasting monuments to the public spiritedness of a noble Highland gentleman in whose veins it is said there flowed the blood of King Robert the Bruce'.

The Inglis tradition lived on in other members of his family, Dr John Inglis Nicol, who died of cholera contracted whilst attending to his patients, was Provost from 1840 to 1843: 'The name of Provost Inglis, the moving spirit and 'vis a tergo' in the proceedings that led to its foundation and opening in 1804, is to be associated with that of Miss K. Inglis, his grand-niece, who since 1887 has been active and untiring in her efforts for its welfare, and particularly in relation to the establishment of the Infirmary Library, to whom the Directors continue to offer their thanks and their congratulations on over 60 years continuous service'.[64] At the age of 92 Miss Inglis was still cycling to the Infirmary to assist in the Library there. The Provost was himself descended, in the female line, from Provost William MacLean, 1738-41 and 1747-50.

It is tempting to connect the Inverness family with two other historical characters of the same name but, alas, no link is evident. In 1707 a Burgh Member of the Scottish Parliament, a Robert Inglis, voted against the Union of

159

Parliaments, but it is not recorded which Burgh he represented. Lord President of the Court of Session John Inglis, son of Dr Inglis who was prominent in the ecclesiastical disputes of 1820, was the leading counsel in the famous Madeline Smith murder trial and had won his first case at the Justiciary Court held in Inverness in 1832. His sister married Dr John MacKenzie, Provost of Inverness 1867-73. A connection must, however, surely exist with Alexander Inglis of Charleston, South Carolina who was admitted a Freeman of Inverness in 1784.

Eden Court Theatre

It is extraordinarily difficult to trace the history of the early theatres in Inverness; our worthy predecessors, doubtless believing them to be the very homes of the Devil, maintained a discreet silence about their existence. Typical is the comment in the *Inverness Courier* of 13 June 1827:

> We notice with great satisfaction the progress of
> *several improvements* in the way of taking down old
> and ruinous houses and building new and handsome
> ones in their room. The turnpike and projecting
> turret which for upwards of a century have disfigured
> our High Street is now giving way for a fine modern
> building of improved construction. An old tenement
> in Bridge Street, opposite the Courthouse, has
> likewise been taken down and a new one is in course
> of being built. The Commercial Banking Company
> have contracted for an elegant building in Church
> Street and *our theatre in Inglis Street has been
> converted into spacious shops.*

A few years earlier, however, the *Inverness Journal* had, on 26 January 1810, condescended to report the presence of 'a theatrical company drawing large audiences in Inverness. One special night the proceeds were £40'.[65]

Cameron Lees records 'the first theatre in Inverness' in 1791, but does not give any location or further details.[66] Suter, however, says that the first theatre, 'the speculation of a private individual', came in 1805,[67] and MacIntosh, who gives the same date, says that 'The first building solely to be used as a theatre was erected, by private speculation, in Castle Raat, which was afterwards called Theatre Lane'.[68] Since this is described as the first building *solely to be used as a theatre* it does not necessarily mean that Lees is wrong; the building referred to in 1791 could have been a 'made-over' building, but this appears most unlikely. Nor is the Castle Raat theatre given a more definite siting, but from the reference to it having been in Inglis Street at the time of its demolition it must have covered an area between Castle Raat (later still to become Hamilton Street) and Inglis Street.

No further record of a theatre in Inverness has been traced until 1822, when the Valuation Roll of that year shows, on Bank Street, a theatre owned by 'The Inverness Theatre and Opera House Co. Ltd.' with occupancy recorded as 'vacant'. In fact it was in the final stages of completion, and was duly opened later that year with Charles Bernard's Company playing *Les Cloches de Corneville*. It stood for over a century with the title Theatre Royal, but was destroyed by fire in the early hours of Tuesday morning, 17 March 1931 when Will Fyffe, whose show had opened the previous night, lost all his props and many of his personal souvenirs. The evening's takings were also lost in the blaze. On Tuesday evening Will Fyffe and his company performed in the Central Hall on Academy Street, hurriedly licensed by the magistrates to enable him to do so, and continued to play there for the remainder of the week.[69]

In the meantime, the Central Hall Picture House, built in 1912, had opened as a cinema in Academy Street and, in 1934, presumably to fill the gap caused by the destruction of the Theatre Royal and because there were three other cinemas in the town (The Picture House in Huntly Street, La Scala in Academy Street and the Playhouse in Hamilton Street), it was transformed into the Empire Theatre. It finally closed on Saturday 28 November 1970 with a Gala Performance at which the Corries were among the main performers. The Provost, William Smith, was in the packed audience and, in a letter published in the *Courier* on the following Tuesday, he wrote thus of the manager for the past nineteen years: 'John Worth, himself an artiste of high calibre, was instrumental in keeping the "Empire" open and by his expertise and tenacity has given great pleasure to multitudes of my fellow citizens, young and old'. His letter ended by expressing 'the need for a well-designed and modern theatre which we have envisaged in our Eden Court complex'.

The same Provost Smith cut the first sod for the new building, the 'well-designed and modern theatre', but not until 1973. The Eden Court complex was eventually opened on 15 April 1976. Probably the originator of the idea of having a theatre there, certainly its most ardent early protagonist, was the Rev. Douglas Baxter, Town Councillor and Convener of the Town's Planning and Development Committee. He worked untiringly, canvassing support from any organisation likely to be able to assist in financing such a project. Once he had obtained a reasonable amount of such support he raised the matter in the Council and received the enthusiastic support of the Provost and a few of the members, the acquiescence of others and the outright opposition of one or two. He pressed ahead and eventually got his way in spite of the vociferous opposition of a number of rate-payers objecting to the anticipated annual deficit in the theatre's accounts and to the high capital cost of the building. One such objector even commemorated the cutting of the first sod by clandestinely performing a similar ceremony on the Provost's front lawn. Unfortunately, Douglas Baxter died before the building was opened.

The objections were not without foundation; the feasibility study produced by John Wyckham Associates showed an anticipated annual deficit of some £50,000 to be met in part by grants from various bodies but also partly from the rates of the Burgh. The estimated cost of the building alone was £600,000 but by February 1974 the cost had risen to £920,000 and by completion considerably exceeded a million pounds. Equipment and furnishings were estimated at nearly £150,000. It was anticipated that some 75% of all these costs would be met by outside bodies set up expressly to assist cultural projects.

However well-founded the opposition there can be no doubt that Inverness, now had a magnificent theatre, designed by Edinburgh architects Dunbar-Naismith. The old Bishop's Palace is used as green-rooms and for other ancilliary purposes. The theatre has an auditorium seating a maximum of 780 with sight-lines of the stage; 570 in the Stalls plus 65 in the Stall boxes; 85 in the Circle and 70 in the Gallery, but an extra 90 seats are available when those sight-lines are not essential as in the case of a concert. The stage can be either a small 9.6 metre opening, a larger 11.6 or, by the removal of the front two rows of seats, a 17-metre concert platform.

Controversy still rages, finance is a constant problem, but a large body of music and drama lovers from a very wide area are highly appreciative of the excellent facilities now available to them at Eden Court.

Inverness Courier

The *Inverness Courier and General Advertiser* is at present an exceptionally popular paper, read in almost every household within its circulation area, still with its front page taken by advertisements in the old-fashioned way, devoid of illustrations, its news columns rarely more than one-sixth of its whole and surely bought not for the restricted news it contains but for its intimations, advertisements and community contact. It is the recognised vehicle for all official notices, and no Inverness baby has been properly born until its arrival has been notified in the *Courier*, no local couple considered truly married nor any departed citizen really at rest until due intimation has been made in this unique institution.

First published on 4 December 1817 as a weekly paper issued on Thursday it was then printed in premises on High Street and produced by John Johnstone as editor assisted by his wife who appears to have been at least his equal in that task. They stayed only until 1824 when the owners apparently found themselves unable to pay their joint wage of £400 per annum. Local stalwart James S. Suter then took over as editor and chief contributor, his 'Memorabilia of Inverness' (which did not appear in book form until many years after it had first appeared in weekly parts in his paper) was but a small portion of the mass of writing he produced.

The issue of 23 April 1828 first bore the imprint 'Printed by R. Carruthers for the Proprietors'; the current issue bears 'Printed and Published . . . by Robt. Carruthers and Sons'. a rare continuity in the newspaper industry. Dr Robert Carruthers, a native of Dumfries, came to Inverness to edit the *Courier* in 1828; he became sole proprietor in 1831 and continued to edit it until his death in 1878. The lowering of the tax on newspapers in 1836 enabled him to reduce the cost from seven to four and a half pence and at the same time he changed the publication day to Wednesday. Two years later the office and printing presses were moved to their present location at the corner of Bank Lane and Bank Street. National and international news filled a large proportion of the news columns about this time, a valuable service when but few national papers reached Inverness and hardly any penetrated the Highland glens. Illustrations were not plentiful but certainly not unknown, and the issue of 4 July 1838, for example, contained pictures of the coronation of Queen Victoria, including one of the scene inside Westminster Abbey.

In 1845 the Free Church Assembly met in Farraline Park from 21 to 27 August and the *Courier* recognised the importance of this event by publishing on 23, 26 and 28 August, though thereafter reverting to publishing on Wednesday only. A speeding of mail from the south allowing it to arrive seven hours earlier than previously allowed by the *Courier*, in 1847, to appear on Tuesday evening but only one year later it changed again, back to its original day, Thursday.

About this time the paper had but one real rival, the *Inverness Journal* which had been running since 1807; and hard-hitting comment, both on public affairs and about each other, was freely indulged in, whilst each angled for such advertising revenue as was available. The *Journal* for example, claimed that it 'has double the circulation of the *Courier* in the parish of Moy and Dalarossie', to which Dr Carruthers responded in his next edition, 'We have made enquiries as to the respective circulations of the *Courier* and the *Journal* in the said parish and we are informed by the postmaster that the circulation of the Journal in the parish is 2 copies per week, that of the Courier 1.'[70]

When Dr Carruthers died in 1878 his third son, Robert, became business manager and his fourth son, Walter, took over as editor. Two years later the *Courier* became a thrice-weekly paper. Walter, who had assisted his father with the editing, did not have long to enjoy his independence in that sphere; he died at the comparatively young age of 56. James Barron, a native of Moray, who had long been associated with the paper, now became editor and on New Year's Day 1886, changed the publication days to the present Tuesday and Friday. James became sole proprietor in 1910 and continued to edit until his death in 1919 when he was succeeded by his second son Evan MacLeod Barron, his first son having been killed in the First World War. With Evan began the third prolonged editorship of the paper; Dr Carruthers reigned for fifty years, James Barron for thirty-four and now Evan was to have forty-six. Dr Barron (he received an LL.D. degree at Aberdeen University prior to World War Two) made a notable contribution to the cultural life of Inverness in many ways, especially with his historical writings, most of which had a strong Highland connection. On his sudden death in 1965 his niece, Miss Eveline Barron, since 1952 his junior partner, became both proprietor and editor, positions which she still holds. So the *Courier* continues one of the very few papers in individual ownership, and even more notably, one not apparently in any financial straits.

Inverness Scientific Society and Field Club

Writing in 1822 James M. Suter listed various desirable establishments and amendments to existing societies and institutions in Inverness and included the creation of a 'Literary, Scientific and Antiquarian Society'.[71] Three years later, largely by the energy of George Anderson, son of the solicitor and factory owner for whom Anderson Street is named, the first General Meeting of the Northern Institution was held and a most imposing set of officials was elected. The Society at once set about the task of accumulating information from all the northern counties on remains of Celtic and Danish antiquities but, most important for the future, it solicited contributions to the museum it had already started to create.[72] Unfortunately by 1834, 'The funds of the institution have, however, been declining for some years and nearly all interest in it has been extinguished. The members have accordingly agreed to break it up and to transfer the Museum to the Academy here.'[73] Eventually the exhibits came into the ownership of the Burgh Council and were displayed on the site of the present Museum in Castle Wynd and augmented by donations from the Inverness Scientific and Field Club.

Miss Mary Ettles of Inverness had bequeathed a sum of money for the purpose of providing annual lectures to be given in the town by lecturers who had devoted attention to some special branch of study. The first of such lectures was given by Rev. Dr MacDonald of the Old High Church in the winter of 1874-75 on the History of Scottish Philosophy, apparently a series of talks not just a single lecture. In the autumn of 1875 Professor Young of Glasgow delivered three lectures in the Music Hall on the Geology of Scotland, and so inspired his audience that on Saturday 6 November a party under his leadership made an expedition to Abriachan to investigate the geology of that region. It was as a direct result of this expedition that the Scientific Society and Field Club was founded holding its first meeting in the Town Hall on 11 January 1876. Its declared objects were 'generally to promote scientific study and investigation and specially to explore the district for the purpose of inquiring into its Geology, Botany, Natural History, Archaeology etc.' and the somewhat cumbersome title indicated these early interests. The Society came to be familiarly known as 'The Field Club', a name more suited to its later activities and one officially adopted in 1973. Its 'Transactions' are of the greatest value to anyone with the slightest concern for the history of the area and are probably the greatest contribution the Club has made to the culture of the town and its environs. Papers of value and interest are still read but, unfortunately, no volume of the 'Transactions' has been published since 1925.

Although the first public meeting was in 1876, preliminary consultations had taken place with the first meeting being on 19 November in the Waverley Hotel, called at the instigation of Dr Aitken and Walter Carruthers. A committee was then appointed to draft a Constitution which was adopted, and the Club formally founded, on 8 December 1875 at a second meeting in the same hotel. The first officers appointed were: President, William Jolly, H.M. Inspector of Schools; Vice-Presidents, Alexander Ross, Architect and Walter Carruthers, Editor; Treasurer, C.A. Hendery; Secretary, Dr Aitken, Inverness District Asylum; Committee, George Galloway, Chemist, Dr Duncan MacKay, Thomas D. Wallace, Rector of the High School, Kenneth MacDonald, Town Clerk and James Melven, Bookseller. The others present, and hence comprising the fourteen Founding Members, were James Barron of the *Courier*, William Banks Forsyth and Ebenezer Forsyth, joint publishers of the *Inverness Advertiser*, and Alexander MacTavish, Ironmonger. Dr Aitken only remained in his office until 1879 when he became President, to be succeeded as Secretary by Thomas D. Wallace who then filled that post with diligence and distinction for many years until he, too, became President.

On the 50th anniversary of the founding meeting, on 8 December 1925, a celebration dinner was held in the Station Hotel attended by only one of the founders — Thomas D. Wallace. One other founder, Mr C.A. Hendery, was still alive but living in Kingussie; he sent his apologies, deeming it unwise at his age to travel at that time of year. In proposing the toast to 'The Founders of the Club' Mr E.M. Barron said, 'The Transactions of the Scientific Society and Field Club are also the bones of history. Anybody who wanted to read or study or write about the history of the Highlands or of Scotland could not afford to neglect the Transactions of the Field Club', words as true to-day as when they were uttered. My own indebtedness to those volumes is obvious from the list of sources at the end of this book and one of the most welcome gifts was that of Volume One to complete my set which came from a friend during the writing of this work.

Another notable contribution to historical interest and knowledge of the Highlands came in 1975 when, as a celebration of its centenary, the Club issued *Hub of the Highlands*, a compendium of geological, archaeological, historical and social matter in the Inverness District.

Northern Meeting

In 1778 a Society of Northern Meeting was formed at a meeting in the Town Hall, with purely social activities in mind. Gatherings were afterwards usually held during the second week in October and the company, always in full evening dress, would dine at Mr Beverley's hotel on the first night, at Mr Ettle's on the second and thereafter at the two inns alternately, dancing following at 8 pm precisely and lasting until midnight.[74] Only two years later, according to Suter, the Society erected its own Rooms on Church Street at a cost of £2500, Rooms which originally had three storeys but which were reduced to two after the explosion of 1801 (see page 93) and which were to remain their premises until 1963. Throughout those years the Ball, or rather Balls since there were usually two held on successive nights, were the central feature of the Society's calendar. Of the varied events which came to be part of that calendar only one survives, the annual Northern Meeting Piping Championship.

The first departure from solely indoor activity appears to have been in 1808 when a hunt was held. The *Inverness Journal* on 14 October that year reports on the:

Northern Meeting and Hunt, with which the Meeting was associated. The Duchess of Gordon and the Duchess of Manchester were present. On the days appointed for the enjoying of the sports of the field the hounds were well attended and had excellent sport. The dinners and balls were also well attended, particularly on Friday, when the convivial powers and marked attention of Lord Huntly were unremittingly and most successfully exerted to increase the pleasure of the company, exertions the more extraordinary as the Marquis had in the beginning of the week attended the Shooting Club in Aberdeen, and rode on Friday morning from thence to Inverness, a distance of about 105 miles, in less than 7 hours, having 8 relays of horses on the road. Lord Seaforth, with his usual politeness and attention, presented the company with a brace of excellent fat bucks.[75]

In 1811, 'about 140 ladies and gentlemen sat down to dinner and there were about 200 dancers in the ball-room. Among the amusements of the week was a trotting match between a pony belonging to the Marquis of Huntly and a horse belonging to Mr Forbes of Culloden. The pony was the winner.'[76] The meeting in 1816 decided, for the future, that a plate of 50 guineas should be given from the funds for any horse carrying 10 stones that had never won a plate, the race to be run on Wednesday of the Meeting week. A special committee was appointed to provide a course, £20 being granted for the expenses they would incur.[77]

In 1821 seven cut-glass chandeliers were erected in the Meeting Rooms at a cost of £700.[78] These magnificent ornaments remained there until demolition when they were carefully removed and given on permanent loan to the then Town Council who used three to adorn their Council Chamber and one on the staircase of the Town House. The remainder are kept in storage and partly used to replace damaged portions.

1822 introduced a new feature; Highland Games were to be added the following Meeting, not forming part of it but to be financially assisted by it. These took place at Dunaincroy under the presidency of Glengarry who, it is said,

> presided in all his glory, and had the field almost wholly to himself, the other judges probably conceiving themselves ill-qualified to decide in matters which lay altogether between the chief and the gentlemen of his tail. The sports included a foot race of eight miles, and the report of it has it that four of the runners, who came in first, arrived at the goal in the costume of Adam. Another item was to lift a boulder 18 stone in weight and throw it over a bar five feet from the ground. The feat was accomplished by 'a mere stone mason' after having foiled all the other 'pretty men'. The most remarkable feature, however, was the tearing of three cows limb from limb after they had been felled and stunned by a blow from a sledge-hammer. The dissection of the poor cows was far from easy. Even the most expert of the operators took from four to five hours in rugging and riving, tooth and nail, before they brought off the limbs of one cow. This achievement was paid at the rate of five guineas per joint, so that we hope this rise in the value of black cattle will make the Glengarry men some small amends for the fall of ewes and wedders at Falkirk Tryst lately noticed by their chief.[79]

At the 1826 Meeting, although dinners were held on three days, as had now become usual, they were attended by men only with no explanation given for the exclusion of women. Six years later, in 1832, a serious outbreak of cholera caused 175 deaths in Inverness between late August and the end of October and led to the cancellation of the Meeting that year. Highland Games as a regular feature appear to have started in 1837 on the Thursday and Friday of the Week and in 1838 were held in the Longman. In 1840 they took place in the Academy Park and, since they were held there in 1852, presumably were always at that location until the Northern

Meeting Park in Ardross Street was specially built to hold them.[80]

Throughout the years of the Meeting, Royalty made several visits, especially to the Ball, the first apparently on Thursday 16 September 1847 when Prince Albert was present. The Rooms were closed for demolition in 1962 although the work did not in fact start until 1966 and since then the only apparent activity has been the Piping Competitions held each autumn.

Post Office

In England the establishment of a regular post dates only from the reign of Edward IV who was then at war with Scotland, and with the cessation of that war the post also ceased. It was partially restored by Henry VIII, continued by his son and daughters and by the time of Elizabeth was costing £5000 annually. The Stewart Kings, commencing with James I and VI, were the first to organise a regular system of postal communication in England, mainly because of complaints by foreigners both in London and abroad. This system was swept away in the Civil War but restored under the Commonwealth and from then has continued to grow without interruption, and extended to Scotland.

In 1667 it was arranged to have a regular horse post to convey letters from Aberdeen to Edinburgh every Wednesday and Friday, returning every Tuesday and Thursday in the afternoon, each single letter to pay 2 shillings, every double letter 4 shillings and every packet 5 shillings per ounce, all Scots money. The definition 'single letter' indicated a single sheet of paper, irrespective of weight, and the difference in charges was the cause of 'crossing', that is writing vertically over the horizontal writing to get the maximum wording on the available space. Two years afterwards the Privy Council, on petition, granted warrant 'to settle a constant foot post between Edinburgh and Inverness for the advancement of trade, correspondence and convenience of the King's subjects, the post to go and return

171

two times every week to Aberdeen from Edinburgh, and once weekly to Inverness and back wind and weather serving'.[81] The rates were much as previously but added to according to distance. In later years, when the foot post was largely superseded, a public announcement was made in Edinburgh to the effect that 'a waggon will leave the Grassmarket for Inverness every Tuesday, God willing, but on Wednesday whether or no.'[82] The first postmaster in Inverness, appointed in 1669, was a William Trent according to Mr Appleyard, his 1973 successor.

Almost a century later, in 1755, the service was increased to thrice weekly, according to Suter still by foot but stated by Hay to be by horse. For a short period from 1715 to 1718 there was a horse post between Edinburgh and Inverness by way of Badenoch and in 1719, following its withdrawal, a plea was made to have two post-horses each week by 'this the Laigh Road' (presumably the coast road) and one foot-post in summer by the 'highland road', that is by Badenoch.[83]

In 1737 Archibald Douglas, Postmaster-General for Scotland, appointed Helen McCulloch to be Postmistress in Inverness. Of this appointment Noble says that it was important 'as the Postmaster in Inverness was responsible for all letters posted to the North of the Firth of Forth,'[84] but this must surely have been an exaggeration since he, or in this case she, could hardly have been responsible for letters addressed to Perth or Aberdeen. Helen McCulloch eventually married Robert Warrand, and so precipitated the most notorious incidents in the history of the Royal Mail in Inverness. On his marriage Robert was officially appointed Postmaster, jointly with his wife, but appears to have taken effective control into his own hands. Noble gives the story of Robert in full; here we can only summarise the main points which reached their culmination in a notorious Court case when the errant Postmaster sued Hugh Falconer of Drakies for damages.

In those days people had to go to the post office to collect their own mail at times which, in the case of Inverness, were indeed very irregular since the horse could not be expected to keep up in all weathers the 'five measured miles in the hour, or four computed'. Even when it did arrive they had to wait until the harassed Postmaster had sorted out the mail, much of it into five different bags for onward transmission to Fort William; Thurso, Kirkwall, Dornoch and Wick; Fortrose and Cromarty; Lochcarron, Skye and Lewis; and Badenoch. He would himself later ride to Nairn, for which journey he would be allowed 'three pence a mile for every time he rides it, including both coming and going'. Once the sorting was finished a horn was blown to signify that all was ready for the collection of individual mail but, in Warrand's day, it was possible that the expectant recipients had been forestalled, their mail was likely to have been given to 'a female letter carrier', Margaret Robertson, then aged 'seventy-seven or thereby' who would demand more than the legal charge if she were fortunate enought to find only the addressee's wife or a boy on the premises. Some letters she carried in her official pouch slung over her shoulder, but any foreign or specially valuable ones were carefully hidden in the breast of her gown. It was stated in Court that she used to call on the Excise man before starting her round and would allow him to examine the incoming mail so that the many successful raids made by his men were not just the result of Highland intuition but to him having had access to the contents of sealed letters.

Love affairs were also the subject of illegal investigation; Betty Fraser, daughter of the Town Clerk, had fallen in love with a dashing young officer stationed at Fort George, and although she took the precaution of having her letters to him addressed by her father's clerk her cousin, who was Postmaster at Ardersier, soon suspected something clandestine and arranged for Warrand to have any letter addressed to her delivered to her father. Other love letters were opened by the Warrand's manservant, William Clark, who used to entertain his fellow servants by reading aloud the contents. On one occasion a letter containing three £10 notes was brought to the Warrand's office/house by the postman from Tain for onward transmission to Nairn. Having his own doubts about the affairs at the Post Office he arranged for two maids to witness his handing over the package to Mrs Warrand whose husband was away at the time. After some time the original sender of the letter heard that it had not arrived in Nairn and approached the postman saying that 'if he had been any other than the man he was he would have been put in prison in Dingwall'. The postman duly accused Mrs Warrand and threatened to fire the office and house if the letter were not produced. At first she seemed surprised but when confronted with the maid's testimony she drew out one drawer after another of two rows of drawers in the lowest of which she found the letter.'[85] Another of Warrand's malpractices appears to have been to frank letters for certain merchants if they sent their goods by a ship, the *Peace* of Elgin, in which he had an interest.

Hugh Falconer held lands at the Longman, as did Robert Warrand, and after Falconer had built dykes round them, he found these protectors damaged, he believed by Robert's cattle. Eventually Falconer did find a cow belonging to Warrand on his land, and duly poinded it. Eventually it was returned but the affair started a feud between the two that culminated in the case before the Court of Session. Affairs at the Post Office had become so bad that Hugh Falconer, on 18 February 1770, wrote a letter of complaint to the Post-master-General in which, amongst other allegations, he said 'I am a merchant here who have suffered greatly by the bad behaviour of your deputy. I have the most convincing proof of his keeping up my letters, and have great reason to fear that he may greatly hurt my interest by such practices'.[85] Warrand, who by this time was a Town Councillor and Burgh Treasurer, promptly sued him for £500 damages. Much of the information already given about the Warrands is from the evidence produced at the consequential trial, but there is no record of the eventual verdict. In June of 1770, St Andrew's Lodge of Freemasons, in conjunction with its sister Lodge of St John's, sent a petition to Lieutenant-General Sir James Adolphus Oughton, a Gaelic speaking Englishman who was both Commander-in-Chief in Scotland and Grand Master Mason of Scotland, to have the 'obnoxious' postmaster removed, although how the General was expected to achieve this desirable end is not made clear. However according to Mr Appleyard, Robert Sharp was appointed postmaster in 1770, so presumably Warrand had departed.

In 1794 a daily post to Aberdeen was started,[86] the post office having moved to 32 Castle Street where it remained only until 1810 when it was moved to the then Police Buildings fronting the Exchange. In 1820, according to Hay, it was moved, this time to the top of Bank Lane — where, according to Noble, it had been since 1772.

A mail coach to Edinburgh taking letters and packets for onward transmission to London was established in 1810 after an earlier attempt to start such a service in 1803 had failed through lack of use. A coach to Aberdeen was started in 1811, and one to Wick in 1819.[87]

Hay records that at this time the whole postal establishment in Inverness consisted of the postmaster and a solitary postman who received six shillings a week plus one halfpenny for every 'country' letter he delivered — letters for Petty, Strathnairn and Strathdearn. For the purpose of delivering these he would stand at the Market Cross each Friday and read out the addresses on the letters, handing them to whoever chose to claim them on behalf of the owner or addressee.

'On 5 July 1836, thanks to the late Mr Ellice MP for Coventry, and Mr Fox Maule, afterwards Earl of Dalhousie, there was inaugurated the greatest improvement which had ever taken place in the communication between north and south, as regards the Highlands, by the establishment on that day of a daily mail coach between Inverness and Perth, the first great advantage being that, in a journey either way, the distance was shortened by eighty-two miles.'[88] Two years later the Courier reported 'A traveller leaving Inverness on Monday morning per mail might with ease reach London on Wednesday evening at eight o'clock by the following route:-Mail to Edinburgh which reaches there at six o'clock next morning; Tuesday per mail to Liverpool where it reaches at six next morning; Wednesday per railroad to London which it reaches at eight in the evening.'[89] There is no indication of the physical state at the end of the road of such an intrepid traveller!

From Castle Street the Post Office moved to High Street in 1844, to what later became the Customs House on the south side of the street at the eastern end. Its legacy is the name still often used for the steps leading up the brae along this site — 'Post Office Steps'. Here it remained until the new building was erected in Queensgate, commenced in 1888 and opened in 1890 only to be somewhat damaged in the earthquake of 15 November of that year.[90] That building was demolished in 1966 and the Post Office temporarily housed next door towards Academy Street until the present building was opened on the same site in 1969. It was a matter of some regret to many people that the chance was missed to set back the new building and so leave a square for ceremonial events — an amenity Inverness sadly lacks.

Sett

In August 1676 Commissioners from the Convention of Royal Burghs met in Inverness and drew up a sett of the Burgh, the rules and management and administration of the Burgh. In this various conditions were laid down:-

1 There must be 21 Town Councillors and no more.
2 Five of these Councillors were to be changed each year.
3 The Provost was to continue in office for 3 years and if he did so for that time without interruption he was not to be eligible for the 4th year. He could, however, be chosen Provost for the 5th year. The Provost was to have two votes in Council, making a total of 22 votes. (In fact the Provost was elected annually and his term of office was for one year only).
4 For the setting of peace within the Burgh and for the encouragement of the traders and tradesmen, the following trades were given permission to incorporate within themselves, provided they consisted of at least seven freemen burgesses of each trade:- Hammermen, Wrights, Shoemakers, Tailors, Skinners, Weavers.

5   Each year the trades were to draw up a leet of three
    of their number and from these leets the Town
    Council were to select a visitor or overseer of each
    trade (later called Deacons).

Thus it was not until 1676 that the trades of Inverness were
legally permitted to have Trade Incorporations, but from the
sixteenth century, if not earlier, there were groups of
tradesmen in the same trade who had banded together for
trade purposes. The weavers and the shoemakers (cordiners)
were such very old trade groups. Restrictions were placed
upon their activities, tradesmen not being permitted to sell
goods direct to the public only to make them whilst the
merchants, to whom alone they could sell, were not allowed
to make goods for sale. The merchants were members of the
Guildry.

In 1709 there was trouble between the craftsmen and
Guildry members, originating in a Guildry member making
some silver spoons, the prerogative of the craftsmen, and a
new sett, or rather an amendment of the original, was made.
By this the tradesmen were given the privilege of having three
of their members elected as Town Councillors, the remaining
eighteen Councillors to be members of the Guildry which had
previously chosen all twenty-one.

The six trades formed themselves into an Incorporation in
1676 called 'The Six Incorporated Trades of Inverness' which
was really a general committee to look after the welfare of the
individual crafts and trades. It consisted of the Deacon (or
chairman) of each craft and the past Deacons and the Secretaries, and their function was to protect the rights and
privileges of their members.

The six crafts covered virtually every trade then carried on
in the Burgh:
1   the Hammermen including Silversmiths, Goldsmiths,
Blacksmiths, Coopers etc.; 2   the Wrights included
Wheelwrights, Squarewrights, Carpenters etc.; 3   the
Shoemakers included Brogue Makers; 4   the Tailors
included all who made clothing; 5   the Skinners included the
Glovers; 6   the Weavers appear to be the only ones not
including crafts not obvious from their title.

Each trade had its own flag, the Weavers' flag is now hung in the Town Hall, and those of the Shoemakers (dated 1676) and Silversmiths in the care of the Museum. The flag of the Tailors is said to have depicted Adam and Eve in the Garden of Eden with the words, 'Our craft is over all weave trust with truth'.

The Act of 1846 which abolished trading privileges in Scotland ended the old rights of both tradesmen and Guild merchants and although the Incorporated Trades continued for several years as a Friendly Society they eventually ceased to exist. The Guildry still exists as such a Society.

Stent

This name, almost forgotten today, was once well known but apparently little understood by those most affected by it. It was a form of taxation having its origins in the earliest periods of Scottish history, from a time when normal royal revenue was obtained from the rents of Crown lands supplemented by a few other contributions and occasional large augmentations by way of confiscation of the estates of rebellious subjects. These sources met all normal needs but the unexpected, the national emergency, wars with the English, rebellions by Highland Chiefs, Border skirmishes and the like called for extra provision and a special tax was imposed to meet these exceptional needs, legalised by Acts of Parliament as in 1424, 1431, 1445 etc. The Convention of Royal Burghs fixed the amount each Burgh should contribute, and it was left to the Magistrates to levy the individual Burgesses to raise this sum. In 1483 Inverness was allocated £10 as was St Andrews, Aberdeen £26 13s 4d, Dundee £26, Perth £22, Forres £6, Banff and Elgin each £3 and Nairn £2, all Scots.[91]

In Inverness, and presumably in other Burghs too, the Magistrates appointed responsible and upright citizens as 'stent-masters' to decide how much each inhabitant should pay according to their 'rents and living, goods and gear, which they have within the Burgh'. Gradually it became more in the nature of a permanent levy, as all taxes appear to do, until finally Protector Cromwell ordered a valuation to be made of all taxable property in Scotland (a task not completed until after the Restoration), which became the 'Valued Rent' as opposed to the 'Real Rent' shown in the Valuation Roll. After this valuation had been enacted in 1667 the principle upon which the Burghs were to pay was 'according to the avail and quantity of each person's living, goods and gear, which he hath within the Burgh'. Although not paying 'stent' the landward areas did not escape; they had to pay land-tax instead. Not long before this enactment, in 1644, the Burgh had been 'stented 4000 merks by the Marquis of Argyll, to be repaid by Parliament'.[92]

Until the Lands Valuation Act of 1854 the tax continued, still allocated by stent-masters until about a dozen years before its end when the task passed to the 'distributor of stamps', at that time the Postmaster Mr Penrose Hay. Latterly the stent-masters had been fifteen in number appointed annually by the Town Council: — three heritors, nine merchants being Guild brothers and three craftsmen from the various trades exercising their crafts in the Burgh.[93]

From a Local Report by the Commissioners on Municipal Corporations in Scotland, written in 1833 in preparation for the Municipal Reform Act of 1834 the stent in Inverness was then divided:—

Owners, on £5958 land rent @	£74 9s 6d
on £14,011 house and shop rent @ 1½d	£87 11s 4d
Occupiers, on £4148 shop rent @ 2d	£34 11s 4d
	£196 12s 2d

Chapter 4 —
The locality and its customs

The Boar Stone; The Broadstone; Drumden; The Islands;
The Longman; Sunday Observance; Thursday Market.

The Boar Stone

At Knocknagael, on the Essich Road, stands the oldest man-made object in the whole Ness Valley, the Boar Stone, now protected by a fence and clearly showing an incised representation of a boar facing to the right with above it two concentric circles with their centres marked by a dot. The stone is of Old Red Sandstone, irregular in shape with its flat surface still in its natural condition, 6 feet 9 inches by 7 feet 2 inches by 1 foot 1½ inches. It is of similar stone to others in the vicinity and hence was probably found and carved at or near the spot where it still stands.

From the fact that no metal appears to have been used in the engraving, and because the flat surface has not been dressed in any way, Butter concludes that it must date from before the Bronze Age and is about 10,000 years old. It has been argued that no stone, even one of its hard-wearing properties, could have withstood the ravages of weathering for so long and still retained the quite clear depiction, but there is a local tradition that it was buried for many centuries and discovered only when the Essich Road was being constructed.[1]

The meaning of the carvings must be considered with those of other stones in the north of Scotland, a wolf at Ardross, an Eagle at Strathpeffer, a stag at Grantown, a bull at Burghead, a horse at Inverurie, and possibly also

24 *Cottage industry*

25 *Laundry bleaching in front of Bank Street homes about 1860*

26 *Tomnahurich and Millerton Bridge*

27 *Torvean and the Caledonian Canal at Millerton Bridge*

28   Academy Street showing the Empire Theatre as a Picture House and the Methodist Chapel in the distance

29   The Post Office of 1820 at the corner of Church Street and Bank Lane. The slot for posting letters was only four inches by a quarter inch!

30 *The Post Office built in Queensgate in 1888 and demolished to make room for the present building in 1966*

31 *Commercial salmon fishing at Friars' Shott*

the fish at Edderton. Except for the fish, all are facing right — the opposite of heraldic usage of later days — all are incised outlines only and on surfaces not dressed, all show creatures apparently progressing forwards and all are on stones common to their locality. Several have extra symbols, different in each case, as the circles of the Boar Stone or the horse-shoe shaped device above the Strathpeffer eagle. 'This consistency of treatment shows that the stones had a common purpose, whatever that purpose may have been, and restricts them to a limited period in the same age'.[2] From all these facts Butter concludes that each stone was a totem, an emblem of a tribe living in that locality, and it is surely significant that no creature is duplicated in another area. He is also of the opinion that the extra symbols contain some message clear to the initiated of the day but, alas, lost to present-day learning. These are at least tenable propositions.

The Broadstone

For many years there was a tradition that an ancient stone, known as 'The Broadstone' was lying buried under Kingsmills Road. It had been mentioned in 1455, in a deed when land belonging to the Auld Castle estate was being apportioned for the use of the Altar of St Michael in Inverness, 'one fifth of the land near to "la Braidstone" and one fifth near the torrent of the Skower Burn as that torrent runs towards the land lying in "le Gairbraid".[3] (Le Garbraid was flat and lying between the present Rose Street and the Longman). When the houses in Broadstone Park were being erected the dry channel of a stream was uncovered so that the Skower (Scourie) Burn must have either flowed into the Ness near its mouth or into the Millburn. It probably disappeared when improved drainage was brought into the area.

The Broadstone was again mentioned in the 'Golden Charter' of 1591. The story of its having been buried was so often repeated without any evidence other than hearsay that it came to be somewhat on par with present-day stories about the Loch Ness Monster — never fully accepted but never wholly denied, generally treated with amused scepticism. Then in 1811, David Carey, the Editor of the *Inverness Journal*, noted that 'not long ago a Stone Cross was dug up on the road to Kingsmills',[4] but nothing appeared to be known about the disposal or present whereabouts of that object. Next, in 1863: 'the spot is still shown where the cross is believed to have stood, and a large stone, with a hole in the centre for an upright pillar, has not long since been discovered underneath'.[5] In spite of previous speculation very little attention seems to have been paid to this discovery for in 1878, as recorded in the first volume of Field Club Transactions, members of the Inverness Scientific Society and Field Club inspected it and found it to be 'half embedded in the road'. That half embedded condition apparently became complete, and doubtless stories of its existence were revived together with doubts about their truth. And then, on Wednesday 18 August 1926, workmen laying an electric cable came upon a large stone which the Burgh Surveyor, A.F. MacKenzie, at once suspected was the Broadstone. He called the Provost, Sir Alexander MacEwen, who wholeheartedly agreed. The Courier of 20 August reported the find, and said, 'The original Broad Stone is supposed to have been a shrine, or guide for pilgrims and wayfarers, or a town cross, but there is no historical evidence regarding the stone or its purpose'.

It is a large flat stone of Old Red Sandstone, roughly oval in shape, 12 feet long, 6 feet 2 inches wide and 18 inches thick with an oblong hole 3 feet 7 inches by 9 inches right through, hence giving rise to the corrupted name it sometimes had of the 'Bored Stone'. It lay in the same direction as many boulders carried by moving ice, and it is assumed that it too was deposited by ice movement in the position in which it was unearthed. It was then, apparently, lying under about a foot of road material, but obviously it had once been exposed because its upper surface was weather-worn.

It is still presumed that the central hole had once supported a pillar, or more likely a cross, and either marked the well from which the 'Skower Burn' flowed as a help to travellers on Via Scotia (the old main track to the south which followed the line of the present Kingsmills Road), or was the Mercat

Cross from the days many centuries ago when the town centre was in that area. Today it lies largely ignored, guarded on three sides by the fencing of the Thistle Football Club and on the front by iron bars as though subject to restraint, hardly noticed by passers-by. Yet whatever its origin or purpose, 'it must surely have been an important landmark for its existence to have lived for so long in the traditions of Inverness'.[6]

Drumden

Drumden was a small property about a mile from the 'Exchange' and overlooking the Islands. It was to earn a place in the history of the town by being the scene of a Provost's murder. It contained an avenue of trees leading to the islands (see page 184) from the town and it was here, in 1618 that the ruthless sons of MacKintosh of Borlum ambushed and slaughtered Provost Junor. The motives for this crime are not clear but the feud between the Gordons (Earls of Huntly) and the MacKintosh Clan was at its height, for 1618 was the year that Huntly assembled 1100 horse and 600 foot soldiers in Inverness to force the Laird of MacKintosh to pay feu duties for the Culloden Estate. Generally the magistrates sided with Huntly, and this may well have been the motive. The result was that the Council passed a resolution that no MacKintosh of Borlum should ever afterwards be elected to their number.

The last 'Baron of Drumden' was a gentleman highly esteemed in the neighbourhood who suddenly disappeared. For long it was assumed that he had been waylaid and murdered at 'Sloc-na-Meirlach' (Thieves' Hollow) which adjoined his property. Eventually it transpired that he had simply taken a pilgrimage to the Holy Land and then gone on to Holland.[7]

A further historical incident at Drumden is that it was here that the Black Watch was first formed into a regiment 'traces of their camp being long visible'.[8]

The Islands

Adjoining what was once the Burgh Haugh and separated only by a narrow branch of the Ness are ' The Islands', described thus by Burt:

> the greatest ornament we have in all the adjacent country, about a quarter of a mile from this town but not seen from it by reason of the Castle Hill. It is an island about 600 yards long, surrounded by two branches of the River Ness, well planted with trees of different kinds and may not inaptly be compared with the Islands in St James Park . . . for I speak chiefly of its outward appearance, the beauty whereof is much increased by the nakedness of the surrounding country and the blackness of the surrounding mountains'.[9]

Whilst his assessment of distances may be at fault, Burt's appreciation of this beauty spot has been echoed through the centuries. In his day there were no bridges to give access, and so it was by boat that,

> Hither the Magistrates conduct the Judges and their attendants when they are upon their circuit in the beginning of May, and sometimes such other gentlemen to whom they do the honour of the Corporation by presenting them with their freedom. If it happens to be in the salmon season the entertainment is salmon taken out just by and immediately boiled and set upon a bank of turf, the seats the same not unlike one of our country cock-pits, and during the time of eating the heart of the fish lies upon a plate in view, and keeps up a panting motion all the while, which to strangers is a great rarity'.[10]

In 1663 the Town Council made an order prohibiting the grazing of goats on the Islands[11] and seventeen years later passed an edict 'for the conservation of the Town's beehives in the Islands of the Ness'.[12] Over a century ago Fraser-Mackintosh recorded that, in 1762, as the trees in the Islands had shown signs of decay, the whole Islands were replanted so that the trees then existing were over a hundred years old.[13] A few years earlier, in 1842, there had been a proposal to cut down these trees and to sell the timber in order to liquidate the Town's debt but such was the indignation evoked by this suggestion it was thrown out with little ceremony. The grass was, however, let annually for the benefit of the Common Good Fund.[14]

It was about 1828 that the real improvement started. In that year nearly £1000 was brought in by subscription for this purpose and as a first stage rustic bridges were erected — bridges that were to be swept away twenty-one years later in the flood of 1849, isolating the Islands once again. Four years after this disaster a sum of £350 had been collected for the erection of new bridges, and a Mr Dredge of Bath was erecting the two at each side. A sum of about £120 was said still to be required for the erection of a lodge and an intermediate bridge connecting the two islands.[15] Dr Ross says that he made the working drawings for Mr Dredge and adds 'these bridges still exist and the Islands are well cared for and are a valuable asset and attraction of the town',[16] echoing the words of Edward Burt. Efforts to popularise the amenity have been made, a tea-room was established and ran for several years but has now disappeared and an open-air auditorium to a covered concert platform, long used by Inverness Amenities Association for entertainments during the summer season, has also been closed. For a period the flat rink provided by the auditorium was used for roller-skating but the demand for this facility fell away. The Islands attract by their natural beauty, and bridges and well-kept paths to enjoy that beauty appear to be all that the citizens really desire.

The Longman

No authority has apparently ever been able to give a satisfactory explanation of the peculiar name for an area of the town which is now its Industrial Estate. At one time it was the place of execution and it has even been suggested that the name is a grim reference to the victim after having been hung; but the name is far older than its use as a gallows. Another suggestion is that the reference by Boece to the discovery of an extraordinary human skeleton of a man some thirty feet tall at the promontory of Petty is in fact a slight misplacement and he should really have said that it was found at what is now the Longman.

By far the most plausible is that the name is a corruption of a Gaelic name, 'long' being one name for a ship in that language and 'mìn' an adjective meaning flat, the whole word therefore meaning 'ship-flat', a place where ships could beach.

At one time it was regularly flooded at high water, and it was only after the building of an embankment in 1738 at a cost of £100 according to Ross,[17] or in 1741 at a cost of £60 according to Suter,[18] that the land could effectively be used. This embankment was further extended in 1768, again at a cost of £100.[19] In 1831 some 7000 to 8000 people gathered at the Longman to witness the execution of the Assynt murderer, and four years later on 15 October, a similar number assembled to see John Adam die, the last public execution in Inverness.[20] In 1838 the Northern Meeting was held at the Longman and in 1844 a well-mounted body of people in hunting dress met there for coursing but failed to raise a hare.[21] In 1849 a perimeter road was built from the Citadel to Longman Road, giving an extra 30 acres of land for future development. The Inverness Golf Club, now located at Culcabock, was founded in 1883 and originally played over a course at the Longman.

During the Second World War the north-western part of the Longman was used as an air-field and the early service flights to Orkney and Shetland flew from here. After the war the development as an Industrial Estate commenced and it is now almost wholly used for this purpose.

Sunday Observance

One of the Charters granted to Inverness by William the Lion gave the right to hold a weekly market, specifying that it should be held on Sunday. The strict observance of the Sabbath, which came to be an outstanding characteristic of the Highlands is of comparatively recent development; only after the Reformation was it enforced with full vigour. In 1564 the Burgh Court ordained that every inhabitant should attend the Parish Church every Sunday at ten in the morning and three in the afternoon.[22] Once established, Sabbath day observance took a remarkably firm hold and, although now being eroded at an increasing rate, it is still of great influence in the life of the Highlands. The first break, on the part of the Town Council at least, with strict observance probably came in 1936 when, with one dissentient, the Council agreed to open the public swimming pool on Sunday mornings. At that time many houses did not have a bath, and the Swimming Bath buildings also had hip baths for the people living in these houses. They wished to use this facility on Sunday before going to church; if the building had to open for them, there seemed little reason not to open the pool also.

In 1952 John Cobb came north to make an attempt on the world speed-boat record, the runs to be over a measured mile on Loch Ness. When he was ready the weather was not. For several days he was delayed until at last a day arrived when the conditions were perfect — but it was a Sunday. Conscious of the susceptibilities of the local people he refused to take this opportunity, and thereby earned their undying loyalty. Early next morning he made his attempt — and was killed in so doing. The memorial cairn standing on the side of the road by the Loch, opposite the measured mile, was a spontaneous tribute from the people whose beliefs he had respected.

In 1975 a Manchester firm were instructed to clean the stone-work of the Royal Bank of Scotland in Union Street.

They did an excellent job, on a Sunday, and returned to their base. On Monday the Manager of that Bank found his building still in a rather grubby condition, whilst the Bank of Scotland, also in Union Street, had a sparkling exterior. English ignorance had not realised the difference between the Royal Bank of Scotland and the Bank of Scotland. 'Serve them right for doing the work on the Sabbath', was the verdict of many Invernessians.

Thursday Market

Not far from Tomnahurich is a knoll 'Cnoc-na-gobhar', the hillock of the goats, and here markets, chiefly for the sale of goats, were once held. Gradually these markets grew into a regular cattle market much frequented by men from the Glens. Later a regular market was held weekly on a Thursday for the sale of all forms of farm produce — the day before the weekly market in the town. Not unnaturally this upset the farmers who used the latter day. Those using the Thursday market were mainly from the Glenurquhart area and, by not entering the Burgh grounds, they managed to avoid paying the Petty Customs charged to those selling at the more orthodox Friday Mart. The latter accordingly petitioned the Magistrates to have the irregular market stopped, but got little sympathy and certainly no assistance. They next approached the Lairds of Grant and of Glenurquhart who responded, surprisingly, by threatening to remove from their estates any farmer who continued to trade at Cnoc-na-gobhar. Thus ended the Thursday Market, to the disappointment of the folk from Glenurquhart who had now to compete on equal terms with their fellows from other areas and pay the same petty customs.[23]

Chapter 5 —
Trade and Industry

The Sea; Other Trades; Brewing and Distilling; Commerce.

The Sea

The late Joseph Cook, for so long a diligent Harbour
Trustee, used to assert that the harbour did not grow
because of the town but that the town grew because of the
harbour, and there is a great deal of truth in his claim.
From the earliest times shipping and ship-building have
played a predominant part in the town's story, not
unnaturally at a time when communicjtion by land was
limited to horse-back conveyance. The importancd of the
Burgh was emphasised and guaranteed by the provisions of
the Golden Charter of 1591 which gave to the town the
'petty customs of all cities, towns and villages within the
Shire, and particularly of the Colleges of Tain in Ross,
Merkinch, Chanonry, Dornoch, Thurso and Wick in
Caithness; that no ship break bulk between Tarbetness and
Inverness'. As early as 1249 a French Count, Hugh de
Chatillon, Comte de St Pol et Blois, had a ship built in
Inverness to carry him to the Crusade with Louis IX. This
was a remarkable circumstance, in that he not only did not
choose a yard in his own country but one so far from his
home, rather than, say, in England, the Netherlands or
even southern Scotland. Ship-wrights of Inverness must
even then have earned a high reputation. The Andersons
state that 'In the year 1280 the town was resorted to by a
French count as a fit place for building a large ship, his own

190

having been wrecked in the Orkneys',[1] an account that raises more questions than it answers. Is this un-named French count a different person or is he St Pol? If he is St Pol why do they say he built his ship 31 years later than every other recorder? They do not elaborate on the subject of the wreck, although such an event would be a logical explanation for the choice of Inverness as a yard in which to build a replacement, but what was a French count going to the Crusades doing in Orkney anyway?

According to the Wardlaw Manuscript, Captain George Scott came to Inverness in 1643, 'and there built a ship of prodigious bignes, for bulk and burden, non such ever seen in our north seas. The carpenters he brought with him north and my Lord Lovat gave him wood, firr and oake, in Dulcattack woods [Glenmoriston], I myself was aboord of her in the rode of Kessock, April 1645, and many more to whom she was a wonder. She set sail the very day before the battle of Aldern . . . This ship rode at ancer in the river mouth of Narden [Nairn] when the battle was fought in view'. Captain Scott took this vessel to fight against the Turks, and eventually became Vice-Admiral of the Venetian Fleet.[2]

In 1655 another ship was built, but with a very different purpose and a totally different future. Cromwell's Army, 'constructed at Inverness a vessel, or frigate as she was called, capable of containing sixty men and carried her over-ground to Loch Ness'. She was about forty tons and drawn for over six miles of land by Captain Pestle's seamen and Colonel Fitch's soldiers, who broke three different seven-inch cables in the progress.[3] Of the same incident the Wardlaw Manuscript records, 'They carried a bark driven upon rollers of wood to the Lochend of Ness and there enlarged it into a stately frigate to sail with provisions from one end of the loch to the other'.[4] What eventually happened to this vessel is not recorded, but seventy years later Lees says of General Wade, 'Upon Loch Ness he placed a vessel of about thirty tons which was named the Highland Galley. She carried six or eight 'patteroes' and was employed to transport men, provisions and baggage from Inverness to Fort Augustus. Cromwell's soldiers, as we have seen, sailed a vessel on Loch Ness but she was built at Inverness and transported overland. That of Wade was built on the banks of the Lake'.[5] Apparently there was no difficulty in obtaining the necessary timber for hulk and rigging and in 1670, 'Captain Phineas Pot came down from London by sea to try all the fir woods in the North for masts'. From Struy and Glenstrathfarrar 'he hath already loaded a great ship with masts in Kessock Roads and is providing to load another'. Captain Pot was overseer of naval provisions at the Royal Naval Dockyard at Chatham.[6]

With this record of ship-building — and these are but a few of the many ships that must have been constructed, it is curious that an article on the trade of Inverness in the *Courier* of 2 April 1828 should state 'that it was only within a few years that this branch of industry had been carried on at the port'. It continues,

> Of late, however, several fine vessels have been built here; one of them, *The Caledonia*, now in the Inverness and London trade, was much admired for the beauty of her model and the excellence of her workmanship. She was built by Mr Munro. We learn that another fine smack, intended for the Inverness and Leith trade, will be launched from his yard in the course of a few days. He has also a brig and a schooner on the stocks pretty far advanced, so that we shall have the pleasure of witnessing not less than three launches from his yard within a very short time of each other.[7]

On 17 May 1849, the same paper reports 'A schooner, *The Lady Ann*, was launched from a building-yard in the Merkinch'. Writing in 1905 John Fraser recalls that, at some unspecified date within his personal recollection, there had been at least two shipyards, John Cook's on Shore Street and Mr Munro's on the Capel Inch side of the river,[8] and in 1847 Cameron wrote, 'Ship-building continues to give employment to a considerable number of inhabitants'.[9] A directory published in 1860 listing the various trades carried on in Inverness mentions that there were then seven boat-builders, a figure that would include small yards only making skiffs and dinghies.

Until 1675 there was no regular harbour, boats either beached on the banks of the river or, if too large, on the beach of the firth at the Longman. 'Cherry Shot' just downstream of the Citadel, where the Ordnance Survey of 1868 shows a ship-building yard to have been, it is thought to derive its name from the Gaelic word for a small boat or skiff *Curach*, and so would mean the place where the small boats beached. Just a little further downstream is 'Ship's Flat' where larger vessels grounded. Similarly 'Scatgate', the old name for Rose Street, is usually taken as meaning 'herring way' — the route by which herring from boats beached at the Longman were brought into town.

It was in this era that at least two actions were taken to preserve the town's right to Petty Customs. In 1609 a Robert Henderson of Leith was charged with breaking bulk at Petty 'as if it were a free Burgh'. Both his ship and its cargo were confiscated,[10] and in 1648 it was the turn of the master of a Dundee vessel who was fined by the Town Council for 'breaking bulk between Tarbetness and Inverness'. In recording this event Suter states that it was the only record of enforcement of the provisions of the 1591 Charter; he obviously was not aware of the record of the previous incident.[11] The town also made a charge for merely beaching vessels — 'shore dues' — which were regularised in 1661. Prior to this they had been levied 'according to the customs in other Burghs'.[12] When the Harbour Trust was established these dues were assessed at £332 annually, and that was the amount the Trust agreed to pay each year to the Common Good Fund of the town, an amount still paid each year to the present day.

In 1675 what Suter calls a pier, really a quay, was built at a cost of £300 paid from the shore dues. It is the Shore Street Quay running northwards from the end of the Railway Bridge, 540 feet long. According to Ross 'till late on in the last [eighteenth] century the fishing boats sailed up to the foot of Chapel Street, thus making the Maggot almost an island',[13] but he does not explain why, when the quay was capable of berthing vessels of 70 to 80 tons. By 1718 the Harbour appears to have reached a desperately dilapidated state, but the Council, assisted by Alderman Sir John Barnard MP, Lord Mayor of London, who persuaded Parliament on their behalf, obtained an Act levying one-sixth of a penny sterling tax on every pint of ale or beer brewed in Inverness or brought in from outside. This income was to be used firstly for re-erecting the parish church and then for improvements at the harbour. The Act was for nineteen years only, and in the first five proved so remunerative that the Magistrates decided to enlarge as well as improve the harbour. To this end they bought land, rented quarries, built boats to carry stone, deepened the channels and built a new quay running north from the old one, the Citadel Quay. The revenue from the tax, however, showed a considerable reduction after its early years, due it was said to a fall in the consumption of ale and beer because of the cheapness of 'rum-tea and brandy'; Parliament granted an extension of a further twenty-one years, eleven years after it first came into operation, making forty years in all. The new quay was opened in 1738 having cost £2790, and allowed for the berthing of vessels of 150 tons.[14] Its length is 674 feet.

The first reference to coal being carried is in 1721,[15] by Bailie John Stuart but he encountered financial troubles soon afterwards, and the turmoil of the Jacobite Rising may have prevented this from becoming a regular event until 1770 when both Suter and MacLean say that the first coal arrived. When consideration was being given to the re-building of Fort George in 1747, two reasons were given for not building at the Citadel. One, as mentioned earlier as also applying to the Castlehill Site, was the need to protect the Inverness maidens from the attentions of the 'wild and licentious soldiery'; the second, the compensation that would be claimed by the Magistrates for the loss of harbour facilities if it were built there.[16] In 1793 it was said,

> the harbour is safe and commodious and kept in
> excellent repair. Seven vessels belong to it measuring
> from 400 to 500 tons, and manned by about 30
> seamen including apprentices. They are chiefly
> employed in carrying to London the produce of our
> manufactures, the fish of our river and skins of goat,

roe, deer, fox, hare, rabbit and otter, with other articles.
They bring in return material both for use and for
luxury. There are 9 boats manned by 6 men each.[17]

These comments emphasise that in those days, and for a further twenty years or so, the only practical method of transporting goods to and from Inverness was by sea, roads being virtually non-existent. The danger of this reliance on only one outlet was demonstrated that same year when mob violence prevented the export of grain from the town when there was an acute shortage of it in both town and county.[18]

Shipping to and from London became more organised in 1804 when a fixed day for sailing was established, at first once every three days[19] and then in 1810, 'The Inverness Packet for London is advertised as "armed by Government", the vessel leaving Inverness on 2nd February, Fort George on the 3rd, Cromarty on the 8th and was to call "off Findhorn and Burghead as soon thereafter as possible" yet, in spite of these delays, she is later reported to have arrived in London on the 15th after a quick passage'.[20] Suter, having said that smacks left for London every third day in 1804, inconsistently states that, in 1815, the number of 'smacks plying to London was increasing to one every ten days'.[21]

Captain Burt says that in his time seldom more than three ships were seen at the quay and 'Nonagenarian' says that about 1761 Inverness could not boast of a single trading ship. Two vessels belonging to parties in London plied regularly between London and Inverness during the season, and in winter a Cromarty vessel or two might be laid up in the harbour, a sad deterioration which was matched by dereliction in the town itself.[22] Even in those days there were complaints made about foreign competition, for Inverness traders objected to Dutch vessels that came to Inverness in vessels called 'busses', and that carried away herrings from the firth and oysters from Petty Bay.[23]

Another Parliamentary Act of 1808 allowed the Magistrates to construct a new quay on the other side of the river, the 512 feet long Thornbush Quay, which Suter says was opened in 1815. The following year the shore dues were first handed directly to the Harbour managers in return for the annual payment of £332, instead of through the Common Good Fund administered by the Magistrates. Some of the items liable for shore dues at the time the Trust was formed in 1847 made odd reading today: 'Caviare 6d per barrel; Elephant's teeth 1/- per hundred weight; Imported spirits 1d per gallon; Exported spirits ¼d per gallon and Cabers 1d per dozen'.[24]

In that same year of 1847 there is a record of steamer sailings:

The North Star sails from Thornbush Pier for London every alternate Monday from 1st March to end of October calling at Fortrose Point, Cromarty, Invergordon, Findhorn, Burghead, Lossiemouth, Banff and Aberdeen. Average length of passage 63 hours. Fares to London — cabin £4, steerage £2 12s 6d. Leaves London for Inverness on the following Monday calling at the various places already mentioned. 'The Duke of Richmond' sails from Kessock Roads for Leith every Thursday at 10 p.m. calling at the ports above enumerated and starts from Leith for Inverness every Tuesday at 6. Fares to Leith — Cabin £1 8s, steerage 16s. During the busiest part of the season a second steamer is put on this station for a few weeks. 'The Maid of Morven' sails from Kessock Roads every Monday and Wednesday morning for the several ports in the Moray Firth already named and the Little Ferry in Sutherlandshire returning every succeeding day. Fares to Burghead — Cabin 5s steerage 3/6d to the Little Ferry 10s and 5s. The steamers between Inverness and Glasgow by the Caledonian and Crinan canals viz. 'The Culloden', 'Dolphin', 'Rob Roy' and 'Helen M'Gregor' sail from Muirtown Locks near Inverness on Monday and Thursday mornings and, communicating with swift steamers which leave Glasgow on Tuesday and Friday mornings at the Crinan Canal, the passage is performed in two days. Fares to Glasgow — Cabin £1 10s, steerage 10s and proportionally for all intermediate places.[25]

The Caledonian Canal had been opened in 1822 as somewhat of an anachronism, having been constructed to save sailing vessels the hazardous voyage through the Pentland Firth. Yet the first ship to pass through was not powered by wind but was a steamer with Charles Grant MP and his father on board. The trip was completed in 15 hours.[26] Thereafter it had many 'teething troubles' and in 1837 was said to be almost derelict with 23 miles on the point of collapse and locks no longer in working order. It was closed for ten years for repairs estimated to cost £300,000.[27]

By 1883, 'Mr Macbrayne's steamers, which ply from Glasgow to Inverness by the Caledonian Canal — twice a week all the year round and during the summer months once a day — connect it readily with the S.W. of Scotland. Since 1875 a steamer has also plied once a fortnight from Liverpool to Inverness, Aberdeen and Leith, and vice versa, going by the Caledonian Canal. This makes Inverness a centre from which all sorts of miscellaneous goods are supplied to the smaller towns and villages throughout a very large tract of country round about'.[28] Since then, improved rail and road transport have considerably affected the traffic through the harbour until it became largely a petroleum importing and timber exporting and importing facility, although of course other cargoes continued to be handled, if only in considerably reduced amounts. By 1975, however, trade, although limited in scope, had increased sufficiently for the Trustees to decide to build a new quay, north of Citadel Quay, at a cost of around a quarter of a million pounds which was paid wholly out of reserves and revenue, not one penny having to be borrowed. This quay, 328 feet long, was opened in 1977.

In 1980 the closure of a pulp mill operating at Corpach near Fort William meant that considerable quantities of timber previously handled there was diverted to Inverness for export to Scandinavia, an increase in trade which caused the Trustees that year to commission a 'feasibility study' on a projected further extension at 'Cherry Shott at a possible cost of £3.5 million.

Other Trades

Malting was for generations the chief employment in the town which enjoyed almost a monopoly in the trade and supplied all the northern counties, the Hebrides and Orkneys with malt. In the end of the seventeenth century half the architecture of the town was a mass of malting-houses, kilns and granaries; but from that time the trade gradually fell off and by 1745 the place looked almost like a mass of ruin from the deserted and dilapidated buildings connected with the malt trade. At the end of last [eighteenth] century an extensive white and coloured thread manufacture that is said to give employment to 10,000 people had its centre in Inverness but is now gone owing to the spirited competition of the towns in Forfarshire. A bleachfield and two hemp manufactories then in operation have also disappeared. A woollen factory on the Ness at Holm, about two miles up river was established about 1798 and is the oldest woollen factory in the north of Scotland. It is worked by both water and steam, employs about 100 hands and produces tweeds, mauds, plaiding and blanketing. There are also the large works in connection with the Highland Railway, ship and boat building yards, two large wood-yards and saw-mills, several polished granite and marble works, a rope work, a tan work, two breweries, a distillery, a tobacco manufactory, several foundries and two nurseries.[29]

Such was the industrial picture in 1883. In 1611 Sir John Hay had been admitted a Burgess and Guild Brother, and at the same time given the right to draw water from the Ness 'up to one-third of the amount running' for his lead and iron works at the Bught. That enterprise apparently disappeared without trace. Although a dismal picture is painted of recession at the time, it was in 1754 that the six Incorporated Trades of Inverness purchased premises in Church Street as a Trades House, the Hammerman's share of one sixth being £25 10s.[30]

The older of the two hemp firms was established at the Citadel in 1765,[31] and the thread manufactory (which at its peak employed about 1000 people, not Groome's 10,000) lasted from 1783 only until 1813 when another wave of depression appears to have enveloped the town. The woollen mill apparently closed about this time but a writer in the Inverness Journal on 9 June 1815 pointed to the change in rural economy from the introduction of sheep, and hence the desirability of re-establishing the mill.[32] If this was the mill at Holm, then his plea must have met with success, for Holm Mills continues to the present day. In November 1818, the 'woollen factory at Inverness belonging to Messrs. Mac-Kenzie, Gordon & Co. is advertised for sale. The houses were in the Haugh, the store room at the Shore, and the carding and waulk mills on the bank of the river'.[33] ('The Haugh' was the Burgh Haugh at Holm, not the Haugh we know today which was then known as the Castle Haugh). It must have been about this time that Provost Dr John Inglis Nicol became owner of Holm Mills.

Two actions of the Hammermen about this time are of interest. In 1800 'At a full meeting of the Corporation there was presented a petition by the Glovers Incorporation setting forth a grievance that they be under in consequence of an interdict issued against them by the Magistrates for steeping their skins and hides in the river'. The Hammermen supported them in their objection to this early attempt at river purification. In 1813 the Trustees of the Methodist Chapel had a demand upon them for £40 sterling, and the Hammermen 'agreed to lend them the above sum . . . the interest of the same to be paid yearly until the Corporation has occasion for the same, the interest to be 5 per cent, and the Incorporation to give three months previous notice before the money is demanded'.[34] The Hammermen, like the other Guilds, were wound up in 1836 when new legislation made their continuance in their existing restrictive form impossible.

Mitchell says that about this time the common people manufactured much of their own clothing and that every house-wife 'spun' the linen, blankets and some of the clothing of her family.[35] The Andersons give an interesting record of prices current in the Inverness of 1863.

Good beef sells at 7d to 9d per imperial pound; mutton from 6d to 7d; veal 6d to 7d; pork (of which no great quantity is exposed on account of the demand for cured pork for export and shipping) 6d to 7d. There is a good supply of excellent haddocks which sell at from three to six for 1s; good whitings about the same price; cod from 7d to 1s 4d apiece according to the size and quantity; superior skate 6d to 9d each; turbot frequently at from 2s upwards. Herrings vary much in price as boats only occasionally leave the fishery ground to dispose of this fish so far up the Firth. They sell at from ten to fifty for 6d. Salmon are as high as 1s to 1s 6d and 2s 6d per lb; the salmon fishers being under an engagement to send almost all that may be caught to the London market. Grilse sell from 6d to 10d per lb.; salmon trout 4d to 8d. The price of oatmeal is 20s to 26s per boll of 10 imperial stones and the same price for a quarter of Angus or potato oats; of flour about 46s per sack of 280 lbs; potatoes 16s to 20s per boll; hay 6d to 1s 6d a stone. Whisky is sold at 12s to 18s the imperial gallon; good strong ale at 17s to 18s an anker which will run five dozen of bottles; table beer half that sum. Fresh butter sells at 1s to 1s 4d per lb; salt butter at 24s to 26s per stone of 23 lbs and 16 ozs to the lb. Honey in the comb at 6d to 1s per lb; warm milk at 1d, cream 6d and skim milk at a half-penny the English pint. A pair of fowls cost 3s to 4s 6d; a pair of chickens 1s 8d to 2s 6d; of ducks 2s to 3s 6d; geese and turkeys bring 3s 6d to 6s 6d; grouse 2s to 5s a brace; hares 2s to 3s each; rabbits 1s 6d a pair; lobsters 1s to 2s apiece. Shop goods sell pretty much as in other provincial towns. House rents average from £10 to £60 and shops the same. The wages of housemaids are £2 to £4 per half year; cooks £6 to £16 a year.[36]

Brewing and Distilling

Probably the oldest reference to inns and taverns in connection with Inverness is in a Charter granted by William the Lion which prohibited the Burgesses from keeping taverns anywhere in the Shire other than within the Burgh itself.[37] The Golden Charter of 1591, which conferred so many benefits on the Burgh, for some unexplained reason stipulated that there should only be one tavern in the Burgh, but by about 1820 this restriction had been very considerably broken. There were by then numerous inns in the town, many bearing names now almost forgotten. Among the more interesting names were *The Roebuck*, *The Star* and *The George and Dragon* in Baron Taylor's Street, or Lane as it was then called; *The Deer's Head* and *The Grapes* in Castle Street; *The Coach and Horses* in Bridge Street; *The Jolly Sailor* at the shore, and elsewhere *The Horse Artillery*, *The Salutation*, *The Highlander*, *The Red Lion*, *The Three Merry Boys*, *The Hole in the Wall*, *The Stag's Head*, and the *Haugh Tap*, all popular places for a convivial evening and all apparently having a good trade with ale as the popular drink.

For home consumption the making of ale was one of the housewife's tasks, as a licence from the Council had to be obtained before brewsters could sell their produce. Oddly there were more brewsters than brewers in the commercial field and the ale they produced was generally light, far too weak for the English soldiers stationed in the town after Culloden. Duncan Grant, a merchant with premises in Castle Street, sent to London for 'strong thick ale to suit the taste of Englishmen' and nearly a century later one local brewery was making a mild ale for local consumption and a heavy one for shipment to London. Of the many breweries in Inverness only two survived until within living memory, the Haugh and the Thornbush which closed only during the First World War, both leaving a legacy in the two inns once adjuncts to them. In 1718 the Burgh received Parliamentary sanction to levy a tax of two pence Scots on every pint of ale brewed for sale or brought in from elsewhere, the revenue to pay for repairs to the Parish Church and for harbour improvements and extensions. Two pence Scots was less than a farthing sterling, somewhat under one-tenth of a modern penny, and a Scots pint equalled an Imperial quart.

Until about the middle of the eighteenth century brandy, usually smuggled from France, was the most popular spirit drunk, but from then onwards whisky rapidly supplanted it. It was distilled throughout the Highlands and very little tax was ever paid, the task of the excise officers being almost impossible because of the number, and often almost inaccessible locations, of the stills. An increase in the number of such officers did eventually almost eliminate illicit stills in the Burgh, but Abriachan, Glenurquhart and Strathglass, as well as many other glens in the vicinity, not only continued their illegal production but cultivated a proficiency in smuggling their wares into the numerous outlets in the town. In 1793 there were '4 stills in the town and parish; 12 brewers of ale, 2 of whom are considerable, carrying on the business to a good amount. The retailers of ale and spiritous liquors are about 70. Of the lower class of people, there are some who love whisky rather much; but not so much it is believed as formerly, their inclination begins to change towards ale and beer, a good and wholesome beverage'.[38] Small stills were legalised in 1816 but abuses continued and a new Act came into effect in 1824 under which no less than £1300 was collected in tax in the Inverness area during the first six weeks of its operation.

Many stories are told of the activities of illicit distillers and smugglers. It is said that a Minister living near the town had his own still hidden away about half-a-mile from his Manse and to it he frequently retired for his own and his parishioners benefit. On one occasion, whilst he was working at his still, an excise officer called and enquired of his whereabouts from his young daughter who, trained by her father always to tell the truth, replied 'He's up at his still'. The officer only laughed at what he took to be a joke and departed saying that he would return later. On doing so he enquired of the Minister if he had done a good day's work at his still and, on being assured that he had, laughed louder than ever. The purpose of his visit it transpired was to seek the Minister's aid in suppressing illicit distilling and to ask him to warn any of his parishioners suspected of indulging in such a practice. This the Minister readily agreed to and, the joke having struck too near home for his comfort, set a good example by first dismantling his own still never to use it again.

In March 1811, 'Three men were conveying several ankers of smuggled whisky across the river opposite Ness Castle. They were pulling the boat across with a rope. The river being very high the rope broke and the boat filled, two of the men were drowned and the third was rescued after being carried down a mile and a half clinging to the stern. The spirits were to have been used at the wedding of one of the men who was drowned'.[39]

An Aird crofter, who eked out his insufficient income from the croft by a little distilling in order to pay his rent, habitually sold his produce to various innkeepers in the town. On one occasion he received an order and promised to deliver on a certain day but the innkeeper concerned, anxious to obtain the good graces of the excise officer, told that official when the whisky was to be smuggled in. The officer duly stopped the crofter who had the spirits hidden under a load of peats and questioned him closely but quickly realised that the innkeeper was really the greater villain. Accordingly he allowed the crofter to proceed and make his delivery. The innkeeper was naturally surprised when his supply arrived apparently undetected but, since he had ordered it, had no alternative other than to accept it. Shortly afterwards he was arrested when the excise officer and his assistants searched the premises and found the hoard.

It is said that there are a few, now a very few, hardy souls who believe that they can make whisky as good if not better than any distillery, but they manage to conceal their whereabouts very successfully. One such enthusiast who managed to turn his skill and 'birthright' to good account was a soldier in the 51st (Highland) Division who was captured during the Second World War. Somehow he managed to produce his native liquor in his prison camp and, by bartering it with the Nazi guards, was able to obtain extra comforts for himself and his hut-mates.

Commerce

At the time of the establishment of the Caledonian Bank there were already branches of four banks in the town; the Bank of Scotland, British Linen, Commercial and National and it was rather quaintly commented that two were Tory and two Whig. The directors of the new bank appointed Mr Charles Waterson of Aberdeen to be manager but he replied that he could not leave Darlington, where he then was, so Mr Gray of Glasgow was appointed as interim manager. Mr Gray died at Perth on his way to Inverness. James Ross, Chairman of the Company, then took over until Mr Waterson could start, but whilst going to Dumfries to collect his family Mr Waterson's coach overturned and his arrival was further delayed for six weeks until the broken leg he had sustained healed sufficiently to allow him to take over on 25 May 1839. By the time Slater's Directory of Scotland was published in 1860, two more banks had appeared in Inverness — the ill-fated City of Glasgow Bank and the Savings Bank. That same Directory gives a list of all the businesses in the town and a few of the categories are of special interest:— There were 37 farmers in the district, no less than 21 within what was to be the bounds of the Burgh in 1906, 3 fishing rod makers, 2 gun smiths, 2 hatters, 13 milliners (all female), 2 nursery men (one being Howdens, a firm which still exists), 5 perfumers and hairdressers, 5 rag dealers, 7 straw bonnet makers, 20 taverns, 43 vintners, a 'permanent manure' manufacturer, a cork cutter and a bird stuffer as well as three engineers and iron founders (one being Smith and MacKay of Rose Street) who eventually united to form Rose Street Foundry, now A.I. Welders, very much still with us. The only names still active today are those two mentioned, yet a similar list from the 1894 Valuation Roll shows many names that were familiar until very recently when the take-over of old-established local businesses really made the commercial centre of the town into a catalogue of national names, and almost identical with any other town in Britain. A few of the 1894 names will interest local people: — MacTavish, iron-monger in Castle Street; Jack's, The Exchange; Tulloch, painter, Church Street; Melville, shoemaker and Medlock, Watchmaker, Bridge Street; John Forbes, draper, High Street; MacDonald and Morrison, coal merchants, Church Street; MacPherson, fishing tackle and gunsmith, Drummond Street; MacRae and Dick, 'postmasters', Academy Street etc.; Melven, bookseller and A. & S. Fraser, draper, Union Street; Morel Bros, Italian warehousemen and Wm. MacLeay, bird stuffer, Church Street; Bookless Bros, fish-merchants, then in Falcon Square; Gilbert Ross, ironmonger, Academy Street; A. Fraser and Co. cabinet makers, Union Street and D. & A. Davidson, stone masons, Waterloo Place — all names familiar in town and county but many, alas, now either gone or owned by multiple concerns.

The development of trade and industry in Inverness has several milestones, some indicating depression, some happily prosperity. There were two at periods of war, around the time of the '45 and towards the end of the Napoleonic era when trade was in a trough, but there were also the increased opportunities immediately following 1815 when the improvements in roads and the building of the Caledonian Canal revolutionised communications followed by the yet more significant improvements in the same field when railways spread like a rash throughout Britain in a remarkably short time. Not only did the latter give direct help to local commerce but the easier access for sportsmen and tourists started what has become one of the staple industries of the area — tourism. In the early 1960s Russell Johnston became prospective Parliamentary Candidate for Inverness-shire, and made one of his first tasks a report on the need for a Development Board for the Highlands. His ideas were adopted by the Liberal Party and their success in the General Election of 1964 when, in George Mackie's picturesque phrase, the Highlands became Liberal 'from Muckle Flugga to Ballachulish', was instrumental in causing the Government to set up the Highlands and Islands Development Board in 1965. That Board has had its successes and its failures, it has subsidised enterprises which failed to 'make the grade' but it has also helped others which appear still to be flourishing. The whole concept is too recent to give a balanced judgement on its overall success or failure but nobody can deny that it has had a tremendous impact on development in the area, as well as itself being one of the larger employers of labour.

The discovery of oil in the North Sea has not made such a great impact in Inverness as in some other areas of Scotland, but it has brought extra employment and has caused Government attention to be given to the needs of the locality, with a consequential further improvement in the main roads reaching the Highlands. Time will tell whether these recent events have been for ultimate good or ill, here they can only be recorded as having happened.

Appendix
Town Charters

1057/1093

The First Statistical Account of Scotland states that the first Charter granted to Inverness was by Malcolm Canmore but presents no proof of this assertion nor is it supported by any other evidence.

1165/1214

The earliest known Charter was not restricted to the Burgh, it was granted to all Burgesses in Moray. However, since there were but few Burgesses anywhere else in that Province, it may rightly be considered as a Burgh Charter. Translated into modern idiom it reads:

William, by the grace of God, King of Scots, to all Sheriffs and Bailies of his whole land, Greetings. Know ye that I have granted this liberty to my Burgesses of Moray, that none whatever in my realm shall take a poinding for the debt of any one, unless for their own proper debt; wherefore I strictly forbid any one in my realm to take a poinding otherwise, upon my plenary prohibition. Witnesses — William de Hay, Philip de Valonüs, Richard my Clerk of the Prebend, at Bonkhill.

In the reign of King William the Lion four charters were
granted to the town conferring on the burgesses freedom
from tolls, the right to hold a weekly market, the exclusive
right of trading within the shire (at that time a very valuable
privilege) and other rights. One of these Charters, granted in
1180, is particularly important because by it the King undertook to make a ditch or fosse round the town and the burghers
were to enclose it with a palisade.[1]

1217

The privilege of freedom from poinding for debts other than
their personal ones, granted in William's earliest Charter,
was renewed by another granted by Alexander II at Scone.[2]

1236

Alexander, by the grace of God, King of Scots. To
all good men of his whole land (clerical and laical)
greeting; know all present and to come that we have
given, granted, and by this our present charter
confirmed to our burgesses of Inverness, the lands of
Merkinch, for the support of our Burgh of Inverness,
to be held by the said burgesses of us and our heirs
for ever, freely and quietly, for sustaining the rent of
our burgh of Inverness, so that they may cultivate the
said lands of Merkinch if they choose, or deal with it
in any other way that may be for their advantage;
rendering therefor one pound of pepper at the feast
of St Michael yearly. Witnesses — Walter, son of
Allan, Steward and Justiciar of Scotland; . . . Earl of
Angus; . . . Earl of Caithness, Hugh de Vallebus;
Walter Byset; Walter de Petyn; David Marischall, at
Inverness, the twenty-sixth day of July, in the
twenty-second year of the reign of the Lord the King.

1250

Alexander, by the grace of God, King of Scots. To all good men of his whole realm. Greeting. Know ye that we have granted to our Burgesses of Inverness that none of them shall be poinded in our Kingdom for any but his own proper debt, forfeit or pledge. Moreover we command and charge our Sheriffs, their Baillies, to poind those who owed debts to our Burgesses, which they could reasonably prove, for rendering payment of such debts as may be justly due to them without delay, nevertheless, we strictly forbid them to presume to detain or oppress any one unjustly with poindings for debts which he owes them contrary to the foresaid grant which we have made to them upon our plenary forfeiture. Witnesses, David, Bishop elect of Dunkeld; David, Abbot of Newbothie; Allan Durward, Justiciar of Scotland; and Gilbert de Hay at Scone the 3rd day of December in the second year of the reign of the Lord the King.

1344

David by the grace of God, King of Scots, to all good men, his subjects, to whom these present letters shall come; Greeting. Know that we have granted to our Burgesses of Inverness, and their heirs, that no Justiciar, or any other servant of ours, except our Chamberlain, to whom it pertains by office (ex officio) shall sit in judgement or investigate as to the correction or punishment of which we commit for ever to our Chamberlain only by these presents: therefore let all, whose interest it is, know that we command and order that no one presume to harrass or annoy our said Burgesses of Inverness in any way in face of this our grant, under the pain of losing all that according to our royal laws (regiam majestatum nostram) he might lose; in testimony of which matter our seal is appended to these presents. Given at

Netherdale the last day of December in the year of our reign the sixteenth.

1369

In a Charter signed at Perth David II granted to the Burgesses and Community of Inverness the lands of Drakies, the fishings, mills, tolls and petty customs of the Burgh. This is the first Charter specifically to grant the power of levying petty customs, for which privilege it stipulates that the Burgh shall pay to the King an annual assessment of 80 merks sterling.

This grant of Drakies was the third such Royal bounty. In 1180 it had been the Burgh Haugh and in 1236 it was Merkinch, the three being, with the petty customs, the foundation of the Common Good Fund. It was this Charter which really made Inverness into a Royal Burgh; until then 'the burgesses had been the King's direct tenants or vassals paying rent to him for their possessions. Now the Burgh itself, as a corporate commuunity, became the King's vassal'. Fifty years earlier Aberdeen had been the first Burgh to be granted this status, Edinburgh following ten years later.[3]

1428

Whilst in Inverness James I declared, 'Whereas on the part of the burgesses of our Burgh of Inverness it has reached our ears, by way of common complaint, that some persons dwelling within the bounds and liberty of the said burgh, usurp and infringe its liberty and privilege by buying and selling merchandise or other saleable goods beyond the said burgh, to the no small loss and prejudice of our said burgh', and he therefore directed that, 'those inhabiting all and singular the bounds of the said burgh and liberty thereof, who have any merchandise or goods whatsoever to be sold, shall assemble at the market place of our said burgh and shall actually present themselves there'.[4] He was thus confirming to the Burgesses the right to collect petty customs.[5] Suter says that this was in 1427, but this could be a difference caused by the old range of the year. The year used to commence on 25 March until 1600 when, for the first time, New Year's Day in Scotland was on the 1 January. Not until 1752 did England follow suit. This has meant that events which happened in January, February and much of March are sometimes said to have taken place according to the year then observed whilst others have used the year it would have been under our present system, a variance made all the easier by so many royal acts being dated 'in the . . . year of our reign'.

1464

James III, whilst in Inverness, granted a new Charter which merely confirmed eight previous ones. One of the witnesses was John, Earl of Ross and Lord of the Isles, who only the previous year had proclaimed himself king and seized the Castle of Inverness.[6]

1514

Yet again a Charter merely confirming the privileges granted by his predecessors, this time by James V.[7]

1567

Queen Mary followed her father in confirming the previous grants and privileges but also granted to the Burgesses all the lands, chapels and churches 'Formerly pertaining to the Dominican or Preaching Friars of our said Burgh'.[8]

1587

Queen Mary's Charter of 1567 confirmed by James VI.[9]

32   Inverness Harbour about 1896

33   Kessock Ferry in the days of sail

34 *Kessock Ferry in its last days*

35   *Replacement for Kessock Ferry in course of construction*

36   *Washing fleeces for the Gilbert Street Tannery*

1591

The Great Charter which gave to Inverness powers to levy
customs throughout the north of Scotland, and so caused
continuing jealousy and animosity from communities
everywhere in the eastern Highlands.

> James, by the grace of God, King of Scots to all
> good men of his whole realm, Greeting; Know that
> we, considering the ancient erection of Inverness by
> our famous progenitors, into a free burgh of this
> kingdom, have ratified, and by this present Charter,
> do ratify, and perpetually confirm, all and sundry the
> Charters, confirmations, rights, liberties and
> privileges granted and confirmed by our progenitors,
> William, Alexander, David and James the first of
> that name, Kings of Scotland, to our said Burgh.
> Likewise the Charter and confirmation lately granted
> by our Grandfather James, fifth of that name; also
> the Charter granted in favour of Divine Service, and
> of the Ministers of God's Word, and of the Hospital,
> by our Mother Mary, Queen of Scots; and the lands,
> houses, churches, chapels, crofts, milns, fishings and
> all others mentioned in that Charter, of date 21st
> April 1567 years; moreover we of new grant and, in
> perpetual feu, set and confirm to the Provost, Bailies
> etc. of our said burgh, the lands territories and
> commonty thereof, with all parts and privileges. As
> also all the lands of Drakies and the forest thereof;
> the lands of Merkinch with the pasturage thereof
> with the parks and woods; likewise the lands called
> Barnhills, Claypots, Miln and Milnfields, the Carse
> and the Carn Laws with the common muir of the said
> burgh; likewise the waters of the Ness on both sides
> from Clachnagaick to the sea, with all fishings, ports,
> havens, creeks, the stell fishing, the red pool, with
> power to begin to fish in the said waters with boats
> and nets on the 10th of November yearly, and to use
> cruives and water kists; with the ferry of Kessock and
> the right of ferrying on both sides. Farther all the

milns called Kingsmilns, the sucken and multures thereof, with the astricted and dry multures of the Castle Lands, and all corns which have, or shall receive fire or water, within the liberty, territory and parish of Inverness, as well out-sucken as in-sucken, to pay multure and knaveship at the said milns; with power and liberty of pasture, peats, foggage, turf etc. in all places used and wont; and particularly in Craig Phadric, Capulach Muir, Daveemont and Bogbayne with power of ferrying on Loch-Ness; with mercats weekly on Wednesday and Saturday, and eight free fairs in the year viz. on Palm Sunday; on July 7th St Andrew's Fair; on August 15th Marymas; in September Roodmas; on November 10th Martinmas; in December Saint Thomas Fair; on February 1st Peter Fair and April 25th Saint Mark's Fair; every fair to be held for eight days; with the Petty Customs of all cities, towns and villages within the Shire, and particularly of the Colleges of Tain in Ross, Merkinch, Chanonrie, Dornoch, Thurso and Wick in Caithness; that no ship break bulk between Tarbetness and Inverness; and our said burgh shall have Coroners and Sheriffs within themselves; and a Guildry with a Dean of Guild; that there be but one tavern; that no one in the Shire make cloth but the burgesses; with power to make statutes and rules for the burgh etc. etc.

I am indebted to the late Miss Margaret O. MacDougall F.S.A. Scot., Burgh Librarian and Museum Curator, for these interpretations of the ancient Charters.

Notes

(Page references denoted thus, 1.74, indicate volume number and page.)

Preface

1. Kenneth MacDonald *Inverness Scientific Society and Field Club Transactions*, Presidential address, Vol V, 1898.

Beginnings

1. Richard Muir *Riddles of the British Landscape* 1981 **141**
2. Robert Carruthers *Highland Notebook* 1843 **36/7**

Chapter 1 — Buildings

1. James Souter *Memorabilia of Inverness* articles in the Inverness Courier in 1822, published in book form by Donald MacDonald, Inverness 1887.
2. Thomas D. Wallace, F.E.I.S., F.S.A. (Scot.) Manuscript notes of which a copy is now in Inverness Public Library Reference Room.
3. James Fraser *Chronicles of the Frasers (The Wardlaw Manuscript)* The Scottish History Society 1905 **447**
4. Richard Franck 'Northern Memoirs' Scottish History Society's Transactions 1899 volume
5. Fraser *op. cit.* **413/416**
6. *ibid* **414 and 447**
7. H.C. Boyd 'The Common Good' Inverness Scientific Society and Field Club Transactions volume 8.
8. *ibid.*
8a J. Cameron Lees *A History of the County of Inverness*, 1897 **55**
8b Eds. W.R. MacKay and H.C. Boyd *Records of Inverness* New Spalding Club 1911 **1.74**
9. Reverend F.J.L. MacLaughlan M.C., M.A., *The Old High Church* a pamphlet.

10. *ibid.*
11. John MacLean *Sketches of Highland Families* 1895 **163/4**
12. MacLaughlan *op. cit.*
13. Captain Douglas Wimberley *The Hospital of Inverness and Dunbar's Hospital* 1893 **6 and 7**
14. *ibid.* **9**
15. *ibid.* **10**
16. *ibid.* **17**
17. Alexander Mitchell *Inverness Kirk Session Records 1661-1800* 1902 **217**
18. eds. W.R. MacKay and H.C. Boyd *Records of Inverness* New Spalding Club 1911 **2.348**
19. Wimberley *op. cit.* **18**
20. *ibid.* **25**
21. Mitchell *op. cit.* **218**
22. *ibid.* **159**
23. *ibid.* **162 and 290**
24. Wimblerley *op. cit.* **45/6**
25. *ibid.* **43**
26. *ibid.* **44**
27. Mitchell *op. cit.* **164**
28. *ibid.* **165**
29. Reverend T.P. Addison *A Thousand Tongues to sing, the story of Methodism in Inverness* 1963 A pamphlet
30. Wimberley *op. cit.* **102**
31. Mitchell *op. cit.* **189**
32. *ibid.* **190**
33. *ibid.* **190**
34. *ibid.* **195**
35. Wimberley *op. cit.* **129**
36. Edmund Burt *Letters from a Gentleman in the North of Scotland* **51/2**
37. Robert Hunter and C. Innes *Local Reports on Municipal Corporations in Scotland* 1833
38. James Barron 'Armed Figure in Greyfriars' Churchyard' Inverness Scientific Society and Field Club's Transactions Volume 4
39. Evan M. Barron 'Inverness in the Middle Ages' Inverness Scientific Society and Field Club's Transactions Volume 7
40. Fraser *op. cit.* **67**
41. Evan M. Barron *Inverness and the MacDonalds* **14**
42. James Barron *op. cit.*
43. Dr Alexander Ross 'Old Inverness' Inverness Scientific Society and Field Club's Transactions Volume 2
44. *ibid.*
45. Wallace *op. cit.*
46. *ibid.*
47. *The Topographical, Statistical and Historical Gazetteer of Scotland* A. Fullerton and Co. Glasgow 1842
48. Architectural description written for the author by W.T. Jack
49. attributed to George Cameron *A History and Description of the Town of Inverness* 1847 **69**
50. Fraser *op. cit.* **95**

51. Wallace *op. cit.*
52. Ross *op. cit.*
53. Fraser *op. cit.* **455**
54. Burt *op. cit.* **75**
55. All references in this section are taken from T.C. MacKenzie M.D., F.R.C.P. (ed.) *The Story of a Scottish Voluntary Hospital* 1946 or *The Further History of a Scottish Voluntary Hospital* 1950

Chapter 2 — Streets

1. Wallace *op. cit.*
2. Suter *op. cit.*
3. Evan M. Barron *Inverness in the 15th Century* 1907 **36**
4. Wallace *op. cit.*
5. Evan M. Barron *Inverness in the 15th Century* 1907 **28**
6.
7. } Wallace *op. cit.*
8. Michael Brander *The Original Scotch* 1974 **50**
9. Wallace *op. cit.*
10. Fraser *op. cit.* **479**
11. MacLean *op. cit.* **169/171**
11a. J.B. Salmond *Wade in Scotland* 1934 **70**
12. Evan M. Barron *Inverness in the 15th Century* 1907 **92/3**
13. Cameron *op. cit.* **352 et seq.**
14. *ibid.* **93**
15. Fraser *op. cit.* **352 et seq.**
16. Wallace *op. cit.*
17. *Inverness Courier* 1 January 1907
18. Dr. Alexander Ross 'Old Inverness' Inverness Scientific Society and Field Club's Transactions volume 8
19. Wallace *op. cit.*
20. Cameron *op. cit.* **99/100**
21. George and Peter Anderson *Anderson's Guide to the Highlands* Part II 1863 **212**
22. *Inverness Courier* 21 October 1846
23. Evan M. Barron *Inverness in the 15th Century* 1907 **59**
24. Wallace *op. cit.*
25. *ibid.*
26. *Inverness Courier* 3 February 1967
27. The Burghs of Inverness District, who elected one member of Parliament, were Forres, Nairn, Inverness and Fortrose
28. Sir John Sinclair *Inverness 1793* A reprint of the First Statistical Account of Scotland.
29. Once again it should be emphasised that Inverness was never a town of Highlanders but of 'Incomers' usually associated with the 'establishment', and usually looked on with scorn or hostility by the indigenous population of the surrounding areas.
30. Kenneth MacDonald, 1898 Presidential address, Inverness Scientific Society and Field Club's Transactions volume 5

31. Burt *op. cit.* **46/7**
32. Donald MacKay *Scotland Farewell* Edinburgh 1980
33. James Barron *Northern Highlands in the Nineteenth Century* **1.55**
34. John MacLean *Reminiscences of a Clachnacuddin Nonagenarian* 1886 **408**
35. Wallace *op. cit.*
36. James Barron *Northern Highlands* **1.146**
37. Wallace *op. cit.*
38. Loch-na-Sanais was at the foot of Torvean to the north between it and Glenalbyn Road, said to have been formed by the extraction of clay for the construction of the Caledonian Canal. Now filled in and part of the Municipal Golf Course.
39. James Barron *Northern Highlands* **2.217**
40. Cameron *op. cit.* **38 et seq.**
41. Wallace *op. cit.*
42. Ross 'Old Inverness' volume 8 *op. cit.*
43. Cameron *op. cit.* **82**
44. John Noble *Miscellanea Invernessiana* 1902 **93**
45. James Barron *Northern Highlands* **3.81**
46. Cameron *op. cit.* **82**
47. James Barron *Northern Highlands* **2.227**
48. Evan M. Barron *Inverness in the 15th Century* **22**
49. Fraser-Mackintosh 'The Chantry Altars and Chaplains of St. Mary's, Inverness, 1359-1593' Inverness Scientific Society and Field Club's Transactions volume 4
50. Fraser *op. cit.* **165** and R. Carruthers *Highland Notebook* 1843 **188**
    50[a] Cameron *op. cit.* **32**
51. Wallace *op. cit.*
52. Fraser-Mackintosh *op. cit.*
53. John Fraser *Reminiscences of Inverness; its People and Places* 1905 **21**
54. Suter *op. cit.*
55. Wallace *op. cit.*
56. Cameron *op. cit.* **81**
57. Barron *Northern Highlands* **1.95**
58. Ross 'Old Inverness' volume 2 *op. cit.*
59. Suter *op. cit.*
60. Wallace *op. cit.*
61. Ross 'Old Inverness' Volume 2 *op. cit.*
62. Cameron *op. cit.*
63. Wallace *op. cit.*
64. *ibid.*
65. Suter *op. cit.*
66. Barron *Inverness in the 15th Century* **102**
67. MacDonald *loc. cit.*
68. Suter *op. cit.*
69. Barron *Northern Highlands* **1.16**
70. Suter *op. cit.*
71. Barron *Inverness in the 15th Century* **102**
72. Church of Scotland *Centenary Souvenir 1863-1963 of Merkinch (St Mark's)* a pamphlet
73. James Barron *The Northern Highlands* **2.196**

74. Sinclair *op. cit.*
75. John Fraser *op. cit.* **56**
76. James Barron *The Northern Highlands* **3.181**
77. *ibid.* **3.237**
78. Alistair and Henrietta Taylor *The Book of the Duffs* William Brown 1914 **13 et seq.**
79. *ibid.* **413**
80. Suter *op. cit.*
81. James Fraser *Wardlaw Manuscript* **86**
82. James Barron *The Northern Highlands* **1.24**
83. Dr Alexander Ross 'Ancient Churches and Chapels in Inverness' Inverness Scientific Society and Field Club's Transactions volume 6
84. Mitchell *op. cit.* **164**
85. Ross 'Old Inverness' vol. 8
86. James Barron *Northern Highlands* **2.30**
87. *ibid.*
88. Ross 'Old Inverness' vol. 8
89. Donald MacDonald 'The Glasgow Bank Disaster' *The Scots Magazine* February 1979
90. *ibid.*
91. Wallace *op. cit.*
92. James Barron *Northern Highlands* **3-274**
93. Alexander MacKenzie 'The Gaelic Origin of Local Names' Inverness Scientific Society and Field Club's Transactions vol. 3
94. James Fraser *Wardlaw Manuscript* **296**
94a. Marc Alexander *Enchanted Britain* 1981
95. Suter *op. cit.*
96. Evan M. Barron 'Inverness in the Middle Ages'
97. Wallace *op. cit.*
98. James Fraser *Wardlaw Manuscript* **xl and 447**
99. *ibid.* **xxxiii**
100. Sinclair *op. cit.*
101. Hugh Barron 'Notes on the Ness Valley' Inverness Gaelic Society's Transactions vol. 43
102. James Barron *Northern Highlands* **2.217 and 2.292**
103. Hugh Barron *op. cit.*

Chapter 3 — Names and Institutions

1. Suter *op. cit.*
2. Fraser-Mackintosh *Invernessiana* 1875 **128**
3. Joseph Mitchell *Reminiscences of my Life in the Highlands* 1883 **1.55**
4. James Barron *Northern Highlands* **1.44**
5. Joseph Mitchell *op. cit.* **1.56**
6. *ibid.* **1.57**
7. James Barron *Northern Highlands* **2.xiii** and **2.96**
8. Joseph Mitchell op. cit. **1.60**
9. W.R. MacKay and H.C. Boyd *op. cit.* **2.309**
10. Rev. Archibald MacDonald 'The Presbytery of Inverness 1632-1644' Inverness Gaelic Society's Transactions vol. 38
11. Ross 'Old Inverness' vol. 8.
12. Ross *Freemasonry in Inverness* 1878 **154/155**
13. Wallace *op. cit.*
14. Evan M. Barron 'More Light on Scottish History' Inverness Scientific Society and Field Club Transactions vol. 9.
15. Wallace *op. cit.*
16. Fraser-Mackintosh *Invernessiana* **56**
17. Suter *op. cit.*
18. *ibid.*
19. John MacLean *Reminiscences of a Clachnacuddin Nonagenarian* 1886 **51**
20. John Noble *Miscellania Invernessiana* 1902 **6**
21. Wallace *op. cit.*
22. *ibid.*
23. Wimberley *op. cit.* **54**
24. James Alexander Gossip 'The Hammermen of Inverness' Inverness Scientific Society and Field Club's Transactions vol. 8
25. Maclean *op. cit.* **96 et seq.**
26. Sinclair *op. cit.*
27. James Fraser *Wardlaw Manuscript* **68**
28. MacKay and Boyd *op. cit.* **2.55**
29. *ibid.* **2.358**
30. Suter *op. cit.*
31. *ibid.*
32. *ibid.*
33. Mackay and Boyd *op. cit.* **2.183**
34. Suter *op. cit.*
35. *ibid.*
36. Walter Carruthers, comments made during a visit by the Inverness Scientific Society and Field Club to Bunchrew, 20 July 1878 printed in their Transactions vol. 1.
37. James Barron *Northern Highlands* **3.251**
38. Suter *op. cit.*
39. J. Cameron Lees *op. cit.* 1897 **157**
40. *ibid.* **149** and Joseph Mitchell *op. cit.* **1.63**
41. Suter *op. cit.*
42. Lees *op. cit.* **287**
43. Joseph Mitchell *op. cit.* **1.62**

44. Carruthers 'Transactions' vol 1. *loc. cit.*
45. Joseph Mitchell *op. cit.*
46. Suter *op. cit.*
47. *ibid.*
48. Lees *op. cit.* **45**
49. Suter *op. cit.*
50. MacCulloch, paper read to members of the Inverness Scientific Society and Field Club on their excursion to Essich on 1 August 1925 and recorded in their Transactions vol. 9
51. T.C. Smout *A History of the Scottish People 1560-1830* 1972 **42**
52. James Fraser *Wardlaw Manuscript* **170**
53. Fraser-Mackintosh *Invernessiana* **264**
54. James Fraser *Wardlaw Manuscript* **247**
55. Suter *op. cit.*
56. Noble *op. cit.* **10**
57. James Barron *Northern Highlands* **2.96**
58. Suter *op. cit.*
59. Rev. A. MacDonald *The Old Lords of Lovat and Beaufort* 1934 **3**
60. James Barron *Northern Highlands* **1.264** and **2.321**
61. *ibid.* **1.187**
62. *ibid.* **1.117**
63. Suter *op. cit.*
64. Dr T.C. MacKenzie *The Further History of a Scottish Voluntary Hospital* **1950 110**
65. James Barron *Northern Highlands* **1.31**
66. Lees *op. cit.* **258**
67. Suter *op. cit.*
68. Murdoch Mackintosh *A History of Inverness* 1939 **147**
69. *Inverness Courier* 18 March 1931
70. Noble *op. cit.* **235**
71. Suter *op. cit.*
72. James Barron *Northern Highlands* **2.3** and **2.5**
73. *ibid.* **2.146**
74. *ibid.* **1.277**
75. *ibid.* **1.18**
76. *ibid.* **1.44**
77. *ibid.* **1.111**
78. Suter *op. cit.*
79. James Barron *Northern Highlands* **1.211**
80. *ibid.* **3.261**
81. A. Penrose Hay (Postmaster) Address, published in book form 1885 **7**
82. *ibid.* **7**
83. *ibid.* **12**
84. Noble *op. cit.* **56**
85. *ibid.* **55**
85a. *ibid.* **58**
86. Wallace *op. cit.*
87. Suter *op. cit.*
88. Hay *op. cit.* **17**
89. James Barron *Northern Highlands*
90. Dr A. Ross 'Ancient Churches and Chapels in Inverness'

91. Fraser-Mackintosh *Invernessiana* **157**
92. Suter *op. cit.*
93. Walter Carruthers 'Stent as an Imperial Tax' Inverness Scientific Society and Field Club's Transactions vol. 9.

Chapter 4 — The Locality and its Customs

1. D. Butter 'The Boar Stone' Inverness Scientific Society and Field Club's Transactions vol. 9.
2. *ibid.*
3. Wallace *op. cit.*
4. *ibid.*
5. Anderson *op. cit.* **214**
6. Wallace *op. cit.*
7. *ibid.*
8. *ibid.*
9. Ross 'Old Inverness' vol 8.
10. *ibid.*
11. MacKay and Boyd *op. cit.* **218**
12. Suter *op. cit.*
13. Ross 'Old Inverness' vol 8
14. *ibid.*
15. James Barron *Northern Highlands* **3.284**
16. Ross 'Old Inverness' vol 8
17. *ibid.* vol. 2
18. Suter *op. cit.*
19. *ibid.*
20. James Barron 'Northern Highlands' **2.175**
21. *ibid.* **2.235** and **3.57**
22. MacKay and Boyd *op. cit.* **1113**
23. Wallace *op. cit.*

Chapter 5 — Trade and Industry

1. G. and P. Anderson *op. cit.* **217**
2. James Fraser *Wardlaw Manuscript* **xii** and **297**
3. Lees *op. cit.* **79**
4. James Fraser *Wardlaw Manuscript* **415**
5. Lees op. cit. **127**
6. James Fraser *Wardlaw Manuscript* **485**
7. James Barron *Northern Highlands* **2.46**
8. John Fraser *Reminiscences* **32**
9. Cameron *op. cit.* **97**
10. MacKay and Boyd *op. cit.* **2.67**
11. Suter *op. cit.*
12. *ibid.*
13. Ross 'Old Inverness' vol.2

14. Wallace *op. cit.*
15. James Barron *Northern Highlands* **3.247**
16. Wallace *op. cit.*
17. Sinclair *op. cit.*
18. Suter *op. cit.*
19. *ibid.*
20. James Barron *Northern Highlands* **1.32**
21. Suter *op. cit.*
22. Francis Groome, *Ordnance Gazetteer of Scotland* 1883 vol. 4
23. Wallace *op. cit.*
24. Inverness Harbour Act 1847
25. Cameron *op. cit.* **100**
26. Lees *op. cit.* **256** and James Barron *Northern Highlands* 1.xxiv
27. Francis Thomson *Highland Waterway* 1972
28. Groome *op. cit.*
29. *ibid.*
30. Gossip *loc. cit*
31. Ross 'Old Inverness' vol. 2
32. James Barron *Northern Highlands* **1.87**
33. *ibid.* **3.154**
34. Gossip *loc. cit.*
35. Joseph Mitchell *op. cit.*
36. G. and P. Anderson *op. cit.* **204**
37. Suter *op. cit.*
38. Sinclair *op. cit.*
39. James Barron *Northern Highlands* **1.41**
40. Joseph Mitchell *op. cit.* **2.69**

Appendix — Town Charters

1. H.C. Boyd *op. cit.*
2. Suter *op. cit.*
3. Boyd *op. cit.*
4. Fraser-Mackintosh *Invernessiana* **104**
5. Suter *op. cit.*
6. *ibid.*
7. *ibid.*
8. MacLaughlin *op. cit.*
9. *ibid.*

Bibliography

ADDISON Reverend T.P. *A Thousand Tongues to Sing*, the story of Methodism in Inverness 1963

ALEXANDER Marc *Enchanted Britain* Arthur Barker Ltd., London 1981

ANDERSON George and Peter *Anderson's Guide to the Highlands* Black, Edinburgh 1863

BARRON Evan MacLeod *Inverness in the 15th. Century* Robt. Carruthers, Inverness 1906

Inverness and the MacDonalds Robt. Carruthers & Sons, Inverness 1930

'Inverness in the Middle Ages' Inverness Scientific Society and Field Club's Transactions volume 7

'An Old Inverness School' *ibid.* volume 9

'More Light on Scottish History' *ibid.* volume 9

BARRON Hugh 'Notes on the Ness Valley' Transactions of the Inverness Gaelic Society volume 43

BARRON James 'Armed Figure in Greyfriars' Churchyard' Inverness Scientific Society and Field Club's Transactions volume 4

Northern Highlands in the Nineteenth Century Carruthers & Sons, Inverness Three volumes 1903 to 1913

BARRON Roderick 'S. Adamnan and his Life of S. Columba' Transactions of the Inverness Gaelic Society volume 41

BOYD Herbert C. 'The Common Good' Inverness Scientific Society and Field Club's Transactions volume 8

BRANDER Michael *The Original Scotch* Hutchinson, London 1974

BURT Edmund *Letters from a Gentleman in the North of Scotland* S. Birt, London 1754 and re-published John Donald Publishers Ltd. Edinburgh 1974

BUTTER D. 'The Boar Stone' Inverness Scientific Society and Field Club's Transactions volume 9

CAMERON George *A History and Description of the Town of Inverness* Kenneth Douglas, James Smith and Donald Fraser, Inverness 1847

CARRUTHERS Robert *Highland Notebook* Adam and Charles Black, Edinburgh 1843

BIBLIOGRAPHY

CARRUTHERS Walter 'Stent as an Imperial Tax' Inverness Scientific Society and Field Club's Transactions volume 1
Comments made during the visit to Bunchrew by members of the Inverness Scientific Society and Field Club on 20 July 1878 and recorded in their Transactions volume 1

CHURCH OF SCOTLAND *Centenary Souvenir 1863-1963* of Merkinch (St Mark's) Church a pamphlet, a copy of which is in the Inverness Public Library

COURIER Inverness File copies of this publication are available in the Inverness Public Library and at the Courier Office

FRANCK Richard 'Northern Memoirs' Transactions of the Scottish History Society 1899 volume

FRASER James *Chronicles of the Frasers*, commonly known as the *Wardlaw Manuscript* Scottish History Society 1905

FRASER John *Reminiscences of Inverness; its People and Places* self-published 1905

FRASER-MACKINTOSH Charles *Invernessiana* 'Forsyth', Advertiser Office; John Noble, Castle Street and J.H. MacKenzie, Highland Club Inverness 1875
'The Chantry Altars and Chaplains of St. Mary's, Inverness 1359-1593' Inverness Scientific Society and Field Club's Transactions volume 4

FULLERTON & Co. *The Topographical, Statistical and Historical Gazetteer of Scotland* 1842

GOSSIP James Alexander 'The Hammermen of Inverness' Inverness Scientific Society and Field Club's Transactions volume 8

GROOME Francis H. (editor) *Ordnance Gazetteer of Scotland*, a Survey of Scottish Topography, Statistical, Biographical and Historical volume 4 1883

HAY A. Penrose Address given and later published in book form. Northern Chronicle, Inverness 1885

INVERNESS HARBOUR ACT 1847

LEES J. Cameron *A History of the County of Inverness* Blackwood & Sons Edinburgh and London 1897

MACCULLOCH Paper read to members of the Inverness Scientific Society and Field Club during their excursion to Essich on 1 August 1925 and printed in their Transactions volume 9

MACDONALD Reverend Archibald *The Old Lords of Lovat and Beaufort* Northern Counties Newspaper and Publishing Co. Ltd. Inverness 1934
'The Presbytery of Inverness 1632-1644' Transactions of the Inverness Gaelic Society volume 38

MACDONALD Donald 'The Glasgow Bank Disaster' Scots Magazine (Thomson, Dundee) February 1979

MACDONALD Kenneth Presidential Address Inverness Scientific Society and Field Club's Transactions volume 5

MACINTOSH Murdoch *A History of Inverness* Highland News Inverness 1939

MACKAY Donald *Scotland Farewell* Paul Harris Publishing Edinburgh 1980

MACKAY W.R. AND BOYD H.C. (editors) *Records of Inverness* New Spalding Club 1911 two volumes

MACKENZIE Alexander 'The Gaelic Origins of Local Names' Inverness Scientific and Field Club's Transactions volume 3

MACKENZIE T.C. *The Story of a Scottish Voluntary Hospital* Northern Chronicle, Inverness 1946
The Further History of a Scottish Voluntary Hospital Northern Chronicle, Inverness 1950

MACLAUGHLIN Reverend Frank J.L. *The Old High Church* a pamphlet, a copy of which is in the Inverness Public Library

MACLEAN John *Reminiscences of a Clachnacuddin Nonagenarian* Donald MacDonald, Inverness 1886
Sketches of Highland Families John Noble Inverness 1895

MITCHELL Alexander *Inverness Kirk Session Records 1661-1800* R. Carruthers, Inverness 1902

MITCHELL Joseph *Reminiscences of my Life in the Highlands* in two volumes first published 1883 and re-published by David and Charles 1971

MUIR Richard *Riddles of the British Landscape* Thames & Hudson London 1981

NOBLE John *Miscellanea Invernessiana* Eneas MacKay, Stirling 1902

POCOCKES *Pocockes' Tours* Scottish History Society volume 1 1887

ROSS Alexander *Freemasonry in Inverness* Courier Office, Inverness 1877
'Old Inverness' Inverness Scientific Society and Field Club's Transactions volume 2
'Ancient Churches and Chapels in Inverness' *ibid.* volume 6
'Old Inverness' *ibid.* volume 8

SALMOND J.B. *Wade in Scotland* Moray Press Edinburgh and London 1934

SINCLAIR Sir John *Inverness 1793* an extract from the First Statistical Account of Scotland Pentland Press, Thurso

SMOUT T.C. *A History of the Scottish People 1560-1830* Collins 1969 and Fontana, London 1972

SUTER James *Memorabilia of Inverness* originally weekly articles in the Inverness Courier 1822 and then in book form Donald Macdonald Inverness 1887

TAYLOR Alistair and Henrietta *The Book of the Duffs* two volumes Wm. Brown, Castle Street, Edinburgh 1914

THOMSON Francis *Highland Waterway* a pamphlet published by 'Graphics', Balloch, Inverness 1972

WALLACE Thomas D. Manuscript Notes a copy of which is now in the Inverness Public Library

WIMBERLEY Captain Douglas *The Hospital of Inverness and Dunbar's Hospital* Northern Chronicle, Inverness 1893

Index

Abban 119
Abban Street 57, 108, 120
Abbey Cottage 120
Abbey Street 120
Aberarder 103, 122
Aberdeen 32, 57, 81, 93, 169, 171, 175, 178,196, 204
Abertarff House 100
Aboyne, Earl of 153
Abriachan 114, 129, 166, 202
Academy, See "School, Academy"
Academy Park, See "Farraline Park"
Academy Street 35, 38, 45, 76, 82, 96, 100, 101, 102, *et. seq.*, 161, 205
Ach-an-Eas 63,
Adair, Sir Robert 79
Adam, John 92
"Advertiser" 167
Aird 119, 154, 203
Air-field 186
Air-raid Shelter 18
Aitken, Dr 167
A.I. Welders 107, 204
Albert, Prince Consort 171
Aldourie 154
Ale 112, 194, 200
Ale Taster 87
Alexander II 19, 20, 21, 115, 209

Alexander III 127, 210
Alexander of Lochalsh, See "Lochalsh, Alexander of"
Alexander Place 20, 45, 121
Altar of Saint Michael 181
Alter (Altyre?), Laird of 128
An Comunn Gaidhealach 100
Anderson, Baker 107
Anderson, George 92, 166
Anderson, Isabel Harriet 158
Anderson, James 7
Anderson, John 70
Anderson Street 158, 166
Angus, Earl of 209
Appleyard, R. 172
Apprentices 45
Aquavite 71
Arbroath 20, 21, 22, 23, 108
"Archaelogia Scotia" 54, 70
Archery 109
Architect, Burgh 55
Ardconnel Street 35
Ardconnel Terrace 45
Ardersier 55, 80, 81, 104, 173
Ardross 63, 121, 142, 180
Ardross Street 63, 114, 124, 171
Ardross Terrace 63
Argyll, Duke of 42,143, 179
Argyllshire Militia 59
Armourers 71
Arms, Burgh 20, 24, 39, 40, 42, 49, 59

Arms, Provost Dunbar 28
Arms, Scottish Royal 40, 42, 49, 76
Army, British 134
Army, Hanoverian 25, 79, 138
Army, Jacobite 111
Army, Parliamentarian 53, 110, 111, 191
Army, Royalist 10, 14, 53, 59, 96, 111, 122, 151
Arran, Earl of 133
Assembly of Free Church 106, 164
Assembly, General, of the Church of Scotland 35, 36, 137
Assynt 77
Atheneum 82
Atholl, Earl of 83, 151
Attadale 121
Auchindoun, Lord 132
Augustus Frederick, Prince 133
Auld Castle 109, 139, 181
Auld Ditch, See "Fosse"
Auldearn 125, 191
Aultmuniach 141, 152
Aultnaskiach 152, 153
Avoch 50, 51

Back Vennel, See "Baron Taylor Street"
Badenoch 19, 57, 81, 141, 172, 173
Badenoch, Lord 132
Bailies 27, 31, 44, 57, 58, 83, 86, 87, 151, 158, 208, 210
Baillie, Provost Alexander 137
Baillie of Dochfour 118, 134, et. seq.
Baillie of Hoprigg and Lamington 149
Baillie, John 138, 156
Baillie, Bailie Robert 137
Baillie, Robert 138
Baillie, William 134, 138
Bailzie, Robert 138

Bain, William 43
Bakers 42
Balbeg 154
Baldwin, Stanley 43
Baliol, King John 50, 134
Ballachulish 121, 205
Ballads 104, 105
Ballifeary 65, 69, 124
Balliol College 134
Balmore, Lord 132
Balnain 155
Balnain House 121, 122
Bane, Donald See "Donald Bane"
Banff 136, 178, 196
Banishment 89
Bank, British Linen 81, 135, 204
Bank, Caledonian 73, 82, 123, 204
Bank, City of Glasgow 123, 204
Bank, Commercial 100, 160, 204
Bank, Lane 26, 94, 164, 175
Bank, National 95, 204
Bank, Royal of Scotland 187
Bank, Savings 204
Bank, of Scotland 73, 123, 188, 204
Bank Street 26, 62, 106, 161, 164
Bannockburn 127
Barbour, Daniel 138
Barbour, James 29
Barmuchatie 29
Barnard, Alderman Sir John, M.P. 112, 194
Barnhill 35, 213
Baron Taylor Street 93, 105, 201
Barron, Dr Evan MacLeod 51, 127, 165, 168
Barron, Eveline 165
Barron, James 120, 165, 167
Bass, Michael Arthur 136
Bass, Nellie 136

Batchen's Lithograph   86
Baxter, Rev. Douglas   162
Beaufort   42
Beauly   17, 58
Beauly Firth   8
Beauly River   41
Beauly Street   119
Becher, Richard   155
Becket, Thomas à   22
Beef   200
Bee-Hives   184
Beer   112, 194, 200
Bell   84, 110
Bell, Dr Andrew   106
Bell's Park, See "Farraline Park"
Bengal   155
Benson   16
Bernard, Charles   161
Berwickshire   126
Bewest the Waters of the
   Ness   92, 114 et. seq.
Bible   148
Big Green   108
Bird Stuffer   204, 205
Birkenhead, Viscount   43
Birnie, Arthur   25
Bishop Eden, See "Eden,
   Bishop"
Bishop of Moray and Ross   62,
   108, 124, 128
Bishop's Road   124
Bisset   154, 209
Black Bridge, See "Bridge,
   Waterloo"
Blackfriars   18 et. seq., 113
Black Isle   20, 116
Blacksmiths   177
Black Vennel, See "Baron Taylor
   Street"
Black Watch   183
Blanketing   198, 199
Bleaching Green   53, 60, 198
Blund, Geoffrey   12
Boar   143
Boarstone   180, 181
Boat-building   198

Boating-pond   130
Boece   186
Boethius   8
Bogbain   214
de Bois, Alexander   143
Bombay   156
Bona   9
Bonkhill   208
Bonnets   148
Bonnet, Straw, Makers   204
Bookless Brothers   205
Book-seller   205
Borlum, See "MacKintosh of
   Borlum"
Borthwick Castle   150
Bow Court   99, 198
Boy Scouts   36
Brahan Seer   61
Brandy   113, 194, 201
Braycroft, Sir William de   50
Brechin   63, 134, 149
Bremner, Alexander   66
Brewers   71, 72, 136, 201, 202
Brewery   198, 201
Brewing   71, 201
Brewsters   201
Brey   138
Bridge, Black See "Bridge,
   Waterloo"
Bridge, Blue   16, 17
Bridge End   38
Bridge, Friars'   20
Bridge, Greig Street   61
Bridge, Infirmary   61
Bridge, Longman - 117
Bridge, Ness   16, 19, 29, 39, 45,
   57 et. seq., 88, 115, 159
Bridges, Islands   60, 185
Bridge Street   10, 20, 29, 53, 59,
   60, 70, 71, 74 et. seq., 160, 201,
   204
Bridge, Tomnahurich
   (Millerton)   129
Bridge, Waterloo   48, 60, 77,
   112, 114
Bristol   135

Broadstone 112, 142, 181
Broadstone Park 181
Brogue Makers 177
Broomtown 140
Bruce Gardens 114, 129
Bruce, Robert I 21, 51, 52, 143, 149, 159
Brude 9, 10, 23
Buchanan 8
Bught 42, 45, 48, 60, 130, 143, 156, 157, 198
Building Standards 69, 71
Bull 180
Bunchrew 129, 145, 148
Burgesses 10, 11, 21, 31, 34, 44, 45, 46, 50, 74, 76, 178, 198, 200, 208
Burgh Arms, See "Arms, Burgh"
Burgh Council, See "Council, Burgh"
Burgh Court, See "Court, Burgh"
Burghead 9, 195, 196
Burgh Officers' 48
Burgh Surveyors, See "Surveyor, Burgh"
Burgh Treasurer, See "Treasurer, Burgh"
Burial Ground 101, 108, 109, 110, 113, 141
Burning (of Town) 57, 70, 71
Burns, Robert 72, 95, 158
Burt, Edmund 38, 88, 146, 184, 185, 195
Burton, Lord 134, 136, 137
Burton-upon-Trent 134
'Buses 106, 116
Butter 105, 200
Byrnaye, Arthur, See "Birnie"
Byset Walter, See "Bisset"

Cabers 196
Cabinet Makers 205
Cabinet Meeting 42, 43
Caiplich 129
Caithness 62, 190
Caithness, Earl of 209

"Caledonia" 82, 192
Caledonian Bank, See "Bank, Caledonian"
Caledonian Canal, See "Canal, Caledonian
Caledonian Football Club, See "Football, Caledonian Club"
Caledonian Hotel, See "Hotel, Caledonian"
Caledonian Road 114
Cambridge 155
Camel 40
Cameron Clan 42
Campbell Clan 42, 59
Campbell, James 99
Campbell, Matthew 60
Campbelltown, See "Ardersier"
Campfield 46, 153
Canal, Caledonian 60, 114, 117, 119, 129, 155, 196, 197, 205
Canal, Crinan 196
Candle Maker 93
Candlemas Fair, See "Fair, Candlemas"
Canmore, See "Malcolm Canmore"
Canterbury, Archbishop of 63
Capel Inch 77, 192
Car, See "Motor Car"
Carding Mill 199
Carey, David 182
Carnarc Point 117
Carn Laws 213
Carpenters 42, 58, 177
Carr Bridge 103
Carriages 59
Carruthers, Dr Robert 11, 164, 165
Carruthers, Walter 165, 167
Carse 108, 119, 213
Carseland 16
Castle 10, 16, 45, 50 et. seq., 60, 61, 72, 74, 91, 92, 107, 111, 127, 149, 150, 151, 152
Castle Haugh 199
Castlehill 10, 45, 55, 91, 110,

136, 139, 149, 141, 159, 184, 194
Castle Leather 49
Castle Raat 75, 161
Castle Street 35, 68, 70 et. seq., 82, 175, 201, 204
Castle Stuart 78
Castle Tolmie 91, 146
Castle Urquhart 50, 143
Castle Wynd 10, 39, 92, 166
"Catch-My-Pal" Hall 107
Cathedral, See "Church, St. Andrew's Cathedral"
Catholic Church, See "Church, Roman Catholic"
Catholic Emancipation 155
Cattle 111, 170
Cava 20, 22
Cavell Gardens 81
Caviare 196
Celts 6, 9, 10, 12, 87, 166
Cemetery 114, 128
Cemetery Road 114
Central Hall Picture House 161
Central School, See "School, Central
Chamberlain, Austen 43
Chamberlain, King's 44
Chamber of Commerce 92
Chancellor, Lord High 43
Chandeliers 49, 169
Chanonry 17, 190
Chanonry Point 8
Chapel of the Green 108, 110, 119
Chapel of the Holy Rood 140
Chapel, St. Mary's 17, 108, 109
Chapel Street 19, 20, 45, 108 et. seq., 193
Chapel Tweedmouth 67
Chapel Yard 20, 72, 109, 111, 112
Charity 26, 137
Charles Edward Stuart See "Prince Charles Edward Stuart"

Charles I 64, 143, 151
Charles II 40, 143
Charleston, South Carolina 160
Charters 26, 31, 83, 111, 116, 138, 139, 181, 187, 190, 193, 208 et. seq.
Chattan Clan 150
Cheap Jacks 105
Cherryble Brothers 157
Cheese 105
Cheeses, Battle of the 72
Chen, Sir Reginald le 50
Cherry Flat 113
Cherry Shott 113, 193, 197
Chevalier, The 'Old Pretender' 49
Chisholm, A. 145
Chisholm Clan 42, 125
Chisholm, John de 124
Cholera 36, 67, 121, 159, 170
Christianity 9, 155
Church Attendance 11, 24, 60
Church, East 105, 106
Church Elders, See "Elders"
Church, Episcopal 62, 63, 101
Church, Free 101, 105, 115, 164
Church, Free North 106
Church, Free West 115
Church Lane 100, 106
Church, Methodist 79, 96, 102, 103, 106, 199
Church, Old High 10, 23 et. seq., 26, 31, 36, 38, 85, 90, 99, 101, 102, 105, 108, 109, 110, 111, 119, 122, 146, 166, 187, 194, 201
Church, Protestant 24, 128, 150, 151
Church, Queen Street 116
Church, Roman Catholic 23, 24, 40, 62, 87, 96, 106, 123, 150
Church, Rood 58
Church, St, Andrew's Cathedral 62 et. seq.
Church, St. Columba's 74, 114

Church, St. John's 62, 99
Church, St. Mark's 115
Church, St. Mark's (Gaelic) 26,
  31, 100, 101, 122
Church of Scotland 106
Church Street 10, 19, 26, 49, 57,
  63, 70, 71, 74, 81, 86, 89, 92, 93
  et. seq., 112, 117, 160, 168, 198,
  204
Church, Trinity 116
Church, West 26, 122
Churchill, Winston S. 43
Cider 16
Cinema 161
Cinema, La Scala 96, 103, 161
Circuit Court of Justiciary, See
  "Justiciary, Court of"
Citadel 14 *et. seq.*, 26, 49, 59,
  110, 112, 113, 158, 186, 193,
  194, 199
City of Glasgow Bank, See
  "Bank, City of Glasgow"
Civic Hospitality 184
Civil War 151, 171
Clach Boys 104
Clach-na-Cuddin 80, 105, 112
Clach-na-Gaick 213
Clachnaharry 57, 69, 110, 118,
  124
Clan Chattan, See "Chattan
  Clan"
Clan Gillean 80
Clanranald 42, 97, 127
Clans 42, 52
Claret 48, 146
Clark, William 173
Claypots 213
Clearances 77, 89
Clerk, Town 6, 20, 22, 38, 48,
  87, 88, 110, 140, 173
Clive 155
Clock 16, 79, 84, 85
Clogie, William 138
Clothing 177, 199
Cluny 42
Clyde 93

Cnoc-na Gobhar 188
"Coach and Horses" 201
Coaches 81, 95, 175
Coal 194
Coal Merchant 205
Cobb, John 187
Cod 200
Colbert 139, 142
College, Technical, See "School,
  Technical (College)"
"Colonel Anne" 96, 117
Colonial Secretary 43
Commander-in-Chief in
  Scotland 174
Commercial Bank, See "Bank,
  Commercial"
Commissary Coup 17
Commissioners on Highland
  Roads and Bridges 61
Commissioners on Municipal
  Corporations in Scotland 46
Commissioners of Supply 56
Common Good Fund 44/48,
  111, 185, 193, 196, 211
Common Muir 213
Commonwealth 16, 17, 125, 171
Comte de St. Pol, See "St. Pol,
  Comte de"
Comyn, Richard 23
Concordia et Fidelitas 40, 41
Constable of Inverness
  Castle 50, 51, 52, 55, 127,
  134, 149
Convention of Royal
  Burghs 143, 178
Cook 200
Cook, John 192
Cook, Joseph 190
Coopers 177
Cordwainers, See "Shoemakers"
Cork Cutter 204
Corpach 197
Corrichie 150
"Corries The" 161
Council, Burgh 11, 14, 22, 24,
  26, 33, 34, 40, 57, 62, 63, 83,

91, 96, 106, 116, 143, 146, 148, 152, 166, 169, 193
Council, Chamber 42, 43, 44, 48
Council, County 56, 82, 91, 96, 136, 153, 157
Council, District 24, 111
Council, Highland Region 116
Councillors, Burgh 24, 62, 81, 82, 95, 145, 174, 176
Councillors, County 82, 137
Count de St. Pol, See "St. Pol, Comte de"
Courier 74, 81, 83, 86, 89, 93, 95, 101, 106, 107, 112, 116, 117, 118, 120, 125, 128, 152, 157, 160, 161, 163 et. seq., 175, 182, 192
Court, Burgh 86, 87, 107, 137, 187
Court, District 56
Court, Head 137
Court-House 40, 55, 56, 86, 89, 91, 153, 160
Covenanters 72, 77
Cradlehall 141
Craig Dunain Hospital 67
Craig Phadrig 9, 10
Crawford, Earl of 134
Cream 200
Criminals 88, 90
Crofts 213
Cromartie, Earl of 147
Cromarty 71, 154, 173, 195, 196
Cromlix, John Hay of, See "Hay of Cromlix, John"
Cromwell 14 et. seq., 25, 49, 110, 111, 179
Cross 10, 16, 69, 78, 80, 81, 142, 175, 182
Crown (District) 10, 70
Crown (Monarchy) 12, 21, 44, 45, 52, 111, 144, 178
Crown o' the Causey 68
Crown Road 75
Crown School, See "School, Crown"

Cruives 213
Culcabock 46, 92, 107, 141, 186
Culcabock Road 74
Culclachy 71
Culduthel Road 71
Culloden 31, 46, 112, 143, 148, 183, 196, 201
Culloden, Battle of 25, 35, 55, 59, 68, 97, 111, 122, 125, 148, 149, 154
Cumberland, Duke of 48, 55, 68, 78, 79, 97, 117, 138, 148
Cumine, John 57
Cumming, William 20, 145
Cunningham, William 89
Curfew 25, 69
Curling 95, 129
Customs 44, 74, 76, 188, 190, 193, 211, 213
Customs House 76, 175
Cuthbert, Provost Alexander 73, 140, 142
Cuthbert, Alexander 142
Cuthbert, Provost George 22, 139, 140, 141
Cuthbert, George 142
Cuthbert, Dr George 142
Cuthbert Family 23, 43, 44, 139 et. seq.
Cuthbert, James 142
Cuthbert, Provost James 139, 140
Cuthbert, John 140, 141
Cuthbert, Lewis 141, 142
Cuthbert, Margaret 110, 141
Cuthbert, Thomas 87
Cycling 83, 159

Dalarossie 165
Dalcross 30, 58
Dalhousie Earl of 175
Dallas Bailie 152, 153
Dalneigh 26, 100, 125
Damisdaille 70, 71
Darlington 204
Daveemont See "Daviot"

David I 50
David II 108, 211
Davidson D. & A. 205
Daviot 214
Deacons 31, 177
Dean of Guild 31, 84, 158
Debtors 86, 88, 90
Deer 10, 81, 195
"Deer's Head" 201
Defe, Matilda 109
"Defiance" Coach 81
Dempster 48, 86
Denain See "Dunain"
Dentist 43
Derwent Lord 43
Devonshire, Duke of 137
Dickens, Charles 157
Dingwall 11, 50, 57, 103, 174
Disruption 105, 160
Distillery 198
Distilling 71, 89
District Council, See "Council,
   District"
District Court, See "Court,
   District"
Dochfour 95, 134, 135, 136, 137
Dochgarroch 129
Dock 113
"Dolphin" 196
Dominican Friars, See "Friars"
Donald Bane 127, 154
Donald, Lord of the Isles See
   "Isles, Lord of"
Doomsdale 70
Doomsday Book 70
Dornoch 173, 190
Douglas, Earl of 52
Dow, Finlay 72
Drainage 101
Drakies 139, 140, 145, 148, 211,
   213
Draper 205
Dredge, Mr of Bath 185
Dromedary 38, 40
Drumden 183
Drummer 46

Drummond 12, 45, 46, 128, 153
Drummond, Captain 125
Drummond Street 96, 205
Drummuir See "Duff,
   Alexander"
Drummuir, Lady 96, 97, 99
Duff, Alexander 96
Duff of Muirtown 117, 121, 149,
   157
Duff Street 45, 92, 118
Duke of Inverness 133
"Duke of Richmond" 196
"Duke of Wellington" 81
Dulcattock 191
Dumfries 136, 164, 204
Dunabban Street 120
Dunachton 83, 151
Dunain 134, 136, 149
Dunaincroy 31, 129, 130, 170
Dunbar (Family) 29
Dunbar (Town) 14
Dunbar, Provost Alexander 27,
   36
Dunbar, James 29, 30, 32, 33
Dunbar, James Roy 30
Dunbar-Nasmith 163
Dunbar's Hospital 19, 26 et.
   seq., 99, 102, 103, 118, 119
Dunbar, Thomas 32
Duncan King 141
Dundas, Doctor Alexander 35
Dundee 178, 193
Dunean, See "Dunaincroy"
Dunhill 144
Dunkeld, David, Bishop of 210
Dunlichity 78
Durward, Allan 210
Dutch Vessels 195
Dyll, Marjory 109
Dymingisdale 70
Eagle 180
Earl of Inverness 132 et. seq.
Earlston 126
Earthquake 85
East Church, See "Church, East"
Eastgate 70, 74 et. seq.

East India Company   155
East Indies   154
Edderton   181
Eden, Bishop Robert   62, 64
Eden Court   64, 160
Edinburgh   14, 20, 40, 49, 57, 65, 77, 81, 85, 148, 171
Edinburgh Castle   132
Edinburgh, Duke of   42
Edoua of the Auldcastle   109
Education See "Individual School"
Edward I   50, 51
Edward IV   52, 171
Elders   27
Election, General   90
Electricity   85, 100, 130
Elephant   39, 40, 41, 196
Elfland   126
Elgin   62, 112, 156, 157, 178
Ellice, Edward, M.P.   175
Embankment   186
Empire Theatre   161, 162
Engineer   14, 53, 204
England   171
English (Language)   100, 106, 115
English (People)   10, 18, 50, 120, 188, 201
Episcopacy   25, 138, 146
Episcopal Church, See "Church, Episcopal"
Episcopal School, See "School, Bishop Eden's"
Escape of Prisoners, See "Prisoners, Escape of"
Essich   150, 180
Established Church, See "Church of Scotland"
Ettles, John   95
Ettles, Mary   166
Eustacius, Master   108
Evenus   8
Exchange   69, 76, 77, 78, 79, 80, 81, 95, 101, 105, 116, 156, 175, 183, 204

Excise   89, 173, 202
Execution See also "Public Execution"   70, 86, 92, 151, 186
Explosion   93
Fair Andrew's   77
Fair, Candlemas   77
Fair, Martinmas   77
Fair, Marymas   77
Fair, Peter   214
Fair, St. Mark's   214
Fair, St. Thomas's   214
Fair, Wool   77
Fairfield   110
Fairfield Road   114
Fairs   76, 104
Falconer, Hugh   172, 174
Falcon Square   205
Falkirk Tryst   170
Farm, Blench   83
Farmers   204
Farraline Park   63, 106, 164, 170
Farrar   8
Feast of St. Andrew   214
Feinn   126, 127
Ferintosh   34, 71, 72, 145
Ferry   116, 117, 122, 213
Fettes, Sir William   116
Feu Duty   20, 22, 45, 115, 137, 211
Field Club   6, 88, 100, 166 st. seq., 182
Fife, Earl of   50
51st Highland Division   203
Findhorn   195, 196
Finsbury   156
Fir   17, 191, 192
Fire   57, 70, 71, 82, 96, 161
Fire Brigade   36, 82, 83
Fireworks   79
First Footing   79
Fish   181, 194
Fishing Rod Makers   204
Fishings   30, 45, 211, 213
Fish Merchants   205
Fitch, Colonel   191

Fitzwarine 51
Flemings 6
Flogging 158
Flood 10, 22, 58, 60, 91, 119, 159, 186
Flora MacDonald, See "MacDonald, Flora"
Flour 200
Fontenoy 148
Football 109
Football, Caledonian Club 119
Forbes, A. 145
Forbes Clan 42
Forbes of Culloden 42, 48, 71, 91, 110, 118, 143 *et. seq.*, 169
Forbes, Doctor 66
Forbes, Donald 34, 119
Forbes, Duncan 78, 143, 145, 146
Forbes, Duncan George 148
Forbes Fountain 81
Forbes, John 143, 144, 145, 146, 147, 148, 205
Forbes, Lord President, See "Forbes of Culloden"
Forest 213
Forfarshire 198
Forres 9, 93, 103, 157, 178
Forsyth, Ebenezer 167
Forsyth, William 154
Forsyth, William Banks 167
Fort Augustus 70, 74, 137, 191
Fort George 55, 74, 80, 173, 194, 195
Fortrose 104, 173, 196
Fort William 14, 173, 197
Fosse 11, 45, 70, 72, 209
Foul Pool 100, 101, 102
Foundry 114, 198
Fox 195
France 14, 49, 150
Franciscan Friars, See "Friars"
Franck, Richard 15
Fraser & Co. A. 205
Fraser, A. & S. 205
Fraser of Achnagairn 65
Fraser, Alexander 92

Fraser, Reverend Alexander 37
Fraser, Betty 173
Fraser, Clan 41, 42, 49, 125, 127, 146, 147
Fraser, Donald 97
Fraser of Fairfield 110
Fraser, James 37, 49
Fraser, James of Brae 72, 138
Fraser, Reverend James 15, 17, 72, 118
Fraser, Jane 155
Fraser, John 117, 192
Fraser of Lovat, See "Lovat"
Fraser-MacKintosh 110, 118, 127, 134, 153, 154, 184
Fraser, Miss May 6
Fraser of Reelig 145
Fraser, General Simon M.P. 152
Fraser, Sir Simon of Inverallochy 58
Fraser Street 100
Fraser, Thomas of Struy 17, 138
Fraser of Torbreck 65
Free Church, See "Church, Free"
Freedom of the Burgh 45, 142, 160, 184
Freemasons 84, 174
Free West Church, See "Church, Free West"
Freskyn, Allan 108
Friars 18 *et. seq.*, 113, 140, 212
Friars' Bridge, See "Bridge, Friars'"
Friars' Croft 20, 22
Friars' Lane 19
Friars' Shott 22, 74, 93
Friars' Street 18, 19, 108
Friary 18 *et. seq.*, 40, 103, 140
Friendly Society 178
Fusiliers Regiment 33
Fyffe, Will 161

Gaelic 12, 26, 100, 106, 111, 115, 122, 126, 157, 174, 186, 193

Gaelic Church, See "Church, St. Mary's (Gaelic)"
Gairbraid 181
Gairloch 42
Gait, See "Gate"
Galloway, George 167
Galloway, Lord of 127
Galloway, Ronald of 127
Gallowmuir 31
Gallows 70
Gardenstone, Lord 94
Gartallie 129
Garter, Order of 49
Garthie, Lord 132
Gas Lighting 100
Gas Works 112
Gate 74
Geddes, Sir Eric 43
Gellions Hotel, See "Hotel, Gellions"
General Assembly of the Church of Scotland, See "Assembly, General of the Church of Scotland"
General Election, See "Election, General"
George IV 156
George V 42, 133
George VI 67, 133
"George & Dragon" 201
George, Duke of Gordon 152
George, Margaret nin 78
Gilzean, Thomas 64
Gingerbread 104
Glasgow 82, 123, 196, 197
Glasgow Bank, See "Bank, City of Glasgow"
Glebe 23, 108
Glebe Street 108
Glenalbyn Road 95
Glencharnich 154
Glenelg 135, 156
Glenelg, Lord (Charles Grant, Junior) 95, 96, 155, 197
Glengarry 42, 145, 170
Glenmoriston 58, 59, 191

Glenroy 135
Glensheil 135
Glenstrathfarrar 192
Glenurquhart 80, 129, 154, 188, 202
Glovers 71, 92, 177, 199
Goats 184, 188, 194
Godsman, Captain 152, 153
Godsman's Walk 152
Goldsmiths 177
Golf Course 186
Gollan, Gilbert 87
"Goodfellow, Robin" 93
Goodfellow, Miss Carol 7
Goodwin, Robin, See "Goodfellow, Robin"
Gordon, Sir Adam 149
Gordon, Alexander 53, 149
Gordon, Alister 112
Gordon Castle 153
Gordon, Clan 183
Gordon, Duchess of 152, 169
Gordon, Duke of 55, 91, 132, 133, 149 et. seq.
Gordon, George 149, 150, 151, 152
Gordon, Sir Robert 68
Grain 195
Grammar School, See "School, Grammar"
Granary 16, 198
Granite 61, 198
Grant, Alexander 154, 155
Grant, Major Alpin 158
Grant Brothers 157
Grant of Bught, Duncan 156
Grant, Charles M.P. Senior 154
Grant, Charles M.P. Junior, See "Glenelg, Lord"
Grant Clan 42, 154 et. seq.
Grant, Colonel 157
Grant, Duncan 42, 201
Grant, James 157
Grant, Reverend John 157
Grant, Laird of 110, 118, 134, 157, 188

de Grant, Lawrence   154
Grant, Robert   155, 156
Grant Street   85, 114, 158
Grantown   180
"Grapes"   201
Grass   111, 185
Gray, Mr of Glasgow   204
Great Glen   56, 57
Green, Chapel of the, See
  "Chapel of the Green"
Green of Muirtown, See
  "Muirtown, Green of"
Greenwood, Sir Hamer   43
Greig Street   114, 123
Greig Street Bridge, See "Bridge,
  Greig Street"
Greyfriars   17, 18 et. seq., 72
Griffiths-Boscawen, Sir
  Arthur   43
Grilse   200
Grocer   91
Grouse   200
Guildry   38, 177, 198, 199
Gundie   104
Gunn Clan   68
Gun-Smith   204, 205

Haco King of Norway   21
Haddock   200
Hairdressers   204
Halifax, Nova Scotia   89
Hamilton Street   75, 161
Hammermen   42, 142, 176, 198,
  199
Hanes, German Engineer   14
Hangman   48, 88
Hanover, House of   49, 53
Hanoverians   53, 79, 96
Hanoverian Army, See "Army,
  Hanoverian"
Harbour   11, 45, 48, 69, 101,
  110, 111, 112, 193, 194, 195,
  196, 197, 201
Harbour Trustees   111, 190, 193,
  197
Hare   186, 195, 200

Harlaw, Battle of   52, 57, 139
Harvest Festival   115
Hats   148
Hatters   204
Haugh Brewery   201
Haugh, Burgh   11, 45, 128, 199,
  211
Haugh, Castle   199
Haugh Tap   201
Hawley, General   79, 146
Hay   200
Hay, Sir John   198
Hay of Cromlix, John   135
de Hay, Gilbert   210
Hay, Penrose   172, 175, 179
de Hay, William   208
Health   120
Hebrew   148
Hedon   136
"Helen MacGregor"   196
Hemp   198, 199
Henderson, Robert   193
Hendery, C. A.   167
Henry VIII   171
Hepburn, Bailie John   26, 27
Herring   107, 193, 195, 200
Hides   87, 199
Higginbottom, Richard   7
Highland Club   82
Highlander   201
Highlanders   52, 59, 71, 87, 124
"Highland Galley"   191
Highland Games   170
Highland Railway, See "Railway,
  Highland"
Highland Regional Council, See
  "Council, Highland Region"
Highland Road   172
Highlands and Islands
  Development Board   91, 205
High School, See "School, High"
High Street   10, 57, 59, 69, 70,
  73, 74 et. seq., 104, 112, 160,
  163, 175, 205
Hogmanay   79, 80
"Hole in the Wall"   201

Holm 31, 198
Holm, MacKintosh of, See "MacKintosh of Holm"
Holm Mills 199
Honey 200
Honorius III, Pope 18
Horne, Sir Robert S. 43
Horns Hotel, See "Hotel, Horns"
Horse 64, 180
Horse Artillery 201
Horse Market, See "Market, Horse"
Horse Racing 109, 125, 129, 130, 169
Hospital 21, 22, 26, 28, 36
Hospitalers 82
Hospital, Royal Northern Infirmary 64 et. seq., 157, 159
Hossack, Provost John 55, 79
Hotel, Beverley's 168
Hotel, Caledonian 81, 93, 95, 96, 100, 137
Hotel, Ettle's 168
Hotel, Gellion's 93
Hotel, Horns 48, 79, 94, 138
Hotel, Mason's 94, 95
Hotel, Palace 136
Hotel, Station 103, 167
Hotel, Union 81, 82
Hotel, Waverley 167
Housemaid 200
Housing 120, 124, 125
Houston, Thomas, See "Howieson, Thomas"
Howdens 204
Howieson, Thomas 24, 25
Hunt 169, 186
Huntly, Earl of 53, 83, 91, 132, 134, 149, 150, 151, 183
Huntly, Marquis of 55, 118, 128, 132, 151, 153, 169
Huntly Place 45, 118, 119
Huntly Street 96, 103, 106, 118, 123, 161
Hurry, Colonel 78, 125
Hutchins & Co., Thomas 61

Ice Rink 130
Illicit Distilling 202
Incorporated Trades 42, 99, 142, 156, 177, 198
Independence, War of 51
India 136, 155
Indigo 121
Industrial Estate 186, 187
Infirmary, Aberdeen 32
Infirmary Bridge, See "Bridge, Infirmary"
Infirmary, Royal Northern, See "Hospital, Inverness Royal Infirmary"
Inglis, Alexander 160
Inglis, Henry 124
Inglis, John 160
Inglis, Miss K. 159
Inglis, Rev. Dr. 160
Inglis, Robert 159
Inglis Street 75, 103, 105, 106, 123, 160, 161
Inglis, Provost William 64, 80, 84, 85, 102, 110, 119, 158, 199
Inn 114, 116, 117, 129, 200
Invergarry 137
Invergordon 196
Inverlochy 14
Inverness Amenities Association 185
Inverness Burghs 85, 121, 135, 136, 147, 156
Inverness Civic Trust 122
Inverness County Council, See "Council, County"
Inverness Courier, See "Courier"
Inverness, Duchess of 133
Inverness, Duke of 133
Inverness, Earl of 132 et. seq.
Inverness Field Club, See "Field Club"
Inverness Golf Club 186
Inverness Hymn 156
Inverness Museum and Art Gallery, See "Museum"

Inverness Public Library, See "Library"

Inverness Royal Academy, See "School, Royal Academy"

Inverness Scientific Society and Field Club, See "Field Club"

Inverness Tartan   133

Inverness Theatre and Opera House Co. Ltd.   161

Inverness, Viscount   132, 152

Inverurie   57, 149, 180

Iona   9

Ireland   42

Irish   140

Irish Language, See "Gaelic"

Iron Foundry   204

Ironmonger   204

Ironpurs, Alexander   109

Iron Works   198

Irrwall, John   112

Island Bank   12, 45

Islands, Ness   19, 60, 183, 184, 185

Isles, Lord of the   52, 57, 69

Italian Warehousemen   205

Jack, William T.   55

Jack's the Exchange   204

Jacobites   48, 49, 53, 59, 71, 133, 147, 148, 152, 194

Jail   11, 55, 56, 60, 84, 86, 88, 89, 91, 153

Jamaica   141

James I   52, 149, 211

James II   40

James III   212

James IV   119

James V   113, 212

James VI and I   127, 171, 212

James, "Old Pretender"   133

Johnston, D. Russell M.P.   205

Johnstone, John   163

"Jolly Sailor"   201

Jolly, William   167

Journal, Inverness   157, 160, 164, 165, 169, 182, 199

Judges   184

Junor, Provost   183

Justice of the Peace   34

Justiciary, Circuit Court of   56, 160

Justiciary, Lords of   94

Kebbocks   105

Keith   103

Kennedy, Doctor   66

Kenneth, MacAlpin   11

Kenneth Street   114, 121

Keppoch   97

Kerr, Doctor   83

Kessock   20, 22, 116, 117, 213

Kessock Avenue   117

Kessock Road   117

Kessock Roads   17, 191, 192, 196

"Kicked Provost", See "Hossack, Provost"

Kilravock, Rose of   53, 146

Kincardine, Lord   132

Kingdom of Scotland   21

Kingsmills   45, 129, 140, 158, 159, 182, 214

Kingsmills Road   31, 74, 181, 182

King Street   45, 114, 119, 124, 125

Kingussie   135, 167

Kinloss   17

Kinmylies   124, 135

Kinnoull, Earl of   133

Kintail   78

Kirkgate   19

Kirking of the Council   24

Kirk Session   25, 26, 29, 30, 31, 32, 34, 36, 37, 38, 122, 156

Kirkwall   173

Knights of St. John of Jerusalem, See "Hospitalers"

Knocnagael   180

Knowles, Alexander   124

Knox, John   24, 71

"Lady Ann"   117, 192

Laigh Council House 38
Laigh Road 172
Laing, Alexander 85
Laing, John 34
Lamington 134
Lanark 134
Land-slide 73
Land-tax 179
Lang, Reverend Gavin 122
Lang, Matheson 123
Larach-an-Tighe-Mhor 10
Largs 21
La Scala Cinema, See "Cinema, La Scala"
Laying, John, See "Laing, John"
Leachkin 57, 114, 129
Lead Works 198
Leather 104
Le Balloch's Hill 70
Leith 18, 192, 193, 196
Levan, Earl of 77
Lewis 173
Leys 71, 134, 136
Liberal Party 205
Library 6, 7, 34, 36, 38, 107, 159
Library, Kirk Session 34, 36, 38
Lilburn, Colonel 19
Linen 199
Lint 33
Literary, Scientific and Antiquarian Society 166
Little Ferry 196
Little Theatre, See "Theatre, Little"
Liverpool 175, 197
Lloyd George 43
Lobster 200
Lochaber 128, 129
Lochaber, Lord 132
Lochalsh, Alexander of 52
Lochalsh Road 120
Loch Broom 89
Lochcarron 173
Loch Dochfour 129
Locheil 42, 97, 128
Lochend 129, 191

Loch Gorm 75, 95
Loch Lochy 127
Loch Maree 43
Loch-na-Sanais 95, 129
Loch Ness 9, 74, 114, 129, 187, 191
Lodge St. Andrew's 84, 95, 138, 174
Lodge St. John's 84, 95, 137, 142, 174
Lollius Urbicus 8
London 36, 65, 84, 112, 154, 175, 195
Longman 75, 101, 107, 111, 174, 181, 186, 193
Lord Advocate 147
Lord of the Isles, See "Isles, Lord of"
Lord Lyon 39, 40
Lord President of the Court of Session 160
Lossiemouth 196
Lotland Place 113
Loudon, Lord 96
Louis IX 190
Louis XIV 139, 142
Lovat 33, 78, 100, 145
Lovat, Lord 38, 49, 109, 111, 127, 128, 141, 147, 150, 152, 154, 191
Lovat, Master of 77, 127
Lower Kessock Street 116
Lowlanders 11

MacAlyshander, Reginald 124
McBean, Gillespie 31
MacBrayne's 197
McCulloch, Helen 172
MacDonald, Clan 42, 52, 57, 144
MacDonald, Flora 42, 56
MacDonald, Reverend Dr. D. 166
MacDonald, Doctor John 88
MacDonald & Morrison 205
MacDonald, Kenneth 110, 167

MacDonald of Keppoch   124
MacDonald, Sir Murdoch,
   M.P.   61
MacDonald of Sleat   145
MacDonell and Aros, Lord   145
MacDougall, Miss
   Margaret   214
MacDuff, Shaw   50
MacEwen, Sir Alexander   42,
   158, 182
MacGregor, Clan   42
MacHenrick   87
MacIntosh, See "MacKintosh"
MacKay, Alexander   89
MacKay, Clan   42
MacKay, Doctor Duncan   167
MacKay, Reverend James   62
MacKay, Roderick   89
MacKay, Provost William
   (Bobo)   158
MacKenzie, Alexander F.   182
MacKenzie, Clan   42, 183
MacKenzie, Gordon & Co.   199
MacKenzie, Hugh Breac   89
MacKenzie, James   34
MacKenzie, Provost Doctor
   John   160
MacKenzie, Murdoch   142
Mackie, George, Lord
   Mackie   205
MacKintosh, Sir Aeneas   54, 70,
   111
MacKintosh of Borlum   53, 183
MacKintosh, Clan   41, 42, 50,
   118, 143, 145, 147, 148, 149,
   150
MacKintosh of Dunachton   83
MacKintosh, Duncan   127
MacKintosh of Holm   110
MacKintosh, John of
   Aberarder   103
MacKintosh, Lachlan   96, 151
MacKintosh, Laird of   150, 183
MacKintosh of MacKintosh   128
MacKintosh, Malcolm   118
MacKintosh, Shaw   127

MacKintosh, Provost
   Phineas   43, 46, 47
MacLean Clan   42, 80
MacLean, John   73, 91, 113,
   194, See also "Nonagenarian"
MacLean, Provost William   80,
   159
MacLeay, Bird Stuffer   205
MacLeod Clan   42
MacLeod, Lord   147
MacLeod of MacLeod   59
MacNamara, Dr. T. J.   43
MacPherson Clan   42
MacPherson, Fishing Tackle
   Maker & Gunsmith   43, 205
MacRae Clan   42, 157
MacRae & Dick   205
MacRae, Duncan   78
MacTavish, Alexander   167, 204
MacWilliam, Donald, See
   "Donald Bane"
Madras Education System   106
Madras Street   115
Maggot   20, 99, 101, 113, 141, 193
Magistrates   19, 22, 24, 25, 32,
   33, 34, 35, 38, 48, 64, 78, 80,
   95, 101, 106, 110, 124, 146, 156,
   178, 183, 184, 194, 199
Magnus King of Norway   21
"Maid of Morven"   196
Major, John   57
Makferry, Cristina   83
Malcolm Canmore   10, 50, 52,
   127, 208
Malcolm IV   50
Malting   198
Malt-kilns   100, 102, 198
Manchester   157, 187
Manchester, Duchess of   169
Manse Place   20
Manure Manufacturer   204
Marble   198
Mar, Earl of   19, 52, 53, 57, 133
Margaret, Saint   64
Margaret Street   96, 105, 106,
   123

Marischal, David   209
Market Brae   75
Market, Cattle   75, 77
Market Cross, See "Cross"
Market, Feeing   76
Market, Fish   75, 76
Market, Flesh   75, 76
Market, Horse   77
Market, Meal   75
Markets   11, 76, 104, 188, 209
Market, Whitsuntide   77
Marquis of Huntly, See "Huntly,
   Marquis of"
Marsh   128
Marshall, Gilbert   29
Martinmas Fair, See "Fair,
   Martinmas"
Maryann Court   121
Maryfield   10
Marymas Fair, See "Fair,
   Marymas"
Mary, Queen of Scots   6, 21, 22,
   53, 58, 91, 92, 113, 150, 212
Masons (See also
   "Freemasons")   16, 17, 40, 42
Mason's Hotel, See "Hotel,
   Mason's"
Master of Lovat, See "Lovat,
   Master of"
Master Mason of Scotland,
   Grand   174
Matheson, Clan   42
Matheson, Sir Alexander   63,
   117, 119, 121
Matheson, Sir James   121
Mauds   198
Maule, Fox   175
May Court   121
May, Reverend Howard   79
Medlock, Arthur   205
Melven, James   167, 205
Melville, William   205
Mental Home   67
Mercat Cross, See "Cross"
Merchants   24, 76, 177
Merkinch   45, 114, 115, 116,

190, 192, 209, 211
Merkinch School, See "School,
   Merkinch"
Methodist Church, See "Church,
   Methodist"
Middleton, General   53
Midmills Road   10, 112
Milcraig   142
Milk   200
Mill   211, 213
Mill Burn   181
Millburn Distillery   85
Millburn Road   74, 141
Milliners   204
Mill-lade   130
Millstone   112
Milnfield   31, 140, 213
Mission Hall   74
Mitchell, Joseph   100, 102, 113,
   135, 137, 199
Moderator (of Presbytery)   138
Monck, General   14
Moncrieff, James   20
Mond, Sir Alfred   43
Money   86
Monster   9, 181
Montague, Edward S.   43
Montague Row   114
Montrose, Marquis of   53, 77,
   78, 140, 143
Moorton   31
Moraine   128
Moray   8, 50, 51, 57, 61, 165,
   208
Moray, Andrew de   50, 51
Moray, Bishop of, See "Bishop of
   Moray and Ross"
Moray, Earl of   22, 52, 68, 83,
   128, 143, 150, 151
Morel Bros.   205
Mote-hill   70
Motor-cars   83
Moy   42, 96, 165
Muckle Flugga   205
Mugging   120
Muirfield   70

Muirfield Hospital   119
Muirfield Road   31
Muirtown   63, 117, 121, 157
Muirtown Basin   119, 120
Muirtown, Green of   34, 114, 119, 120, 121
Muirtown Hospital   119
Muirtown Locks   196
Muirtown Street   118, 119
Mulldearg   29
Municipal Reform Act   1833
Munro, Clan   42, 118, 150
Munro, Donald   89
Munro, Elspet   66
Munro, Sir Hector   85, 89
Munro, Janet   118
Munro, John   92, 118
Munro, Robert   43
Murray, Sheriff   110
Museum   70, 89, 166, 178
Music Hall   96, 103, 166
Mutton   200

Nairn   81, 97, 103, 154, 157, 173, 178, 191
Nairne, Sir Ade de   109
National Bank, See "Bank, National"
National Portrait Gallery   49
National Trust for Scotland   100
"Neath the Cock"   84
Ness Bank   60
Ness Bridge, See "Bridge, Ness"
Ness Castle   136, 203
Ness House   136
Ness Islands, See "Islands, Ness"
Ness, Loch, See "Loch Ness"
Ness River, See "River Ness"
Netherdale   211
Newbothie, Abbot of   210
Newsroom   38
New Street, See "Academy Street"
New Year   79, 212
Nicol, Dr. John Inglis   66, 158, 159

Noble, John   104, 172, 175
Nonagenarian   91, 113, 122, 142, 195, See also "MacLean, John"
"No Popery"   95, 156
Normans   10
North Church, See "Church, Free North"
North of Scotland Hydro-Electric Board, See "Electricity"
North Sea   206
"North Star"   196
Northern Institution   166
Northern Meeting Park   171
Northern Meeting Piping Championship   168, 171
Northern Meeting Rooms   49, 93, 94, 168, 171
Northern Meeting Society   49, 93, 129, 168 *et. seq.*, 186
Norway   21
Norwich   35, 156
Novar   85
Nova Scotia
Nursery Garden   119, 198, 204
Nurses' Home   64

Oak   58, 191
Oatmeal   142, 200
Ochiltrie, Andrew, Lord of   83, 151
Oil   206
Old Edinburgh Road   71
Old High Church, See "Church, Old High"
Old Quay   112
Olifrad, David   23
Ordnance Survey   112, 114, 117, 118, 122
Orkney   20, 21, 186, 191, 198
Otter   195
Oude   136
Oughton, General Sir James A.   174
Oysters   195

Painter   205

Palace Hotel, See "Hotel, Palace"
Palisade   11, 70, 209
Palm Sunday   214
Parish Church, See "Church, Old High"
Parliamentary Army, See "Army, Parliamentary"
Parliament, Member of   85, 121, 135, 136, 146, 155, 156, 157
Peat   88, 214
Pension   21
Pentland Firth   197
Pepper   45, 115, 209
Perceval Road   121
Perfumers   204
Perth   14, 81, 103, 133, 137, 172, 178, 204, 211
Perth Road   141
Pestle, Captain   191
Peter Fair, See "Fair, Peter"
Petroleum   197
Petty   37, 50, 51, 74, 143, 157, 175, 186, 193, 195
Petty Customs, See "Customs"
Petty Street   74, 75, 76
de Petyn, Walter   209
Phopachy House   122
Picts   9, 11
Picture House   161
Pier   116, 193
Pigs   121
Pilche, Alexander   51, 158
Pilgrims   182
Pinkie, Battle of   139
Plaiding   105, 198
Plainstones, See "Exchange"
Planning, Town   162
Playhouse   161
Poinding   209, 210
Pol, Comte de St., See "St. Pol, Comte de"
Police   48, 92, 120
Police Station   56, 92, 107, 175
Polla Criadh   119
Pont, Robert   24

Poor   21, 22, 29, 31, 32, 33, 34, 36, 64, 115, 120, 140
Poor-house   26, 31, 33, 35, 36, 37, 118
Pork   200
Portland Place   112
Porter (Beer)   66
Porterfield   56
Ports   213
Port Wine   66
Post-chaise   59
Post-master   172, 174, 175, 179, 205
Postmaster-General   172, 174
Post Office   73, 75, 76, 81, 94, 104, 164, 171 et. seq.
Post Office Steps   75, 176
Pot, Captain Phineas   192
Potatoes   96, 200
Poultry   200
Powder-magazine   16, 17, 54, 93
Presbyterianism   143, 146
Presbytery, Inverness   23, 34, 78, 138
Prices   200
Priests   87
Prime Minister   42, 121
Prince Andrew   134
Prince Charles Edward Stuart   42, 53, 96, 97, 117, 146
Princess Elizabeth Tartan   133
Priory, See "Friary"
Prison, See "Jail"
Prisoners, Escape of   88, 89
Privy Council   145, 171
Privy Seal, Keeper of   43
Protestant Church, See "Church, Protestant"
Provan, David Lees   43
Provost   22, 24, 31, 48, 52, 58, 63, 64, 67, 78, 79, 80, 83, 86, 87, 103, 110, 115, 117, 143, 145, 148, 151, 157, 158, 159, 161, 176, 183
Ptoroton   8
Public Execution   92, 186

Public Works 47

Quarries 194
Quay 111, 113, 193, 194, 197
Queensgate 76, 96, 101, 176
Queen Street 115, 140

Rabbit 195, 200
Rag, David 241
Rag Dealers 204
Ragged School, See "School, Ragged"
Raigmore 46
Railway, Highland 121, 198
Railway, Invergarry-Fort Augustus 137
Railways 103, 108, 113, 121, 137, 193, 205
Raining, Doctor 35
Raining's School, See "School, Raining's"
Raining Stairs 35
Randolph, Earl of Moray, See "Moray, Earl of"
Rangemore 136
Rangemore Road 114, 137
Rateable Value 92
Real Rent 179
Redcastle 116, 135
"Red Lion" 201
Red Pool, "See Rood Pool"
Reed, John 73
Reform 136, 156
Reformation 18, 21, 24, 31, 45, 63, 108, 140, 187
Reid, Captain 84
Rent 179, 200
Restoration 144
Richmond, Duchess-Dowager 153
Riot 120
Ritchie, Thomas 82, 92
River Banks 91, 122, 193
Riverdale 63
River Ness 8, 9, 41, 57, 61, 91, 129, 181, 184, 198

River Purification 199
Robert I, See "Bruce"
Robertson Clan 42
Robertson, Doctor 153
Robertson of Inshes 71, 92, 145
Robertson, Margaret 173
"Rob Roy" 196
Rodez, Bishop of 142
Roe 195
Roebuck 201
Roller-skating 185
Roman Catholic Church, See "Church, Roman Catholic"
Romans 9
Rood Church, See "Church, Rood"
Roodmas 214
Rood Pool 213
Rope Works 198
Rosehaugh 117
Rose of Kilravock, See "Kilravock, Rose of"
Rosemarkie 104
Rose Street 103, 105, 107, 181, 193
Rose Street Foundry 60, 204
Ross, Dr. Alexander 18, 63, 64, 100, 105, 112, 119, 121, 122, 167, 185, 186
Ross Clan 42
Ross, Counties of 52
Ross, Earl of 21, 51, 57, 109, 212
Ross, Gilbert 205
Ross, James 115, 204
Ross, John 112
Ross, Bailie John 22
Ross, Malcolm 89
Ross-shire 89, 97, 116, 121, 136, 147, 154
Rout of Moy 96, 118
Royal Academy, See "School, Academy"
Royal Burgh 44, 132, 211
Royal Engineers 122
Royalist Army, See "Army Royalist"

Roy, Alister McThomas 112
Royal Mail, See "Post Office"
Royal Northern Infirmary, See
  "Hospital, Inverness Royal
  Infirmary"
Royalty 171
Royal Visits 115, 209, 211, 212
Rum-tea 113, 194

Sacrement 111
Saddler 91
Saidhe Chuimein 74
Saint Andrew 109
Saint Andrews 23, 178
Saint Andrew's Cathedral, See
  "Church, St. Andrew's
  Cathedral"
Saint Andrew's Church,
  Edinburgh 85
Saint Andrew's Fair, See "Fair,
  St. Andrew's"
Saint Andrew's Lodge, See
  "Lodge, St. Andrew's"
Saint Behan 127
Saint Catherine 119
Saint Catherine's Aisle 58,
  109
Saint Columba 9, 23, 127
Saint Columba's Church, See
  "Church, St. Columba's"
Saint Dominic 18
Saint Finane 78
Saint Germains 134, 135
Saint John's Church, See
  "Church, St. John's"
Saint John's Kilwinning Lodge,
  "See "Lodge, St. John's"
Saint Margaret 64
Saint Mark's Church, See
  "Church, St. Mark's"
Saint Mark's Fair, See "Fair, St.
  Mark's"
Saint Mary's Chapel, See
  "Chapel, St. Mary's"
Saint Michael 115, 140
Saint Michael's Mount 9, 23

Saint Pol et Bois, Comte de 41,
  190, 191
Saint Thomas' Fair, See "Fair, St.
  Thomas"
Salmon 87, 88, 94, 184, 200
Salutation 201
Sanitary Inspector 124
Saw-mills 198
Saxons 6, 10, 87
La Scala Cinema, See "Cinema,
  La Scala"
Scallags 104
Scandinavia 197
Scatgate 107, 193
Scavenger 48, 125
School 19, 22, 33, 119, 124
School, Academy 19, 20, 35, 37,
  60, 102, 103, 141, 166
School, Bell's 63, 106
School, Bishop Eden's 64
School, Central 115, 125
School, Crown 35
School, Female 36, 37
School, Grammar 26, 28, 29,
  34, 35, 36, 37, 119
School, High 6, 35, 125
School, Kindergarten 38
School, Merkinch 115
School, Ragged 124
School, Raining's 35
School, Technical (later
  "High") 125
School Lane 99, 101
School Master 19, 34, 36, 48
Scot, Captain George 191
Scots 8, 9
Scott, John 108, 109
Scourie Burn 181
Seaforth 128, 169
Sea-shells 10, 81
Seceeder Congregation 106
Second World War 62, 125,
  137, 186, 203
Senior Citizens 36
Session Library, See "Library,
  Kirk Session"

Sett   176 *et. seq.*

Sewing   38

Shap   61

Sharp, Robert   174

Shaw   118

Shaw MacDuff, See "MacDuff, Shaw"

Sheep   89, 170, 199

Sheriff   51, 53, 110, 141, 148, 149, 150, 151, 154, 208, 210

Sheriffmuir   132

Shetland   186

Shewglie   154

Shinty   60

Ship-building   41, 190, 192, 198

Shipland   20

Ship Flat   109, 186, 193

Shipping   16, 41, 112, 190

Shoemakers   176, 178, 205

Shoes   104

Shooting   81

Shore   112, 142, 199, 201

Shore Dues   45, 111, 193, 195

Shore Street   108 *et. seq.*, 192, 193

Shortt, Edward   43

Shrine   182

Sibbald, William   85

Sick   64

Silversmiths   177, 178

Simpson, Provost William   43

Skate   200

Skeletons   107

Skinners   42, 176

Skins   194, 199

Skye   21, 173

Skyner, Stephen   109

Slate   121

Slater's Directory   204

Sleat   42, 145

Slezer   84

Sloch Dunache   141

Sloc-na-Meirlach   183

Smith & MacKay   204

Smith, James   40

Smith, Madeline   160

Smith, Sandie   104

Smiths   92

Smith, Provost William   161

Society for Promoting Christian Knowledge   35

Solemn League and Covenant   138

Soldiery, "Wild and licentious"   55, 194

Soup Kitchen   36, 93, 121

Southside Road   99

Spean Bridge   137

Spey   50

Speyside   154

Spinning   38

Sportsmen   81

Squarewrights   177

Stag   180

"Stag's Head"   201

"Star"   201

Station Hotel, See "Hotel, Station"

Steele, George   119

Steeple   39, 79, 83, 84, 89, 151, 159

Stell Fishings   87, 213

Stent   45, 58, 144, 178, 179, 211

Stephen's Brae   74, 75

Stevenson, Miss Frances   43

Stewart, Alexander, Earl of Mar, See "Mar, Earl of"

Stewart of Appin   42

Stills   202

Stirling Bridge   51

Stone of Inverness   112

Stone Masons   205

Strathaven, Lord   132

Strathbogie   149, 150

Strathdearn   175

Stratherrick   140, 154

Strathglass   202

Strathpeffer   81, 180, 181

Strathnairn   175

Strathspey   157

Stratton, Sarah   148

Street Lighting   48, 69

Street Sweeping   68
Strother's Lane   103
Struy   17, 192
Stuart, Bailie John   194
Sunday Observance   11, 187
Sunday School   155
Surgeon   145
Surveyor, Burgh   182
Susanna of the Auldcastle   109
Suspension Bridge, See "Ness
  Bridge"
Sussex, Duke of   133
Suter, James   111, 112, 118, 127,
  147, 154, 155, 159, 160, 164,
  166, 172, 186, 193, 194, 195
Sutherland   112
Sutherland, Andrew   110
Sutherland, Earl of   132
Swimming Pool   187

Tailors   42, 94, 176, 178
Tain   81, 190
Tallow   93
Tanner's Lane   121, 124
Tannery   114, 115, 198
Tarbetness   190, 193
Tarradale   135
Tartan, Inverness   133
Tartan, Princess Elizabeth   133
Tavern   200, 204
Taxation   76, 112, 178, 194, 201
Taylor, John   94
Teaching Friars, See "Friars"
Technical School, see "School,
  Technical"
Telephone Exchange   18
Telford Street   114, 119
Thatched Houses   68, 69, 124
Theatre   107, 160
Theatre Lane   75, 161
Theatre, Little   107
Theatre Royal   161
Theft   120
Thistle Football Club   183
Thistle, Order of the   49
Thomas the Rhymer   126

Thomson, John   117
Thornbush   113, 117, 158
Thornbush Brewery   117, 201
Thornbush Road   117
Thornbush Quay   48, 195
Thread Manufacturers   198, 199
"Three Merry Boys"   201
Thursday Market   188
Thurso   173, 190
Tilting   109
Timber   105, 197
Times   89
Tobacco   66, 198
Tolbooth   39, 83
Tolls   45, 60, 114, 209, 211
Tomnahurich   95, 125, 126, 127,
  128, 129, 188
Tomnahurich Street   114
Tomnahurich Bridge, See
  "Bridge, Tomnahurich"
Torbreck   134, 136
Torture   84
Torvean   10, 95, 127, 128, 129
Tory   204
Tourism   205
Tourists   81
Town Band   79
Town Clerk, See "Clerk, Town"
Town Council, See "Council,
  Town"
Town House   24, 38 *et. seq.*, 69,
  93, 96, 99, 101, 105, 112, 142,
  157, 166, 168, 169, 178
Town Treasurer, See "Treasurer,
  Town"
Trade   10, 198 *et. seq.*
Trades Hall, See "Bow Court"
Traffic   73, 83, 86, 101
Transportation   59, 89, 195, 197
Traverne, William   109
Treasurer, Town   31, 87, 158,
  174
Trees   183, 184
Trent, William   172
Trinity Church, See "Church,
  Trinity"

Tuff, H. T.   79
Tulloch, Painter &
   Decorator   205
Turbot   200
Turks   191
Typhus   66
Tweeds   198

Underwood, Cecilia Letitia   133
Union Hotel, See "Hotel, Union"
Union of Parliaments   159
Union Street   63, 96, 103, 187,
   205
Urquhart   66, 129
Urquhart Castle, See "Castle,
   Urquhart"
Urry, Colonel, See "Hurry,
   Colonel"

Vacomagi   8
de Vallebus, Hugh   209
de Valonus, Philip   208
Valuation Roll   161, 179, 204
Valued Rent   179
Vararis   9
Vassals   211
Vaus, Robert   140
Veal   200
Venetian Fleet   191
Via Scotia   182
Victoria Drive   75
Victoria, Queen   164
Victoria Terrace   10
Viewmount   70, 71, 144
Vintner   91
Virgin Mary   23, 40, 108
Virgin Mary's High Altar   140

Wade, General   74, 191, 192
Wages   66
Walker, Sir Francis   136
Wallace   50
Wallace, Thomas D.   6, 110,
   124, 127, 128, 167
Wardlaw   72
Wardlaw Manuscript   15, 109,
   191

Warrand, Robert   172, 173, 174
Watchmaker   205
Watchnight Service   79
Water Kists   213
Waterloo, Battle of   85
Waterloo Bridge, See "Bridge,
   Waterloo"
Waterloo Place   20, 205
Water Supply   48, 71
Waterson, Charles   204
Watson, T.   145
Waverley Hotel See "Hotel,
   Waverley"
Waulking Mill   199
Wause, Martin   71
Weavers   176, 177, 178
Weighouse   28, 29, 31, 35, 36
Well   56
Wesleyan Methodist, See
   "Church, Methodist"
Wesley, John   35, 102
West Church, See "Church,
   West"
Western Isles   21, 67
West Indies   134, 135
Wheel   59, 64
Wheelwrights   177
Whig   79, 204
Whin Island   130
Whisky   89, 200, 202
Whitings   200
Whitsuntide Market, See
   "Market, Whitsuntide"
Wick   173, 175, 190
Wig Maker   92
William the Lion   11, 21, 23, 41,
   45, 70, 74, 100, 102, 154, 187,
   201, 209
Wilson, Robert   95
Windmill   117
Witch   141
Witchcraft   146
Wolf   180
Wolfe, Lt. Col. James   25, 35
Wood, John   75
Wood-yard   198

Wool Fair See "Fair, Wool"
Woollen Factory   198, 199
Worth, John   162
Worthington-Evans, Sir
   Laming   43
Wotherspoon, Provost
   Robert   94
Wrights   176

Wyckham Associates, John   162

Yet, Donald   88
York, Duke of   67, 133, 134
York Ward   67
Y.M.C.A.   73
Young, Professor   166
Young Street   20, 108, 124